IMAGES
of America

YARMOUTH REVISITED

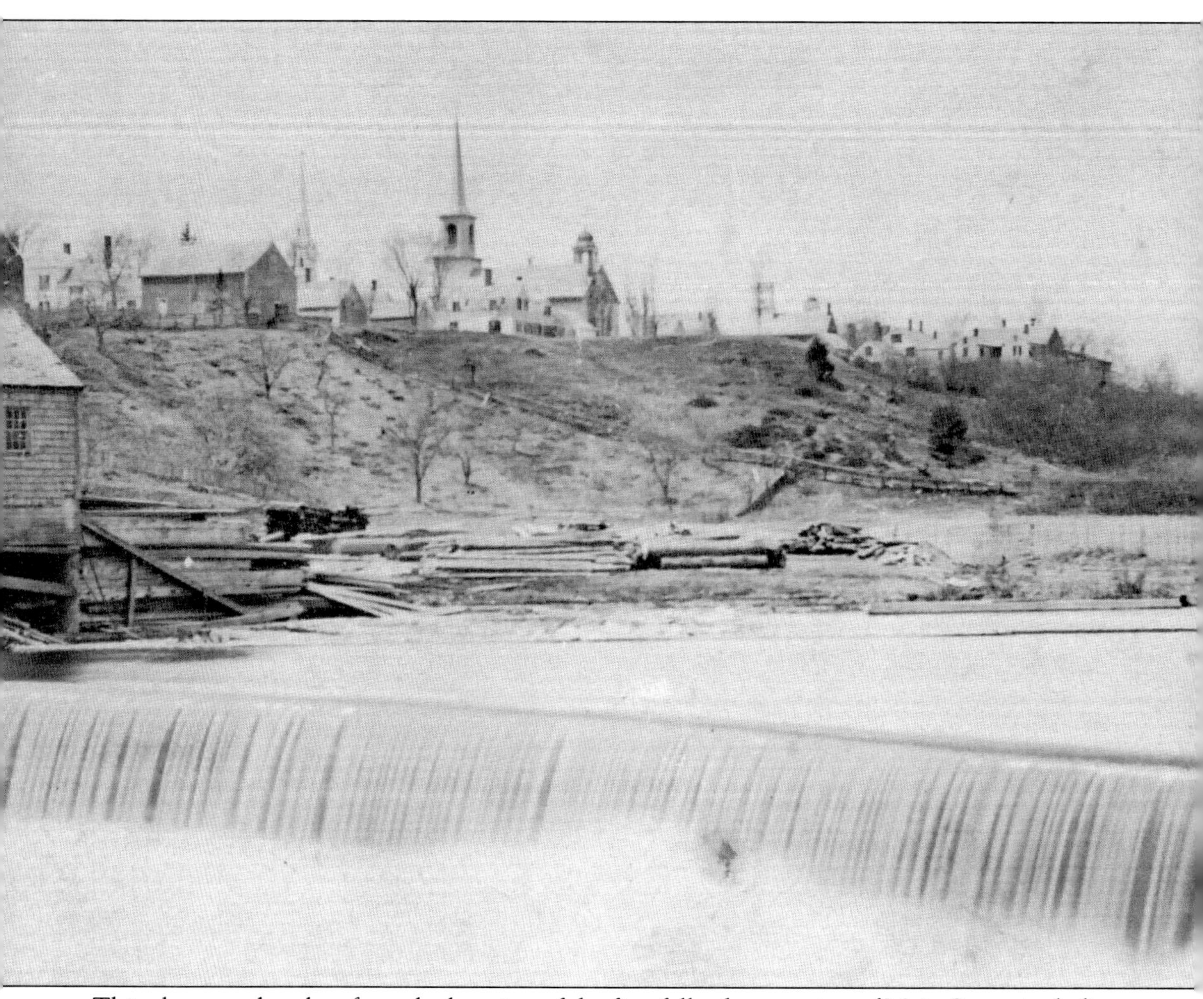

This photograph, taken from the location of the first falls, shows a view of Main Street including three church steeples. The third and present First Parish Church on the left was completed in 1868 to replace the "Old Sloop" at the right. In 1859, 45 prominent members of the Congregational church withdrew over internal issues. The Central Parish Church was built and operated as an orthodox Congregational church until November 1886, when the Universalist church relocated to the building shown in the center. (Courtesy of Yarmouth Historic Society.)

On the Cover: This photograph, dated August 12, 1897, is one of six taken on this day in the collection of the Yarmouth Historical Society. The men in this photograph as well as the other photographs are taking part in a firemen's muster to celebrate the implementation of the town's water system. The 1 on their shirts indicates that they are members of Hose Company No. 1. Hose Company No. 2 is represented in a similar fashion. Look closely at their faces; they will appear in other photographs, as these men represented all segments of the population. In the background is the Universalist church that is located at the intersection of Portland and Main Streets. (Courtesy of Yarmouth Historical Society.)

IMAGES
of America

YARMOUTH REVISITED

Amy Aldredge

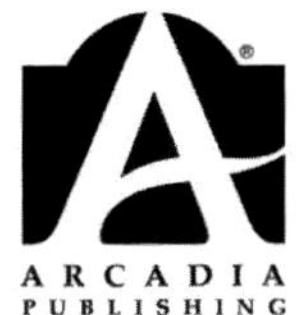

ISBN 978-0-7385-9903-8

Published by Arcadia Publishing
Charleston, South Carolina

Printed in the United States of America

Library of Congress Control Number: 2012951108

For all general information, please contact Arcadia Publishing:
Telephone 843-853-2070
Fax 843-853-0044
E-mail sales@arcadiapublishing.com
For customer service and orders:
Toll-Free 1-888-313-2665

Visit us on the Internet at www.arcadiapublishing.com

Contents

Acknowledgments

This book would not be possible without the resources and support of the Yarmouth Historical Society and the board of trustees, the executive director Michael Chaney, and the expertise and knowledge of research assistant Jennifer MacDowell. Unless otherwise noted, all photographs are from the Yarmouth Historical Society. The photographs in this book that are from the collection of Dick Knight are in honor of his parents, Frank and Frances Mann Knight.

INTRODUCTION

The area of Ancient North Yarmouth attracted both Native American and later European settlers because of the natural features that surrounded the coastal land. Rivers provided a variety of resources including food, fertile soil, hydropower for mills, and transportation links connecting inland areas with the sea. This ability to access both the river and the sea along Broad Cove made this area desirable for Native American tribes, such as the Wabanaki, and European settlers, who were primarily English.

North Yarmouth was settled three times, beginning with William Royall and John Cousins, who were among the first European settlers. The "North" in the name was intended to differentiate it from Yarmouth, Massachusetts, which had already been established on Cape Cod. The first settlement began in the 1630s and lasted until 1676. King Philip's War commenced in 1675, and the settlers were forced to leave the area. In the fall of 1679, settlers returned. The following year, the town was officially incorporated as North Yarmouth and became the eighth town in the province of Maine. This second settlement lasted 10 years before it was destroyed again. The death of Capt. Walter Gendall and the beginning of King William's War devastated the coast and left the area desolated for a generation. After settlers were driven out twice, the third and permanent resettlement began in 1715. By 1722, the population was close to 100 people. The old Meetinghouse under the Ledge was built in 1729 to serve as the church and town house. The settlement also had a school, tavern, and a cemetery but was fined for not having stocks and a dunking pool. The original territory of North Yarmouth in 1680 was repeatedly subdivided, with Harpswell being set off in 1758, Freeport in 1789, Pownal in 1808, Cumberland in 1821, and Yarmouth in 1849.

When the third settlement was laid out, the heirs of Henry Saywood and Bartholomew Gedney asserted ownership of two miles on each side of Royall's River. This dated back to the Indian deed known as the Steven's claim of 1673 and was acknowledged on the proprietors' map. After several court battles, in deference to the deed, the committee in charge of resettlement reserved 100 acres of land on each side of the river.

The proprietors' map was a survey of land divisions made with 103 original proprietors, each with a "home lot" of 10 acres. If the home lot was occupied and improved, the settler was given a chance to draw for varied land lots in 120- and 100-acre "after divisions." This was done to prevent the home lots from being held for speculation.

Between 1715 and 1810, North Yarmouth's population grew rapidly. In 1821, Cumberland split off, and only North Yarmouth and Yarmouth remained as the town of North Yarmouth. As the town grew, settlers moved closer to what is now the present village. Falls Village, the area near the harbor, was the location of Union Wharf, North Yarmouth Academy, and the Second Congregational Church (Old Sloop), which was constructed in 1818. Some members of the original meetinghouse opposed building the new church and incorporated themselves as the Chapel Religious Society. The two sections of town developed in different directions. Shipbuilders, captains, and merchants populated Falls Village along the coastal section. Corner Village, later Yarmouthville, was the location of the Meetinghouse on the Hill. The inland portion, extending all the way to the New Gloucester border, was mainly agricultural and populated with small family farms. The town voted in 1849 to split, with the inland section taking the name of North Yarmouth.

Starting in 1674, when the earliest known mill was erected, the Royal River has had a lasting impact on the community of Yarmouth. There are four falls along the river and the energy produced by them led to the development of the town. Grain, lumber, carding, and cotton mills along with iron foundries were among the earlier types of mills found along the river. Later, industries that utilized Yarmouth's hydropower included a shoe factory and a poultry processing company. At its peak, Yarmouth was a thriving mill town, employing hundreds of workers in a variety of industries.

Papermaking started in Yarmouth in 1816 when William Hawes and George and Henry Cox built their mill on Bridge Street. This mill lasted in various forms until about 1840. In 1874, S.D.

Warren and George W. Hammond bought the Yarmouth Paper Company on the third falls and renamed it the Forest Paper Company, which became known worldwide for producing high-quality soda pulp fiber. Because of its great success, Forest Paper Company was able to expand its production over the course of its existence, and what started as a humble wooden mill building became an industrial complex, sprawling over 10 acres with 10 brick buildings and numerous smoke stacks and chimneys. The Royal River Manufacturing Company, incorporated in 1857, was one of the most prominent industries in town. This was a textile mill for spinning a variety of coarse and fine yarn and seamless grain bags. The mill employed an average of 50 people, many of whom were of French Canadian descent. Weston's Machine Shop and Hodsdon Shoe Company were mills along the fourth falls of the river. With the closing of the Forest Paper Company in 1923, Yarmouth suffered economic hardship that lingered until the 1950s.

The protected harbor at the mouth of the Royal River provided an ideal location for shipbuilding. Throughout Yarmouth's shipbuilding history, vessels were built for different kinds of trade—sloops and schooners for coasting, brigantines and barks for trade with the West Indies, and barkentines and ships for world trade. In the early days, vessels built were generally sloops with broad beams and large sails. These sloops were built by the merchants of the town and used in the coasting trade. It was normal for a captain to own a share of his vessel. Insurance was expensive and owners spread the risk by taking small shares in many vessels. Quite often, the responsibility of finding cargo was the duty of the captain. When a captain was unable to get a cargo, he loaded ballast at the bottom of the hold in order to keep the vessel upright. The weight of the masts, yards, and rigging, along with the pressure of the wind on the sails, would otherwise have capsized the vessel. The height of Yarmouth's shipbuilding occurred between the years 1850 and 1875. In 1874, there were 12 vessels launched from the harbor. Four major shipyards built vessels during this time. On the western side of the river, Henry Hutchins and Edward Stubbs operated from 1851 to 1884. Sylvanus Blanchard and his three sons, Perez, Paul, and Sylvanus Jr., owned the Blanchard Bros. shipyard. Lyman Walker's shipyard launched 40 vessels of all sizes. On the eastern side of the Royal River, Giles Loring had a shipyard where the last major Yarmouth ship was launched in 1890.

Yarmouth at the turn of the 20th century was growing and changing. Brickyard Hollow was filled in with the black ash from the paper mill in an effort to unify the two villages. A grammar school was built in 1890, and a high school was built in 1900 replacing most of the nine separate one-room schoolhouses. Merrill Memorial Library was built in 1904. Taxes from the mills helped finance many of the town's improvements. Changes in transportation, such as the trolley lines and steamboats, made Cousins and Littlejohn Islands tourist destinations. The trolley system ran from Portland to Bath with stops in Yarmouth. In 1955, a bridge was built to Cousins Island to facilitate the construction of a power plant. With the bridge, residents could live on the islands year-round. In 1961, despite unanimous disapproval by the town, the state built Route 295 across Yarmouth harbor, separating the waterfront from the town. Suburban home developments began to appear, and Yarmouth has consistently grown in population. One of the best-known events in Yarmouth is the Yarmouth Clam Festival held every July since 1965. Its roots date back to militia musters in the early 19th century when large crowds of spectators would come to watch from all over the state. By 1900, this tradition had evolved into the firemen's musters that featured competing teams from all over the state. The tradition of the muster continues today.

Yarmouth has maintained its village characteristics primarily by maintaining a Main Street that is reminiscent of earlier days. The Village Improvement Society, founded in 1911, has been active in preservation and education in the town. To celebrate the 100th anniversary of the organization, interpretative signs were placed along the Royal River to bring attention to the industrial nature of the area. The Yarmouth History Center at 118 East Elm Street adjacent to the river has an interpretive gallery that focuses on the history of the region, ranging from the early pre-settlement days to current topics with changing exhibits. Yarmouth is a vibrant town that has an arts center, a music center, and a public school system that consistently ranks in the top tier. In addition, North Yarmouth Academy is centrally located in the town and has a program that attracts students from all over the world.

One

Settlement Patterns

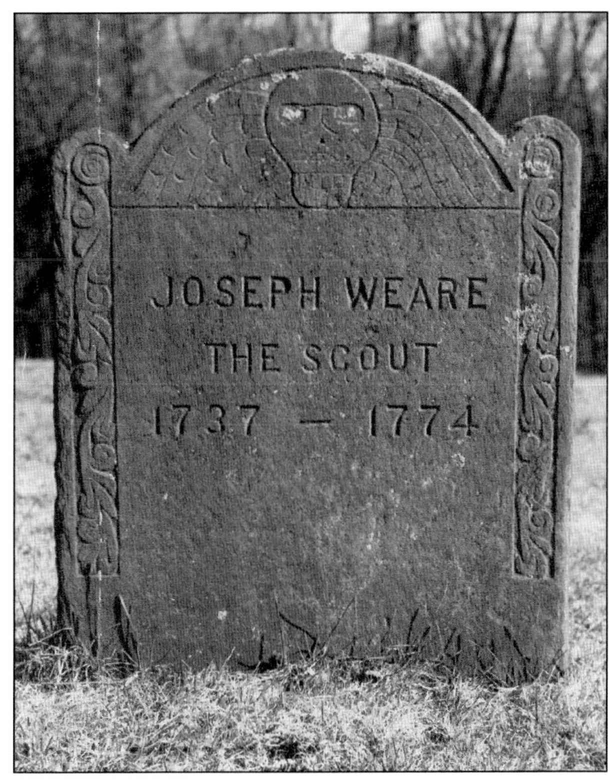

Pioneer Cemetery was the first public burial place in Old North Yarmouth. The members of the third settlement established the cemetery in the early 1730s. Joseph Weare was buried here and may be the reason this cemetery has also been known as the Indian Fighters Burying Ground.

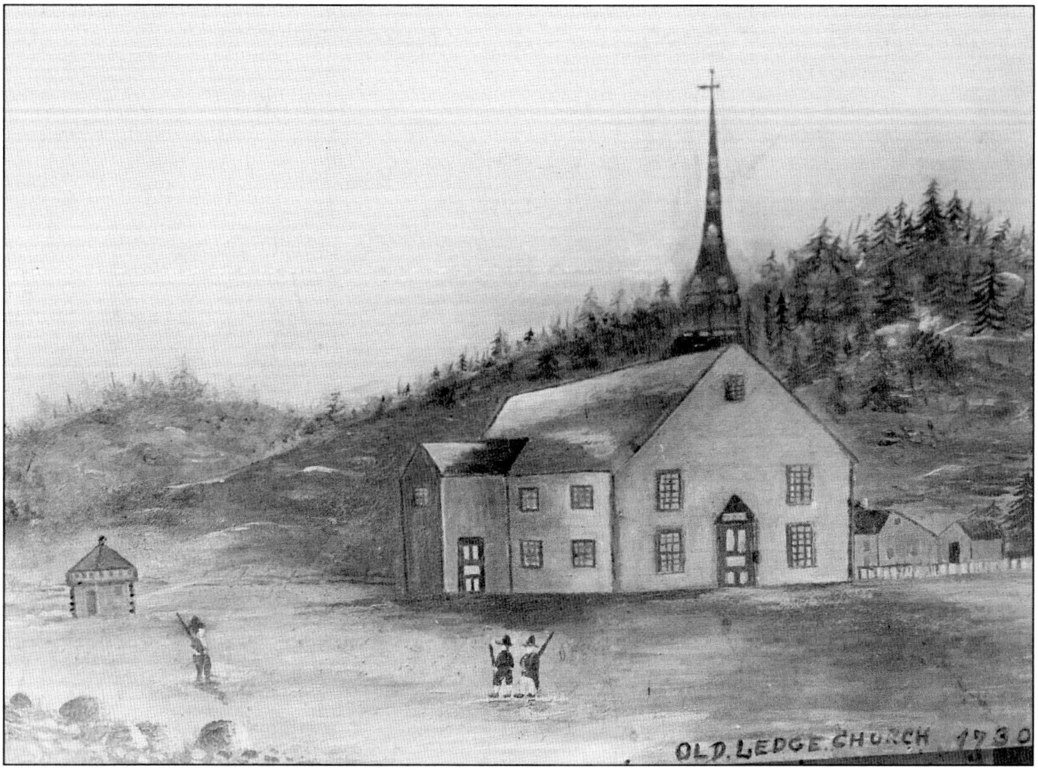

This is a painting of the Meetinghouse under the Ledge by George A. Allen around 1880. The meetinghouse was built in 1729 to serve as the church and town house. North Yarmouth also had a school, tavern, and a cemetery. Next door to the meetinghouse was the home of Ammi R. Cutter, the first minister in the town; his home still stands today.

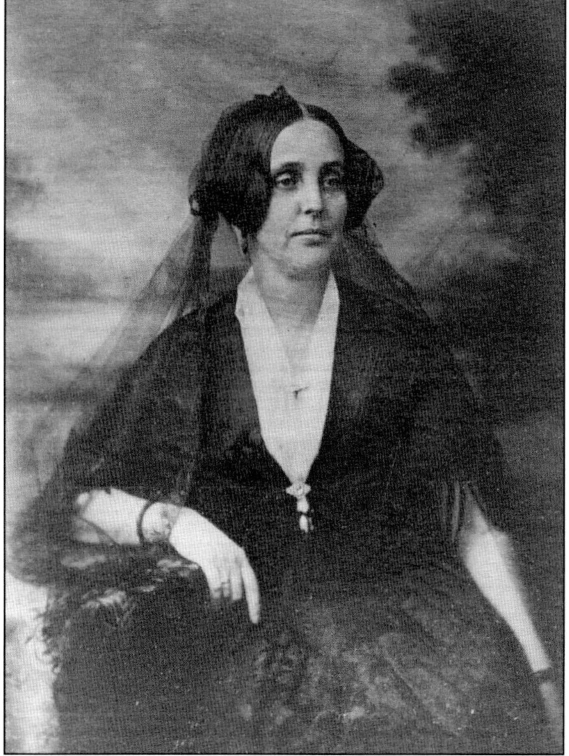

Elizabeth Oakes Smith was born August 12, 1806, in North Yarmouth to David Prince and Sophia Blanchard. A prolific writer, she was a well-known literary figure. Smith published a poem about the old Meetinghouse under the Ledge in which she wrote, "It was a church low-built and square, with belfry perched on high; And no unseemly carving there, to shock the pious eye."

In 1836, when the old Meetinghouse under the Ledge was torn down, Solomon Winslow preserved the weathervane as a relic. Two years later, a group purchased it and mounted it on the ledge. By 1968, the ledge had become overgrown by trees and the vane was removed and now stands in the Yarmouth History Center.

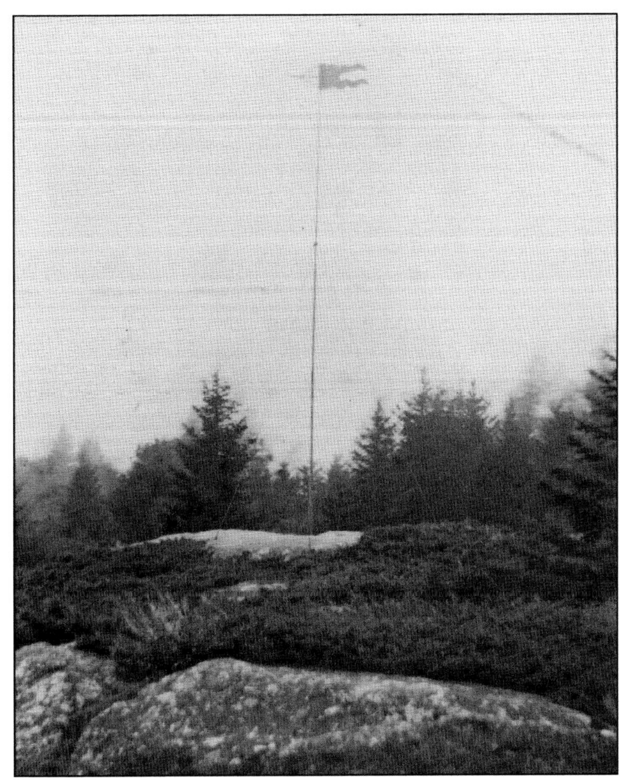

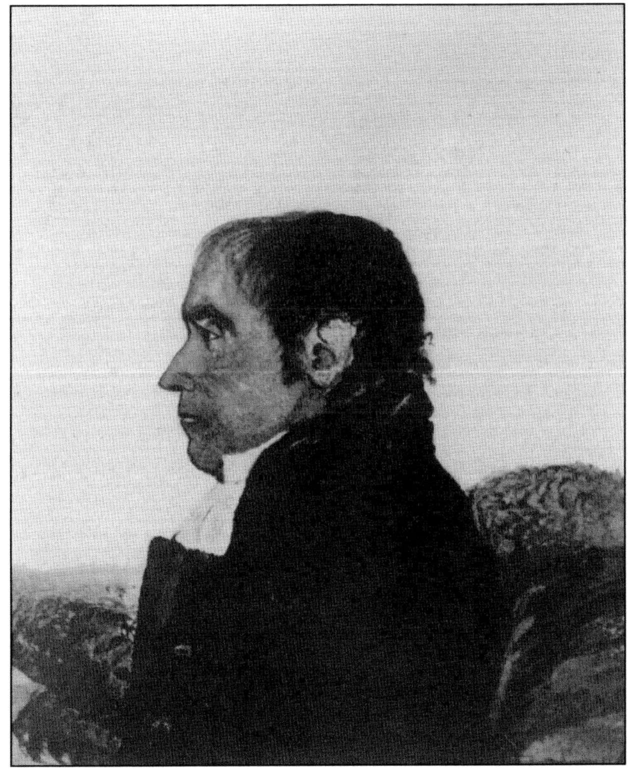

Thomas Green was the first pastor of the newly incorporated Baptist Religious Society of North Yarmouth and Freeport. The first appearance of the Baptist religion came in 1780 when Hezekiah Smith started preaching his newly found Baptist views. Thirteen years later, other Baptists traveled to North Yarmouth. From the start, the parish faced problems gaining members. In 1886, a chapel was built in the center of town designed by John Calvin Stevens.

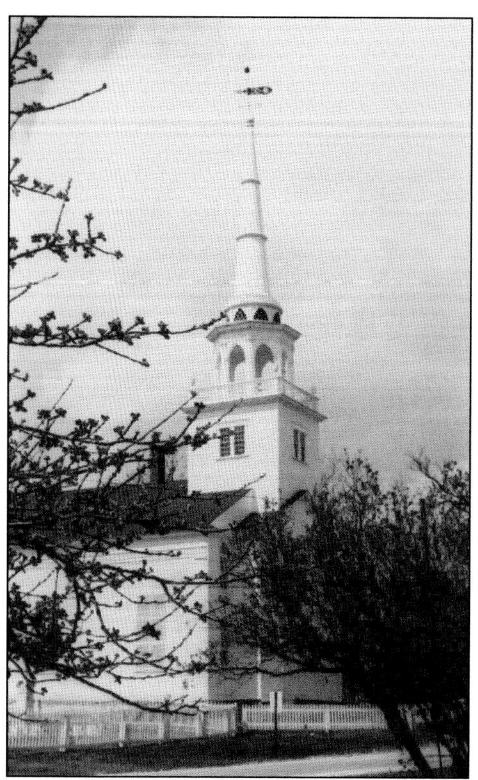

The Meetinghouse on the Hill was constructed in 1796 and sold to the Baptist Religious Society that formed in 1795. The house was built on Byrams's Hill and remained the meetinghouse for the Baptist church until 1886. The Meetinghouse on the Hill became the center of Corner Village.

Francis Brown, a graduate of Dartmouth in 1805, was invited to preach before the Congregational church upon the death of Tristram Gilman. Only 26 at the time, Brown accepted the position of pastor on the condition that the halfway covenant, which had been in use for nearly 80 years, be discontinued. Francis Brown married Elizabeth Gilman, the eldest daughter of the former pastor. Under his pastorate, the church membership increased by 35 people who joined by public profession. Brown resigned to become president of Dartmouth College in 1815 as a result of a theological controversy at the college involving John Wheelock.

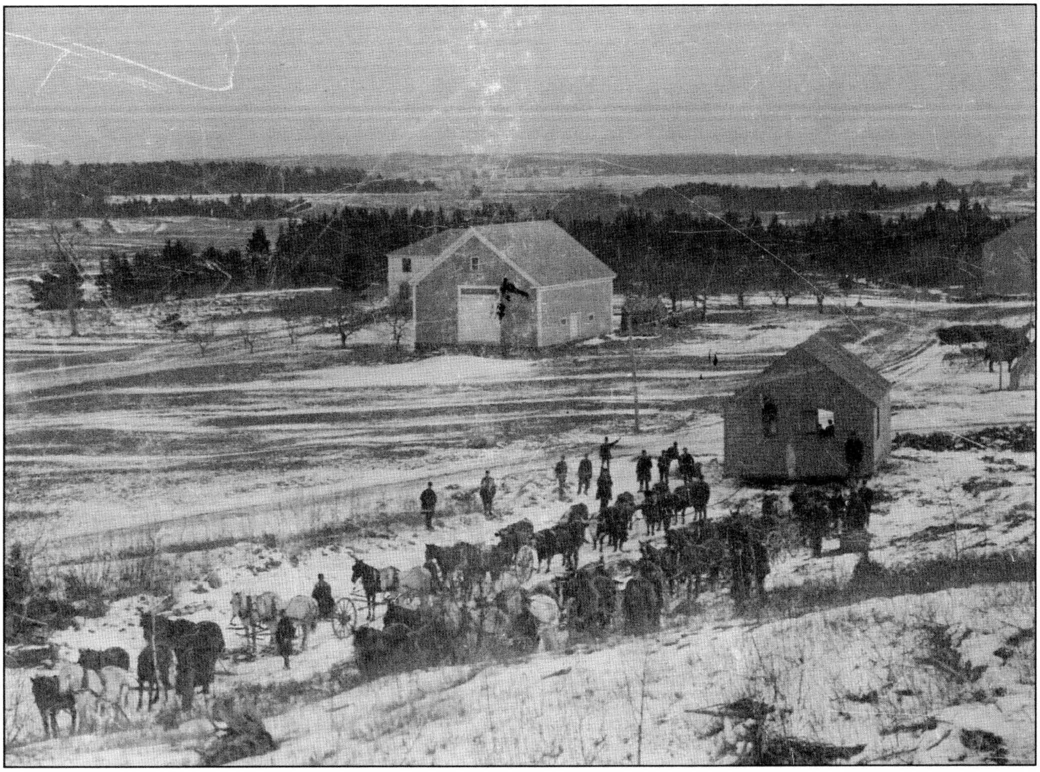

This photograph, taken around 1847, is of the Ledge School being moved from Gilman Street to the ledge. The schoolhouse was moved to the area from its original spot for the photographer C.G. Gooding. Gooding used the building as a tourist attraction. The schoolhouse was later reconstructed and moved to West Main Street. The Yarmouth Historical Society currently owns the Old Ledge Schoolhouse.

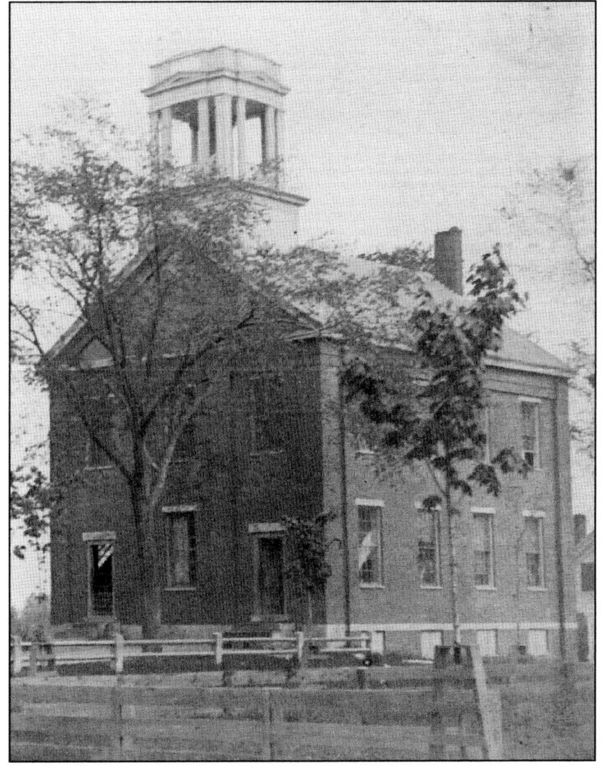

North Yarmouth Academy, incorporated in 1814, is one of the oldest private schools in Maine. Academy Hall was constructed in 1848 to replace the academy's original wooden building. In 1824, tuition was fixed at $4 a term for classical students and $3 for all others. The first alumni reunion took place in 1894 in Academy Hall, led by Maj. Gen. Oliver Otis Howard. Along with Howard, nine other future Civil War generals graduated from North Yarmouth Academy.

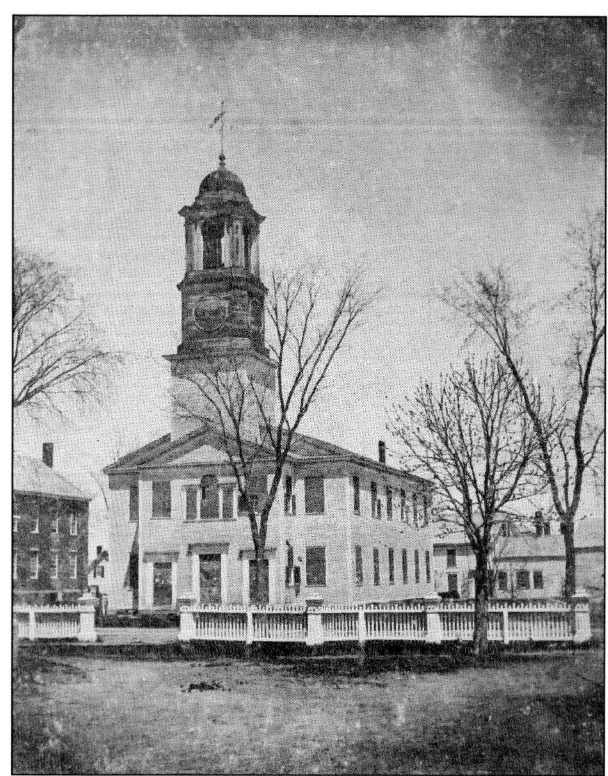

The Second Congregational Church or Old Sloop was built in 1818 in the lower falls section of the village. This was an example of the shifting settlement patterns as townspeople moved into the village. It took two days for the body, roof, and steeple to be raised. The building operated as Union Hall until 1878, when it was torn down.

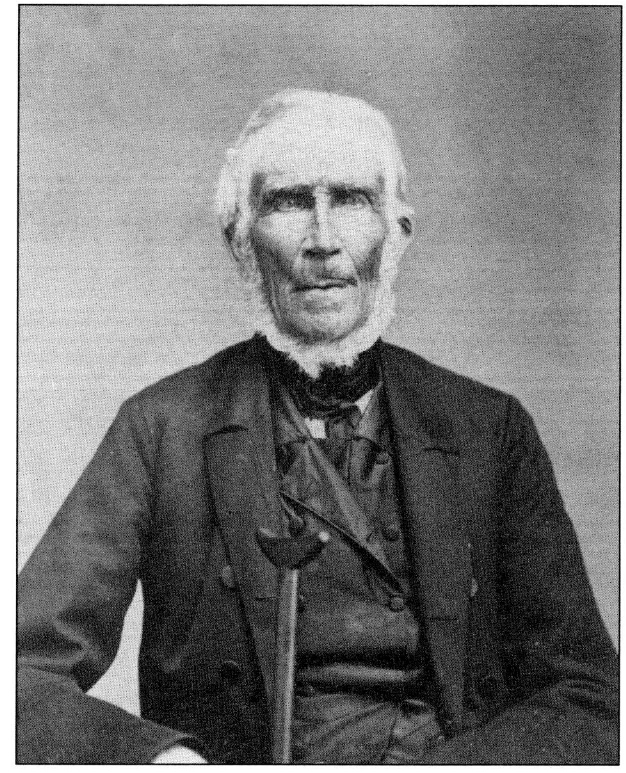

Bradbury True served as first lieutenant in the Cumberland County regiment known as Col. Edmund Phinney's 31st Regiment of Foot. The company in North Yarmouth was raised May 6–14, 1775. True was appointed to a committee whose purpose was to ensure that any vessels belonging to the town not be allowed to contract to carry fuel or lumber of any kind to British troops blockading Boston harbor. Owners of vessels in violation were to have their names published in order that they be known as enemies to their country.

This photograph of the East Main Street Bridge around 1875 was taken from the harbor side with a mill on the left side. The first falls can be seen under the bridge near the mill. Mills were located in this area beginning with the first settlement. Henry Sayward built a sawmill on the east bank of the Royal River in 1674. That mill was abandoned in 1676 due to conflicts with the Native Americans. Walter Gendall, who owned extensive timber operations between 1681 and 1688, also owned and operated a sawmill. Captain Gendall cleared, fenced in, and improved eight acres on the river, four on each side.

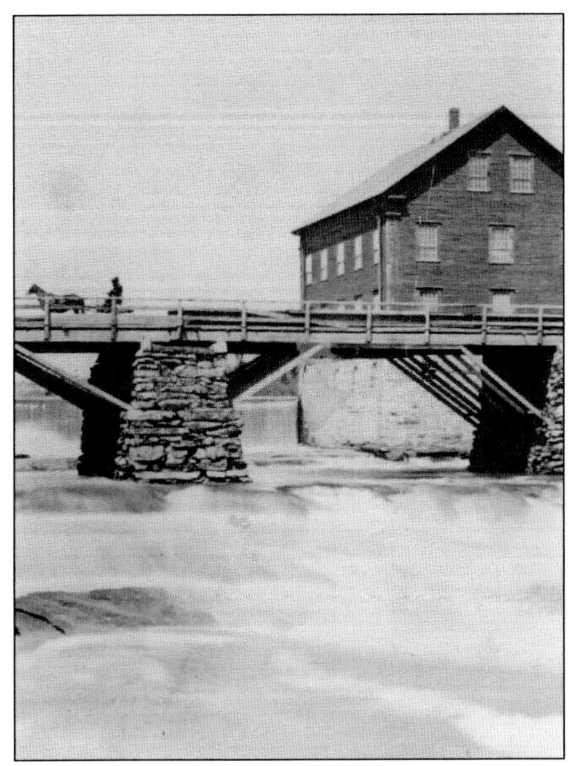

Lower Falls Bridge was built across Royall's River around 1801. Stephen L. Harris, Samuel P. Russell, Ebenezer Corliss, and David Jones were among the members of the committee who commanded that a bridge be built and drew warrants upon Deacon Jacob Mitchell, the town treasurer, for the expense of labor and material.

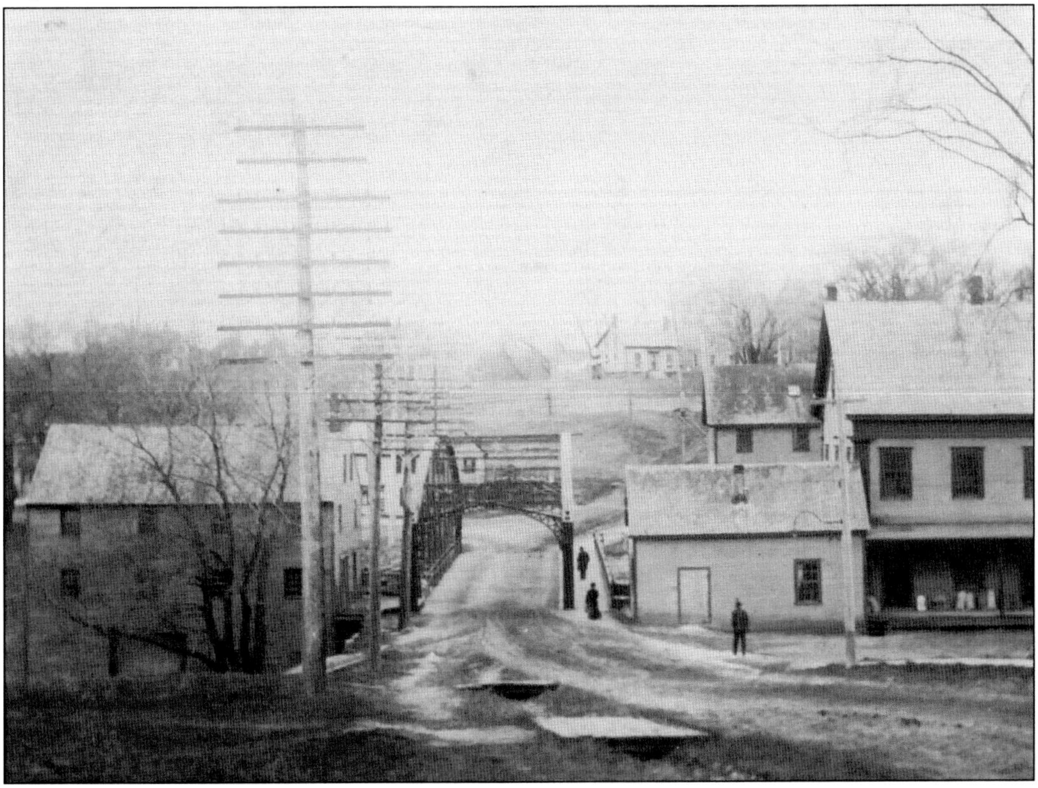

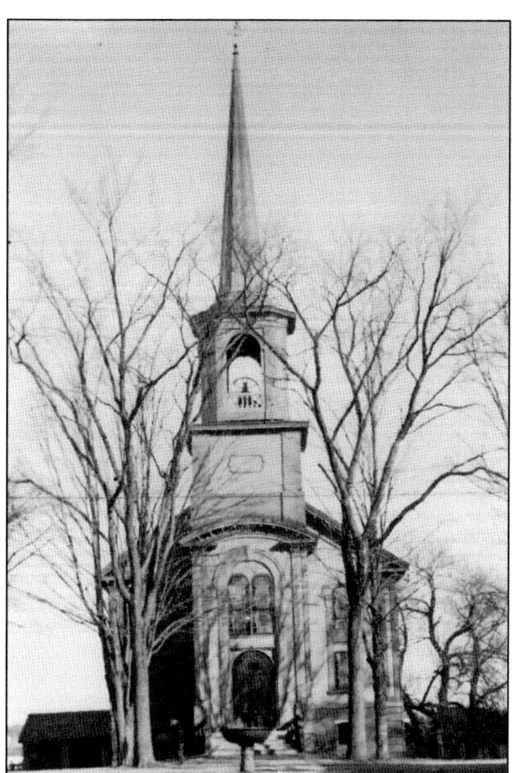

Universalism began in Yarmouth in 1832 in schoolhouse meetings and later in a small chapel on West Elm Street. In 1886, the Universalist church established a Unitarian church in what had been the Central Parish Church on Main Street. The Central Parish Church was formed when members of the Congregational church split from the parish, believing that it was too liberal.

This photograph is of Portland Street as it intersects with Main Street. The Central Parish Church was built on the former site of Jenks tavern. On the left is an 1833 Federal-style cape that was owned by Davis Mocxey, a local shipwright in the early years of shipbuilding. Its features include a center chimney and symmetry in design, as well as a fan over the entry door.

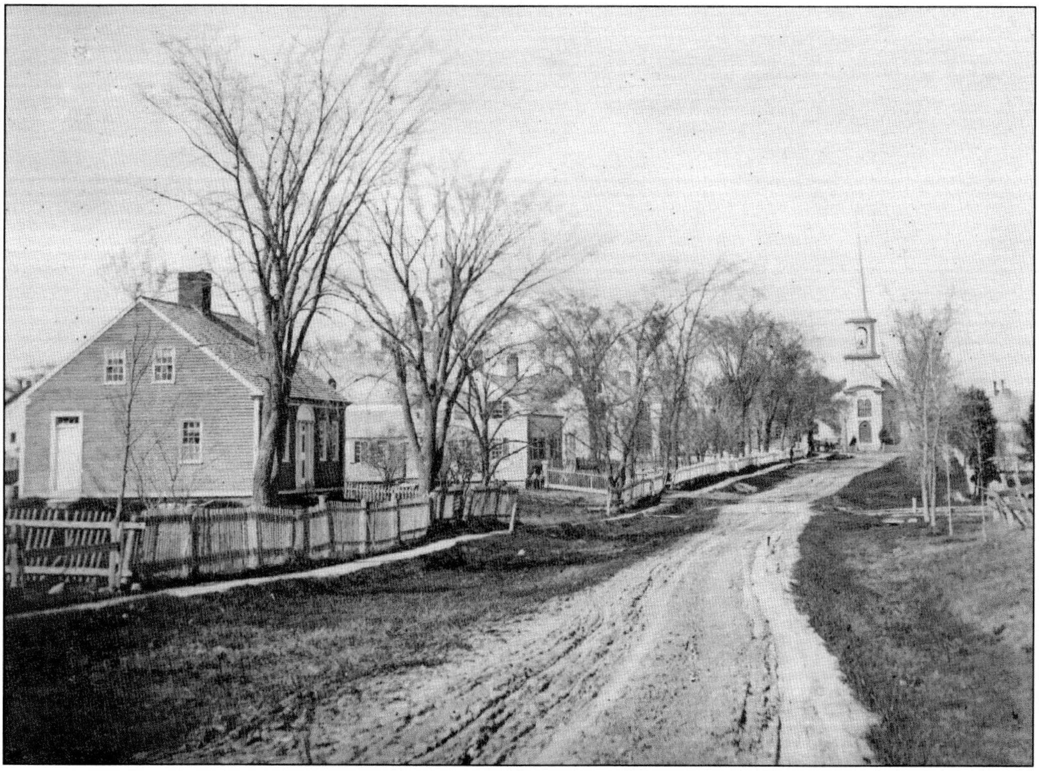

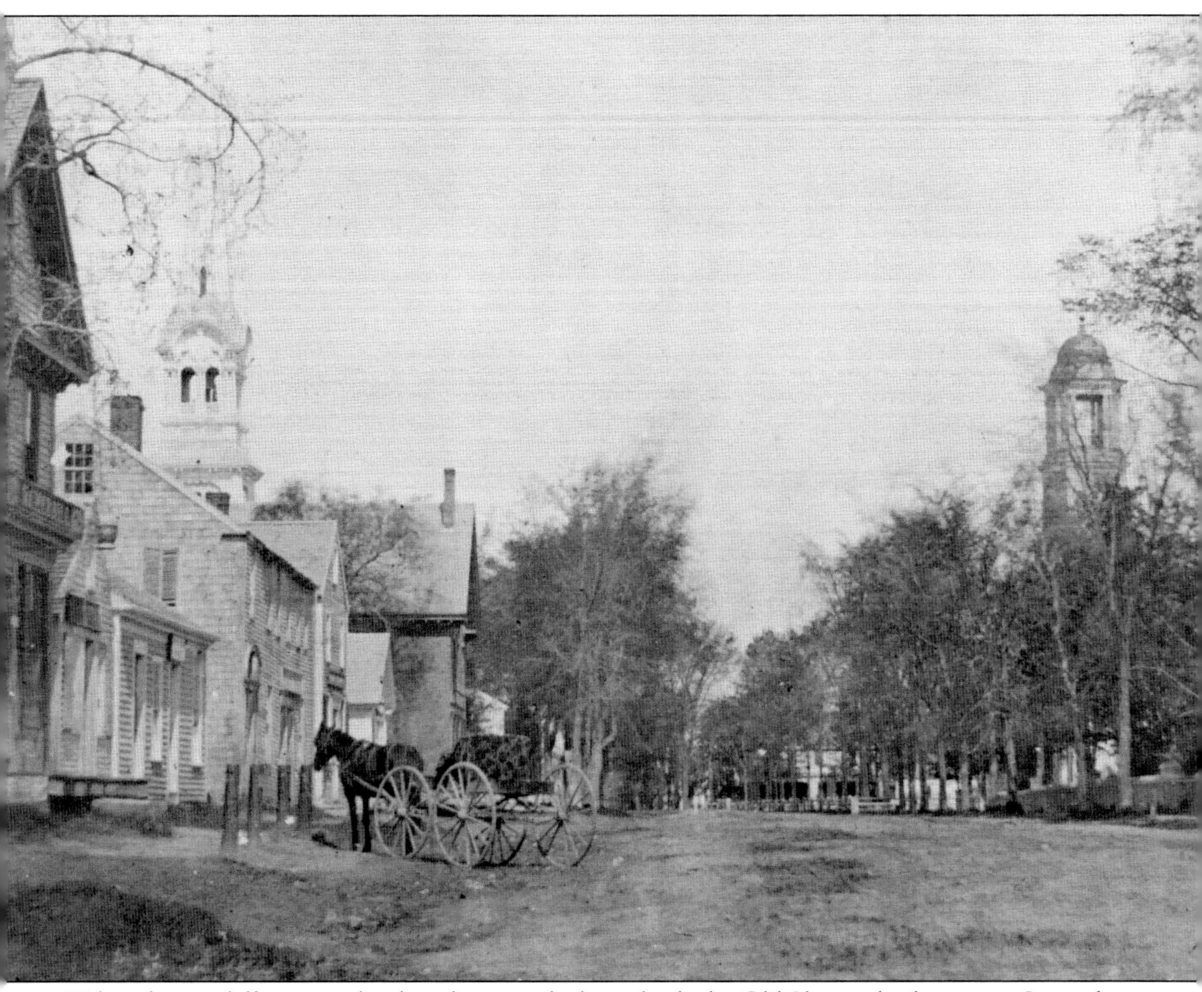

Taken from a different angle, this photograph shows both the Old Sloop, also known as Second Congregational Church, on the right and the third church, now known as the First Parish Church. Old Sloop was later used as Union Hall until it was torn down, and L.L. Shaw, owner of the Royal River Manufacturing Company, had a house built on this location.

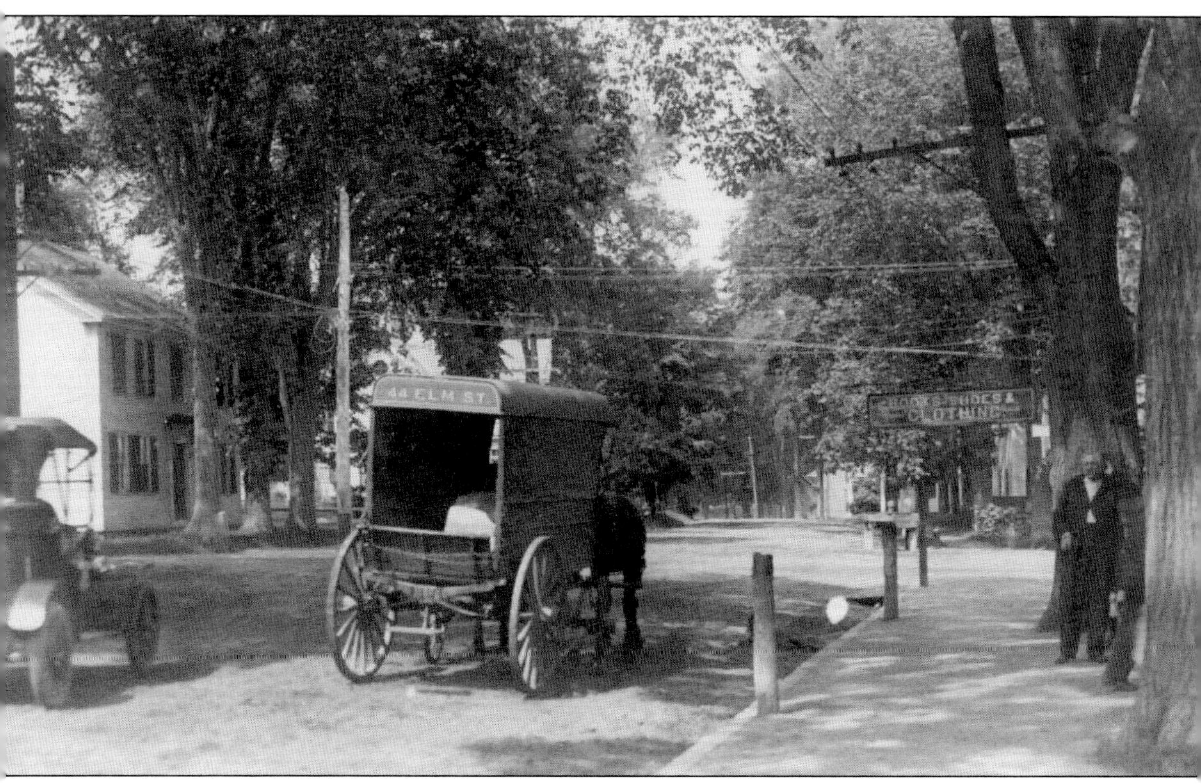

This photograph of Main Street is a lovely example of how elm trees dominated the street, forming a canopy over the road. To the right, George Joy is standing. Note the sign for boots, shoes, and clothing.

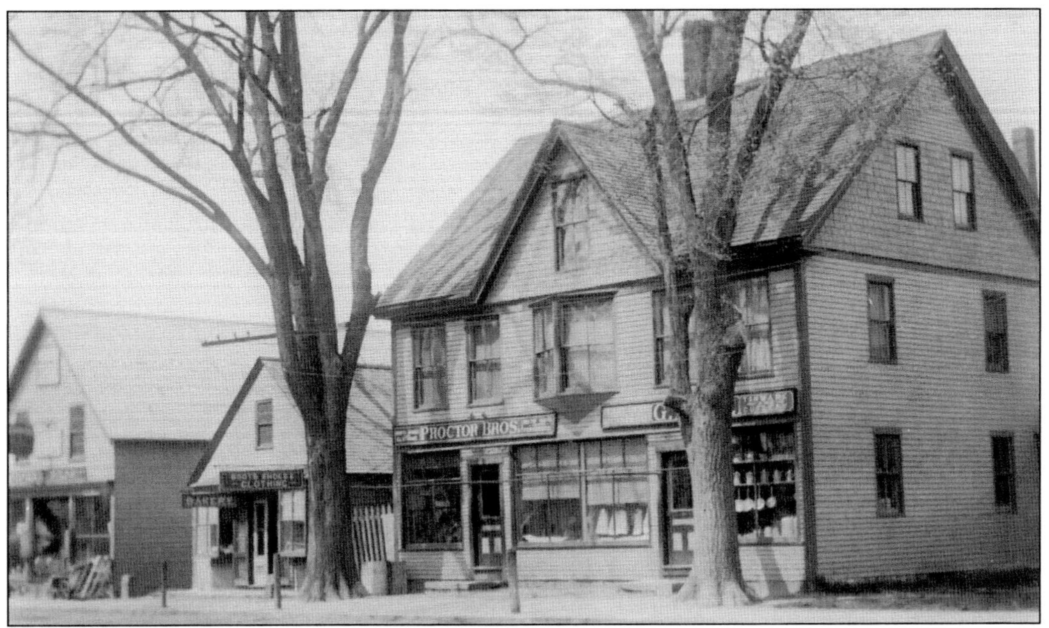

Both Corner Village, later called Yarmouthville, and Lower Village had shops that sold similar goods such as boots, shoes, and clothing, which are advertised in this photograph. There was a separate post office in each section as well.

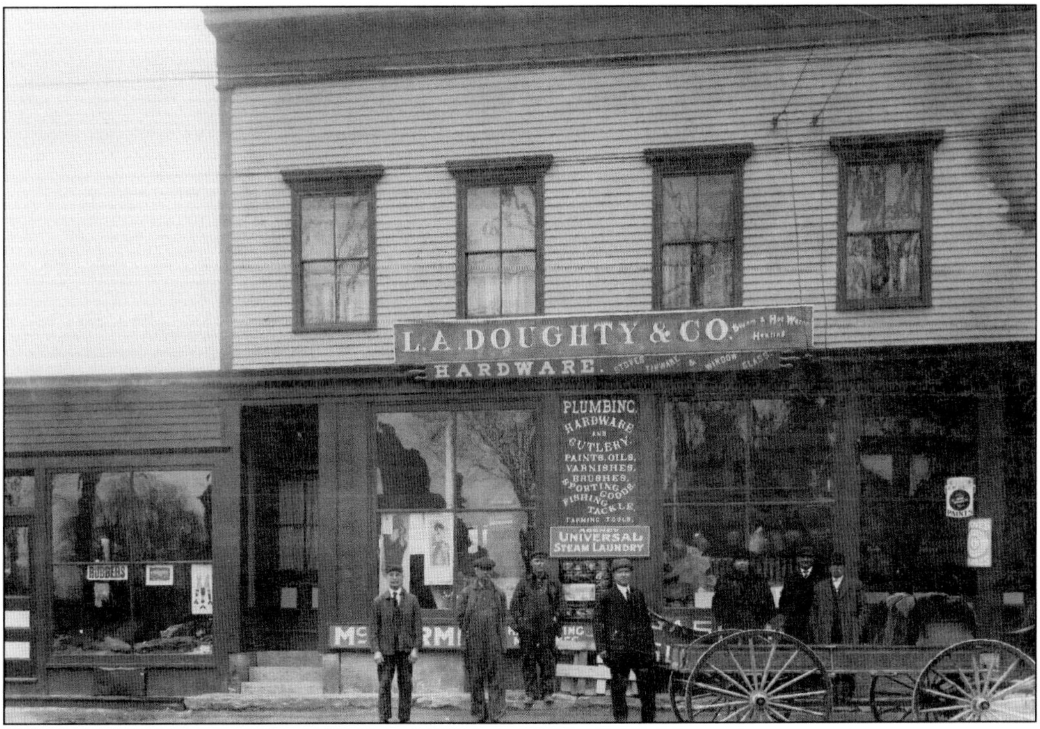

Between 1895 and 1929, L.A. Doughty & Company sold a variety of household goods in Lower Village. Hardware and bicycles were among Doughty's most popular items.

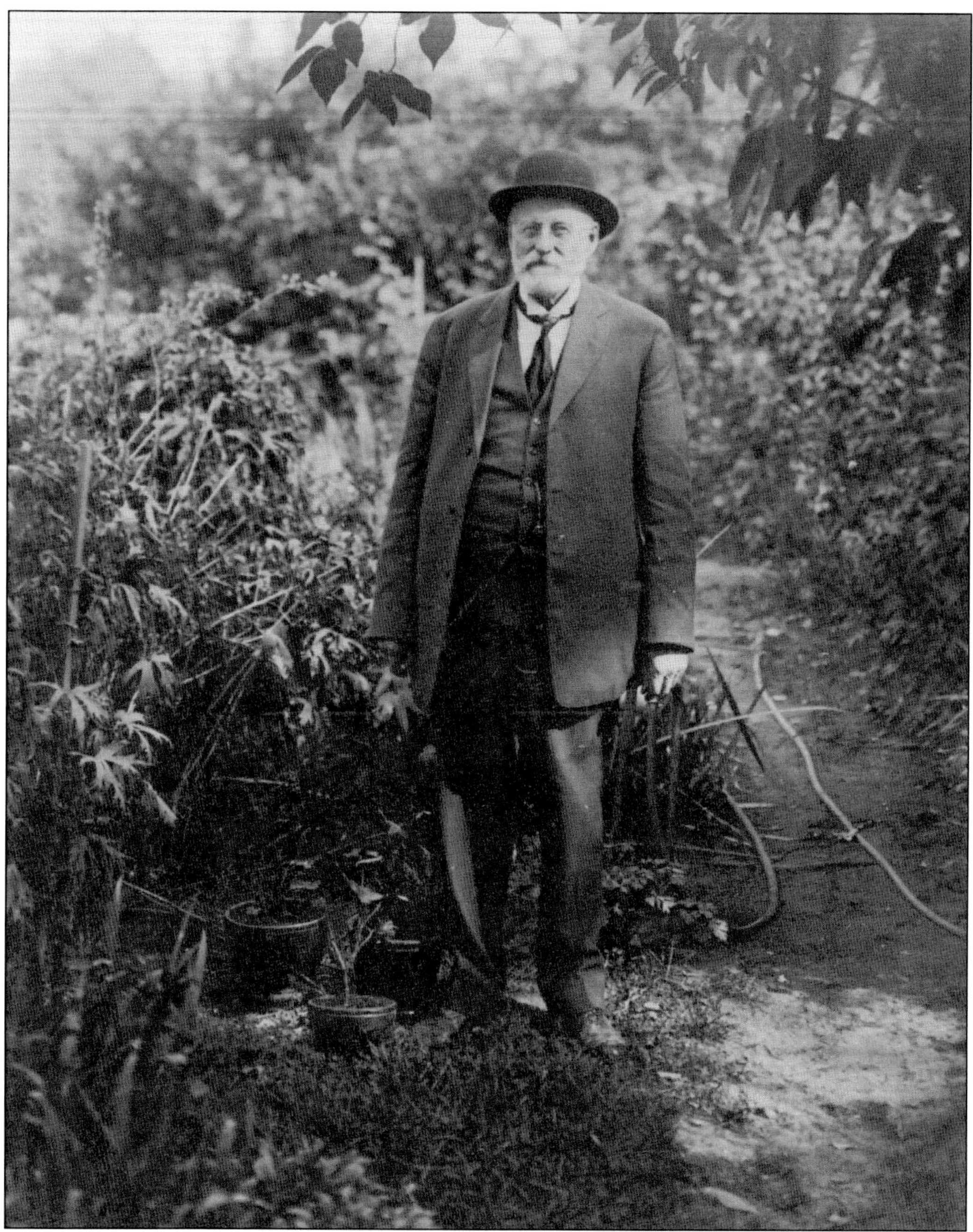

L.R. Cook served two years as a member of the Maine legislature and was highly esteemed as a businessman and town clerk for 28 years. In addition, he was a member of the Casco Lodge, the Independent Order of Odd Fellows, and the Knights of Pythias in Yarmouth. Cook was also president of the Yarmouth Poultry Association.

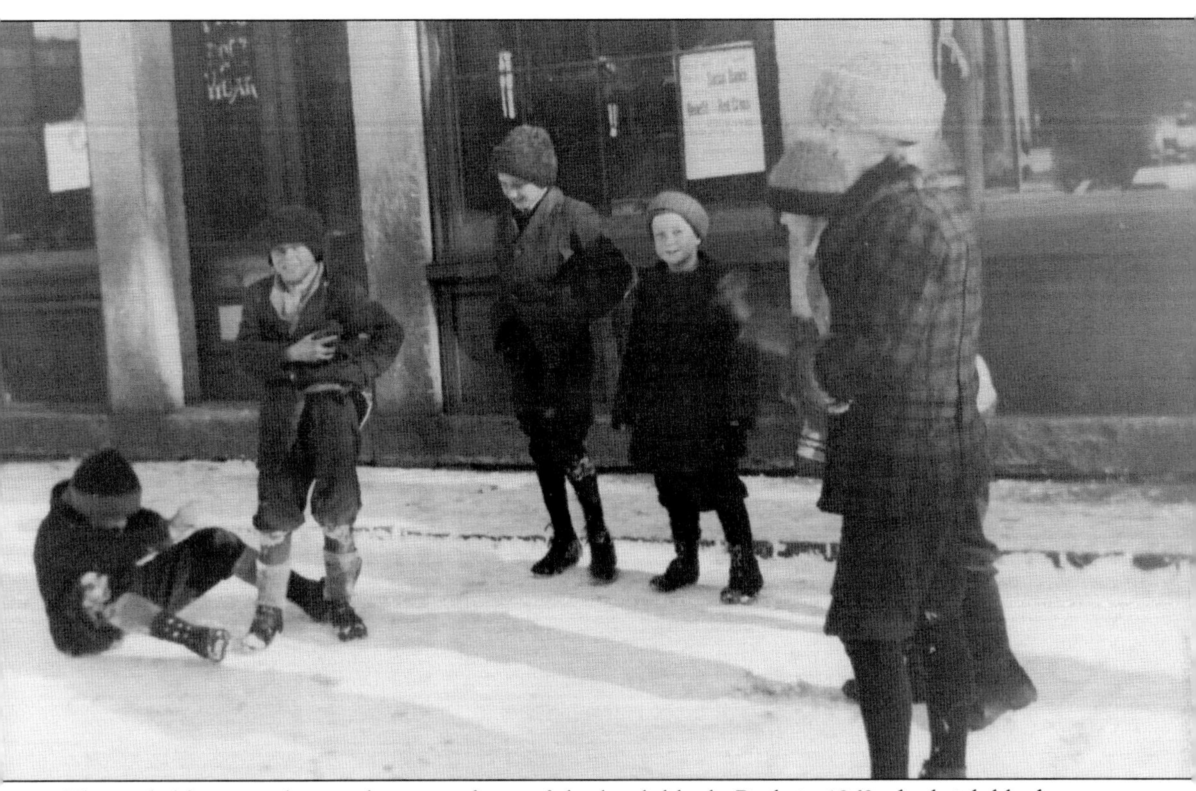

These children are shown playing in front of the brick block. Built in 1862, the brick block was the location of Marston's and L.R. Cook's at the time of this photograph. Marston's occupied the site for over 100 years as a dry goods and clothing store. William H. Marston served as town treasurer of Yarmouth from 1883 to 1900.

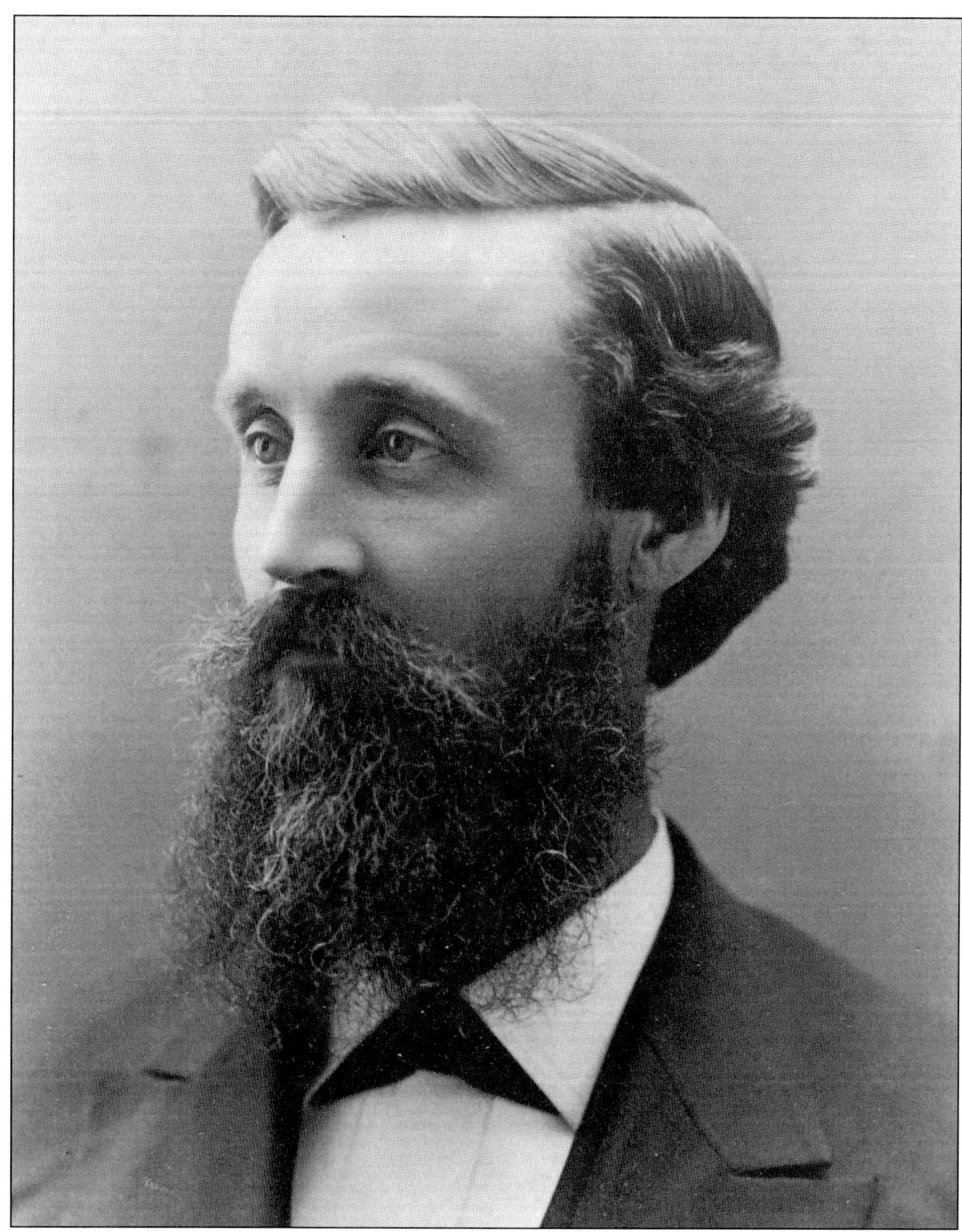

Julius Alphonso Dresser was born in Portland, Maine, in February 1838. Dresser was a follower of Phineas Parker Quimby, one of the founders of the New Thought movement. It was in Quimby's office that Julius Dresser met Annetta Seabury, the daughter of Albion Seabury and Dorcas Pratt of North Yarmouth. Albion Seabury had been a worker in the Pratt shipyard and went on to establish his own shipbuilding yard on the eastern side of the Royal River. Annetta and Julius spent their married lives espousing the teachings of Dr. Quimby.

Annetta Seabury Dresser of North Yarmouth, along with her husband, Julius, took up the practice of mental healing, teaching the Quimby system. They clashed with Mary Baker Eddy, the founder of the Christian Science movement, in what became known as the "Quimby" controversy. The Dressers had two sons who went on to recognition in their respective fields, Horatio W. Dresser and Phillip Dresser. Phillip changed his name to David Seabury to distinguish himself from his brother's writings and to reflect his grandparent's heritage.

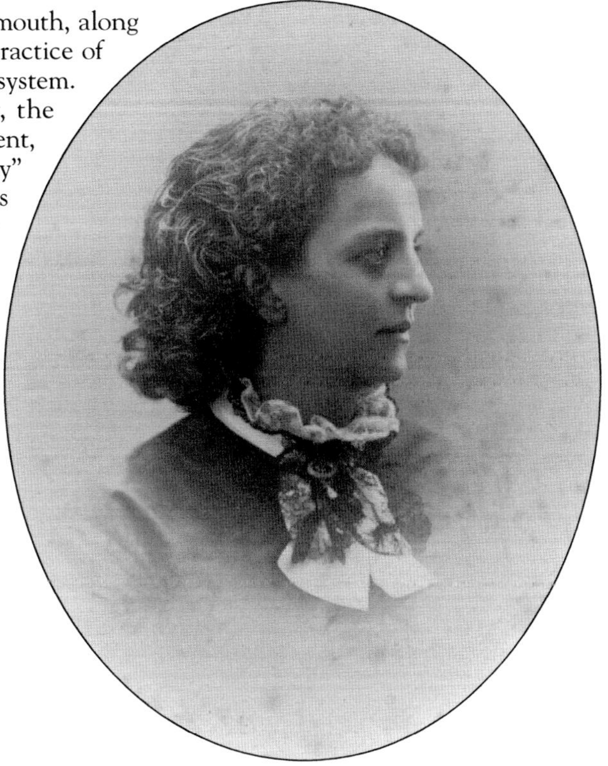

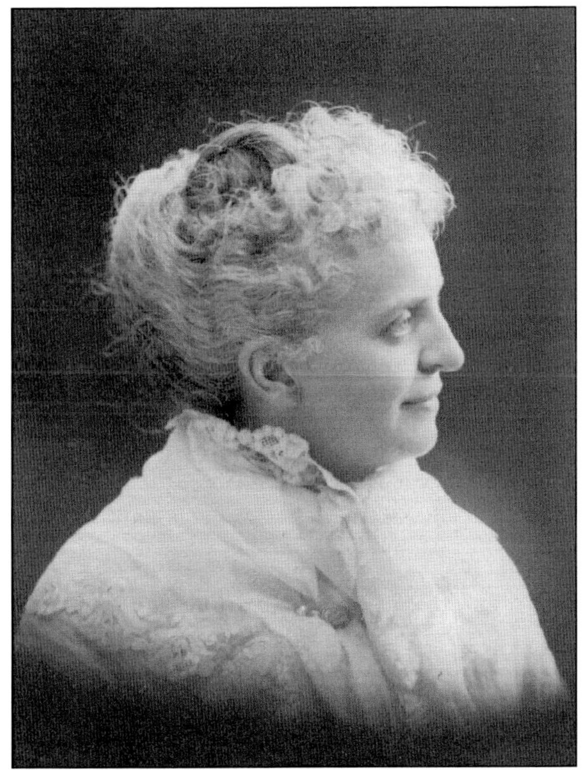

Annetta S. Dresser wrote *The Philosophy of P.P. Quimby*, which was "dedicated to the sick everywhere." Mrs. Dresser stated, "Mr. Quimby claimed that 'mind was spiritual matter, and could be changed'; that we were made up of 'truth and error'; that 'disease was an error,' or belief, and that the Truth was the cure. And upon these premises he based all his reasoning, and laid the foundation of what he asserted to be the 'science of curing the sick' without other remedial agencies than the mind."

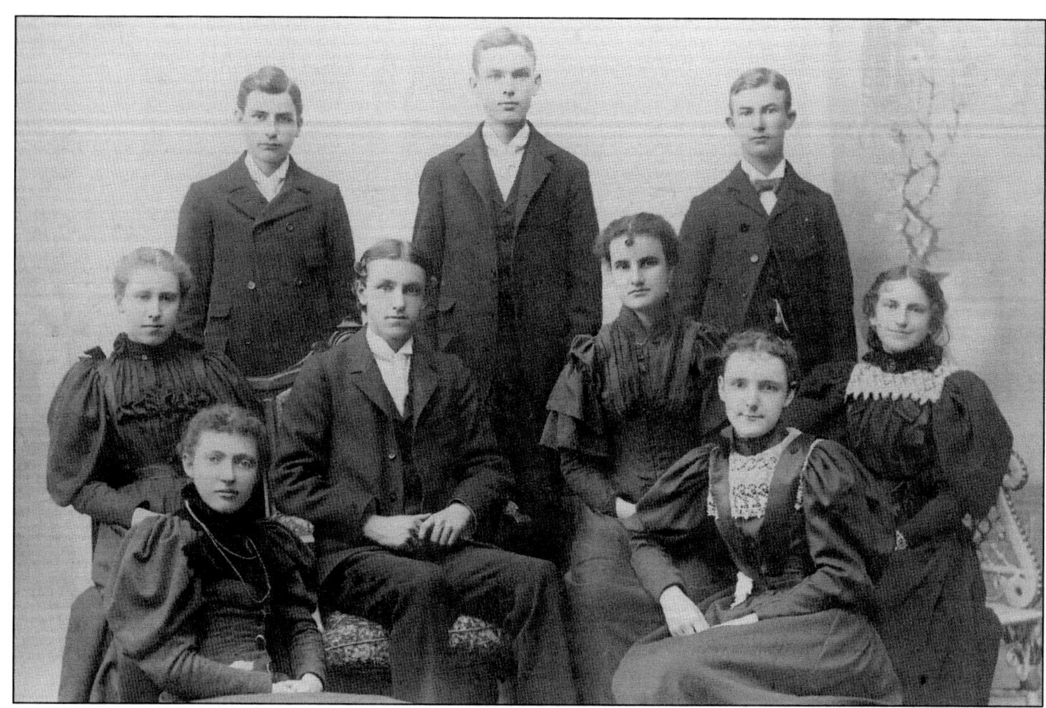

Shown in this photograph is the 1895 graduating class of Yarmouth High School. From left to right are (first row) Elizabeth Mountfort and May Leighton; (second row) Lena Skillings, Roy Johnson, Margaret Walsh, and Georgia M. Titcomb; (third row) George Raynes, Arthur Walker, and Alfred B. Small. (Courtesy of the collection of Dick Knight.)

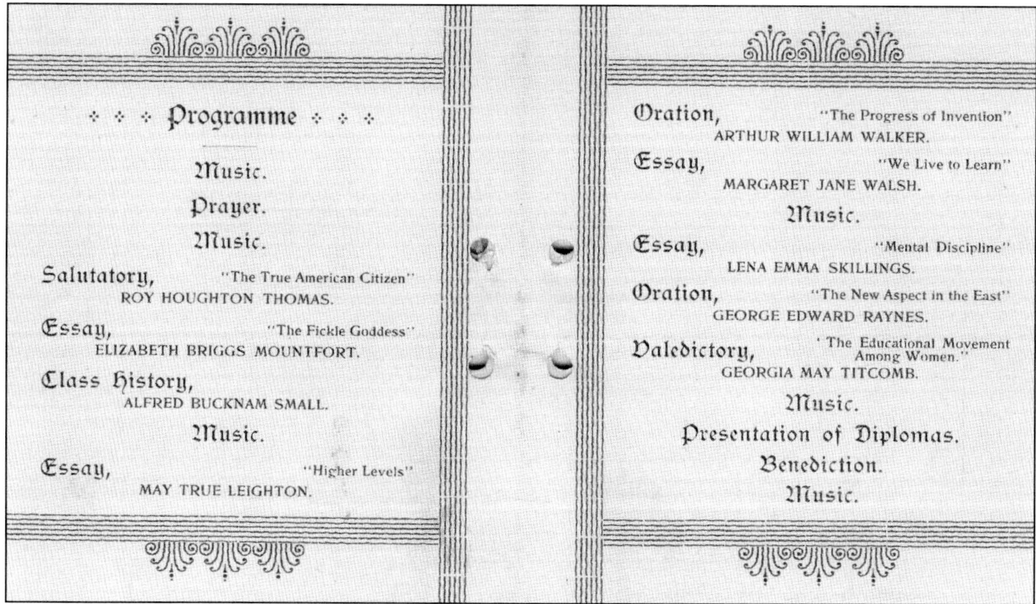

Programme

Music.

Prayer.

Music.

Salutatory, "The True American Citizen"
ROY HOUGHTON THOMAS.

Essay, "The Fickle Goddess"
ELIZABETH BRIGGS MOUNTFORT.

Class History,
ALFRED BUCKNAM SMALL.

Music.

Essay, "Higher Levels"
MAY TRUE LEIGHTON.

Oration, "The Progress of Invention"
ARTHUR WILLIAM WALKER.

Essay, "We Live to Learn"
MARGARET JANE WALSH.

Music.

Essay, "Mental Discipline"
LENA EMMA SKILLINGS.

Oration, "The New Aspect in the East"
GEORGE EDWARD RAYNES.

Valedictory, "The Educational Movement Among Women."
GEORGIA MAY TITCOMB.

Music.

Presentation of Diplomas.

Benediction.

Music.

This is the program for the commencement exercises for the class of 1895 of Yarmouth High School. The class's graduation was on June 21 at 8:00 p.m., and Georgia Mayall Titcomb gave a valedictory talk on "The Education Movement Among Women." (Courtesy of the collection of Dick Knight.)

Georgia Mayall Titcomb is shown in her graduation photograph in 1895. Yarmouth High School students attended North Yarmouth Academy until 1890, when the town erected a new Central School. High school students attended classes on the second floor of this building for 10 years, when the growing number of students proved the need for a separate high school building. This school was located alongside the original building, which became the grammar school, on the site of the current town hall. (Courtesy of the collection of Dick Knight.)

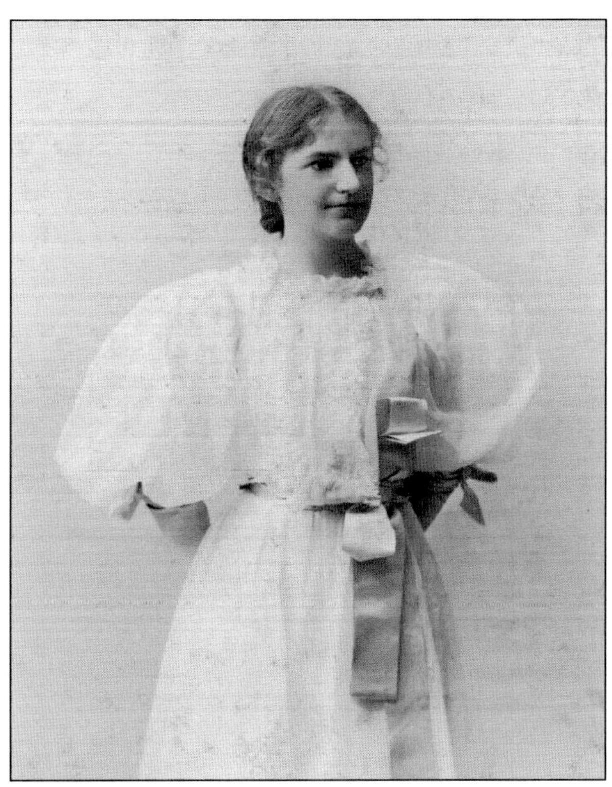

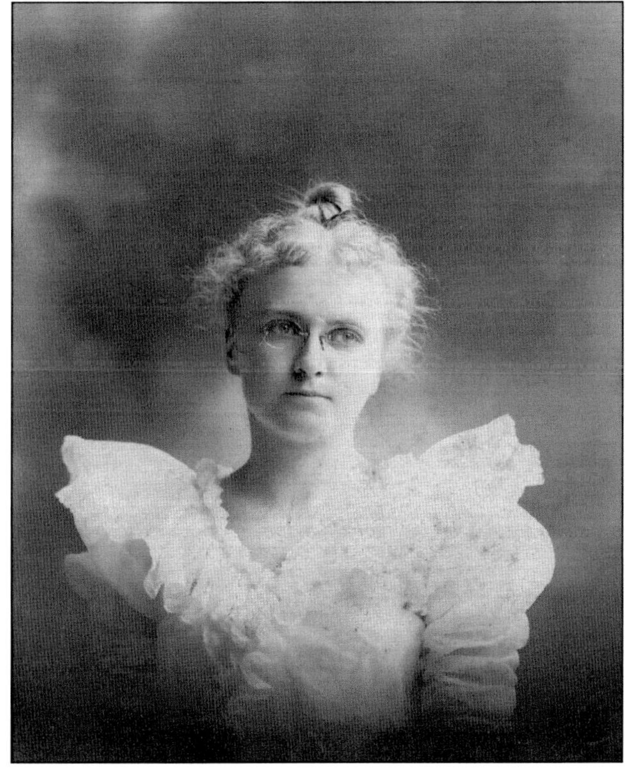

Lucy Loring Ring was born in Yarmouth in September 1875. She was the daughter of Ansel and Martha Dennison Loring. After graduation from Yarmouth High School, Lucy taught school on Cousins Island. Her father rowed her over to the island every Sunday evening. She received $7 a week, with $2 going toward room and board. After attending Kent's Hill school and working in Massachusetts, Lucy Loring married Harry Ring in 1905. (Courtesy of the collection of Dick Knight.)

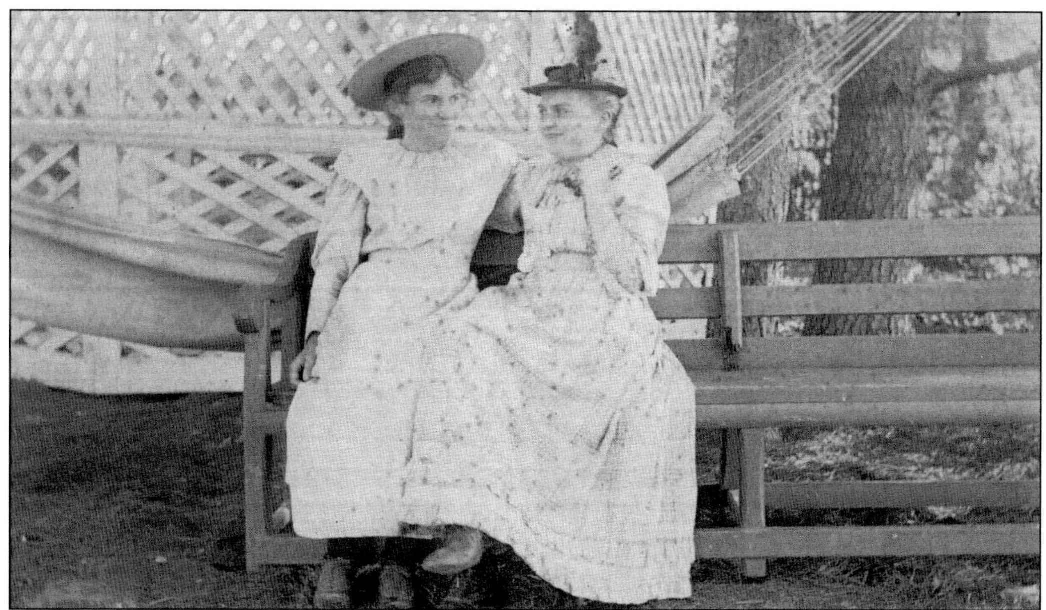

Georgia Mayall Titcomb and Lucy Loring Ring are shown here as juniors at Yarmouth High School in September 1893. Georgia Titcomb and Lucy Ring were longtime members of the Fortnightly Club, a women's club formed in 1896. In a history of the club, Georgia Titcomb recorded a short list of topics covered including geographical outline and history of China to Confucius, architecture in the 19th century, a discussion of the 1922 "Yarmouth Tax Rate," highlights in Russian history to Nicholas II, contemporary painters, and the "ideal woman." (Courtesy of the collection of Dick Knight.)

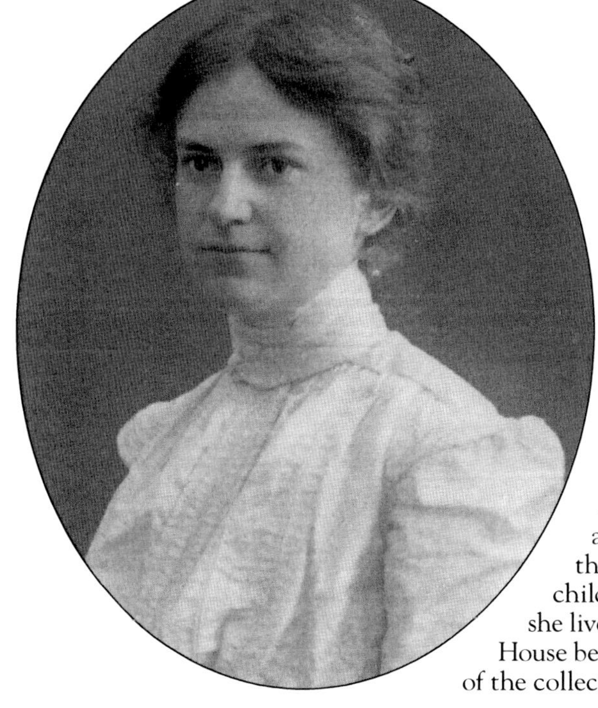

After graduation, Georgia M. Titcomb attended Wellesley College for a year. She then spent six years as a tutor for the Ricker children in South Poland, Maine. As a tutor, she lived in the Mansion House at Poland Spring House between the years 1896 and 1902. (Courtesy of the collection of Dick Knight.)

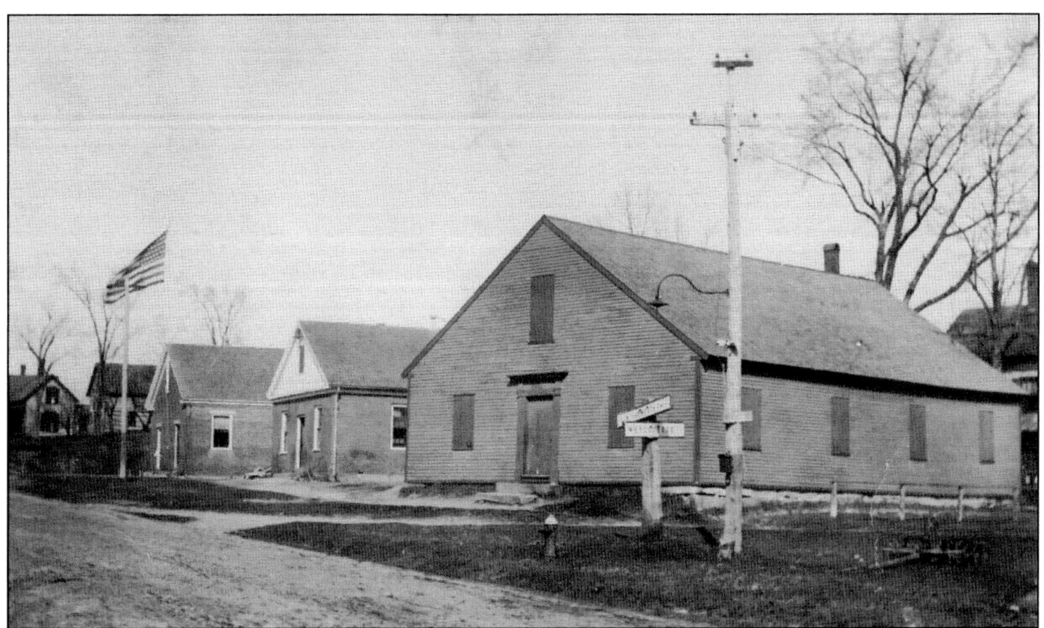

The old town house was located on the corner of West Main Street and Sligo Road from 1833 to 1910. In this building, the town of North Yarmouth, which was made up of today's Yarmouth and North Yarmouth, voted to split into two towns in 1849. Because the meeting was so large, the voters had to assemble on the street with the ayes on one side and the nays on the other side. Next to the building are the two brick schools built in the 1840s. The buildings were improved with electric lights in 1937 and used as schools until 1992. The old town house was removed in 1910.

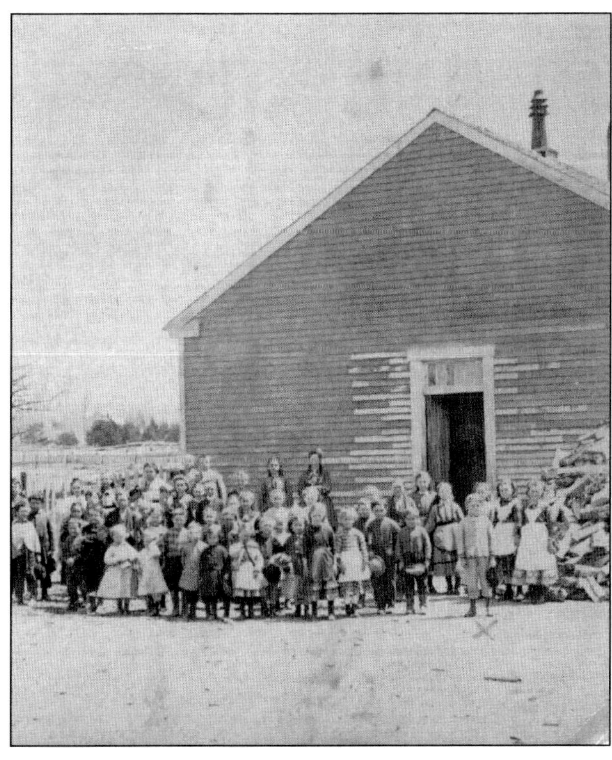

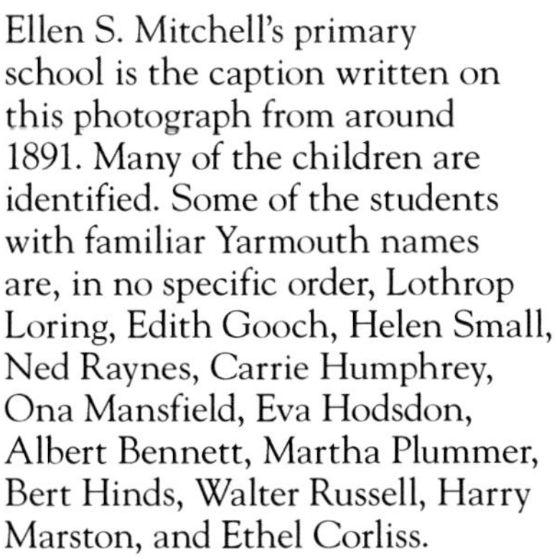

Ellen S. Mitchell's primary school is the caption written on this photograph from around 1891. Many of the children are identified. Some of the students with familiar Yarmouth names are, in no specific order, Lothrop Loring, Edith Gooch, Helen Small, Ned Raynes, Carrie Humphrey, Ona Mansfield, Eva Hodsdon, Albert Bennett, Martha Plummer, Bert Hinds, Walter Russell, Harry Marston, and Ethel Corliss.

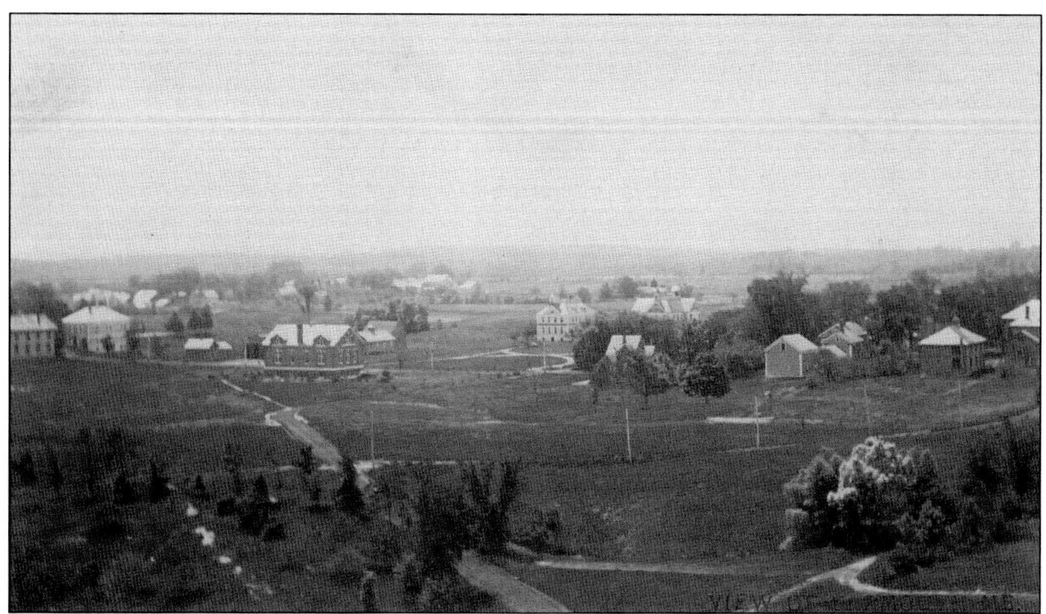

Shown in this photograph is a view from the Forest Paper Company with Merrill Memorial Library in the foreground and the Central Grammar School on the other side of Main Street. The Masonic Hall, built in 1878, is to the left.

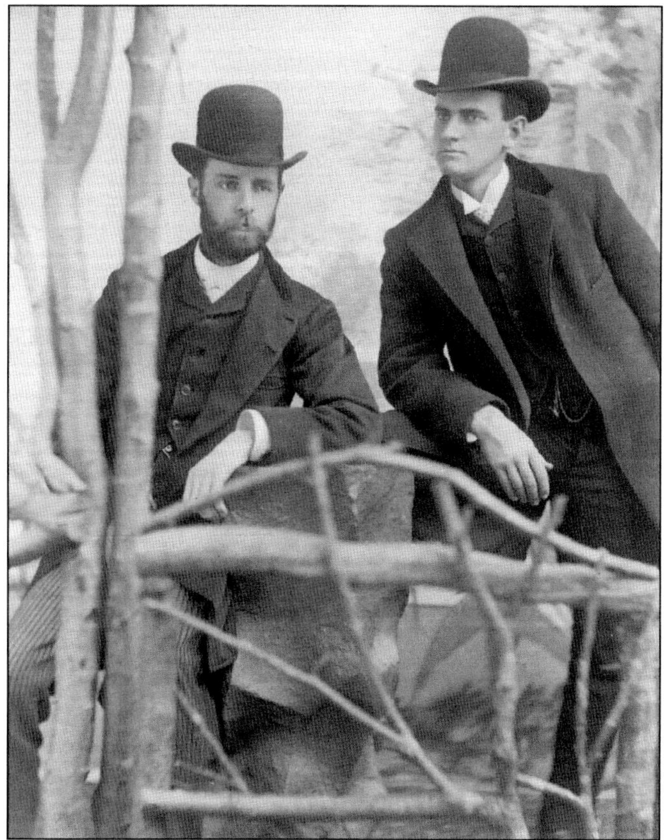

This photograph of Charles G. Gooding (left) and Byron Allen is notable because Gooding is the one being photographed. C.G. Gooding was a well-known photographer and had studios in Yarmouth and Old Orchard Beach.

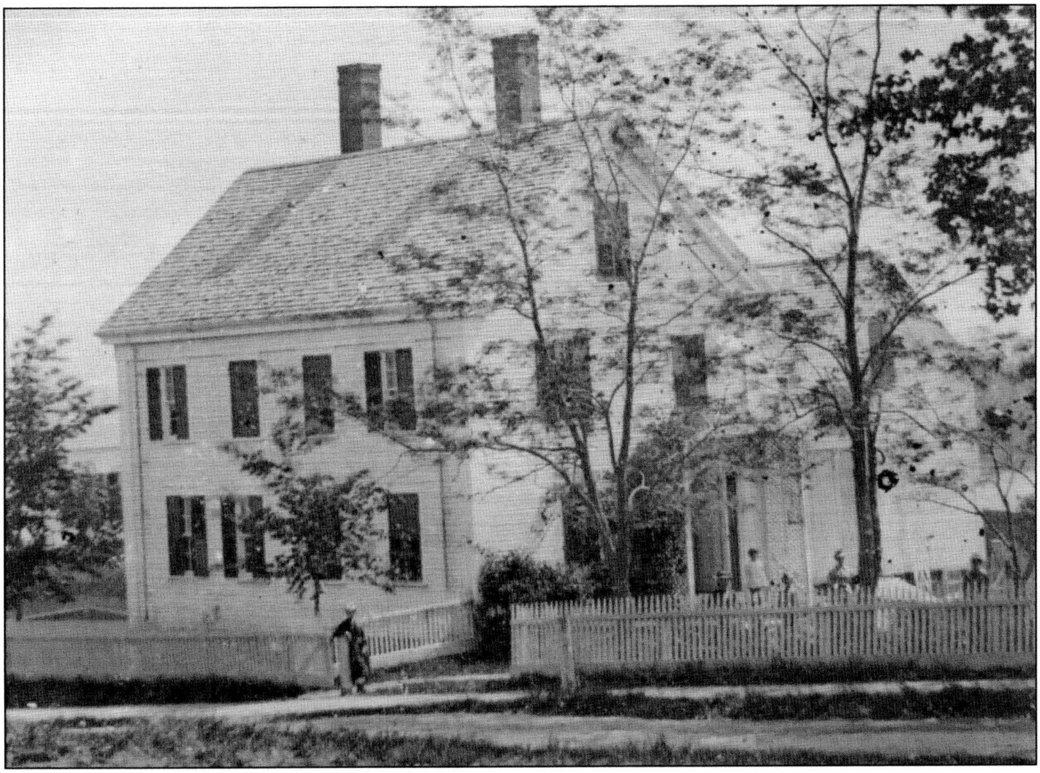

Gooding was from a family of boatbuilders, and his home on Pleasant Street gave him a superb vantage point to the shipyards. C.G. Gooding took many of the shipyard photographs in the Yarmouth Historical Society collection.

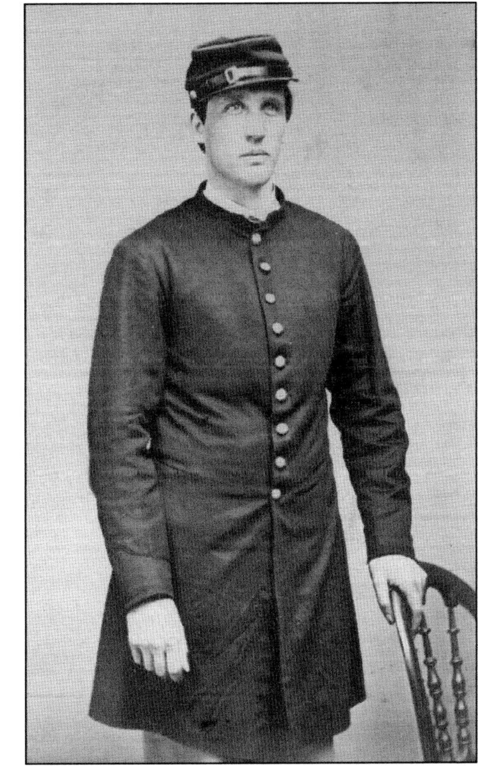

In response to President Lincoln's call in August 1862 for 3,000 volunteers, the 17th Maine raised 24 Yarmouth men. Shown here in his uniform is Pvt. Ammi D. Seabury of Company E. A total of 170 Yarmouth citizens went off to fight in the war.

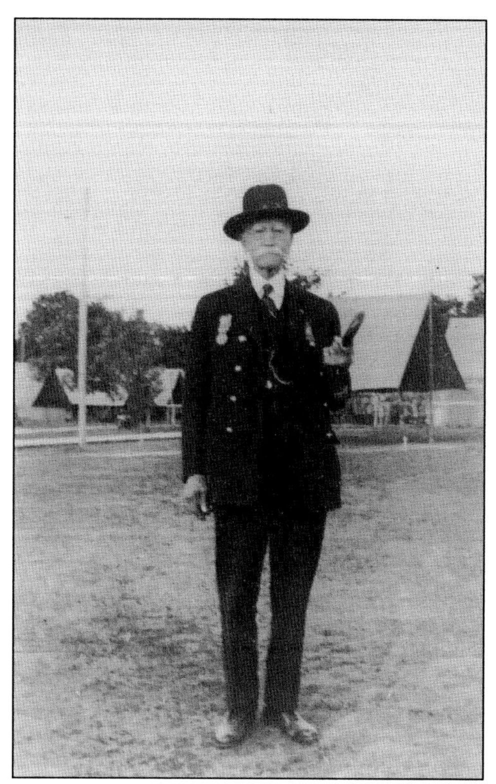

Charles Levi Marston is shown visiting the Gettysburg battle's site on the 75th anniversary. Marston, a Civil War veteran, was born in North Yarmouth in May 1846. He enlisted in the Union army in 1864 and became a sergeant in the 1st Maine Cavalry. Marston was taken prisoner in the battle of Sycamore Church, yet managed to escape and make his way back to the Union lines. Marston was the last surviving member of the W.O. Haskell Grand Army of the Republic. (Courtesy of the collection of Dick Knight.)

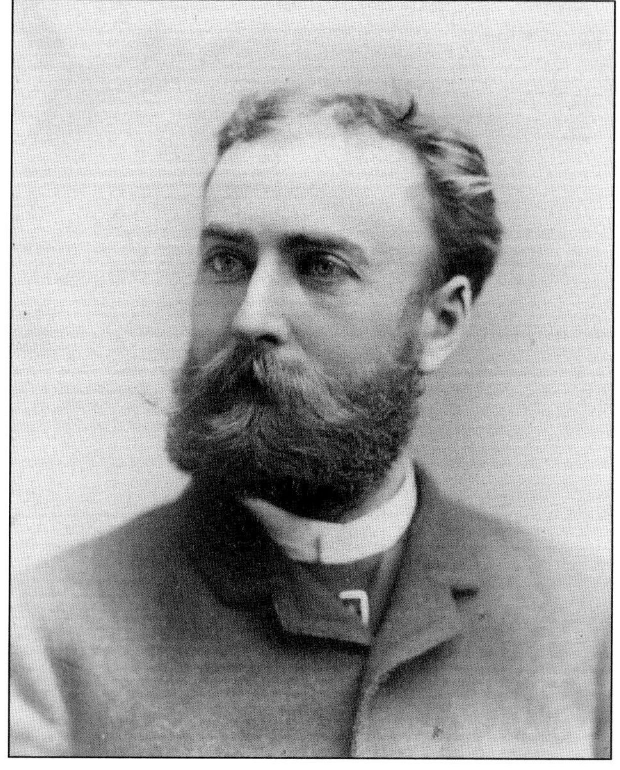

Elias Dudley Freeman attended North Yarmouth Academy and later served as a trustee for 20 years. He was elected to serve in the Maine senate from 1889 to 1891 and was a member of the governor's council from 1895 to 1898. Freeman was a passenger on the steamer *Portland* when it sailed from Boston to its Maine port in November 1898 and was lost with all on board.

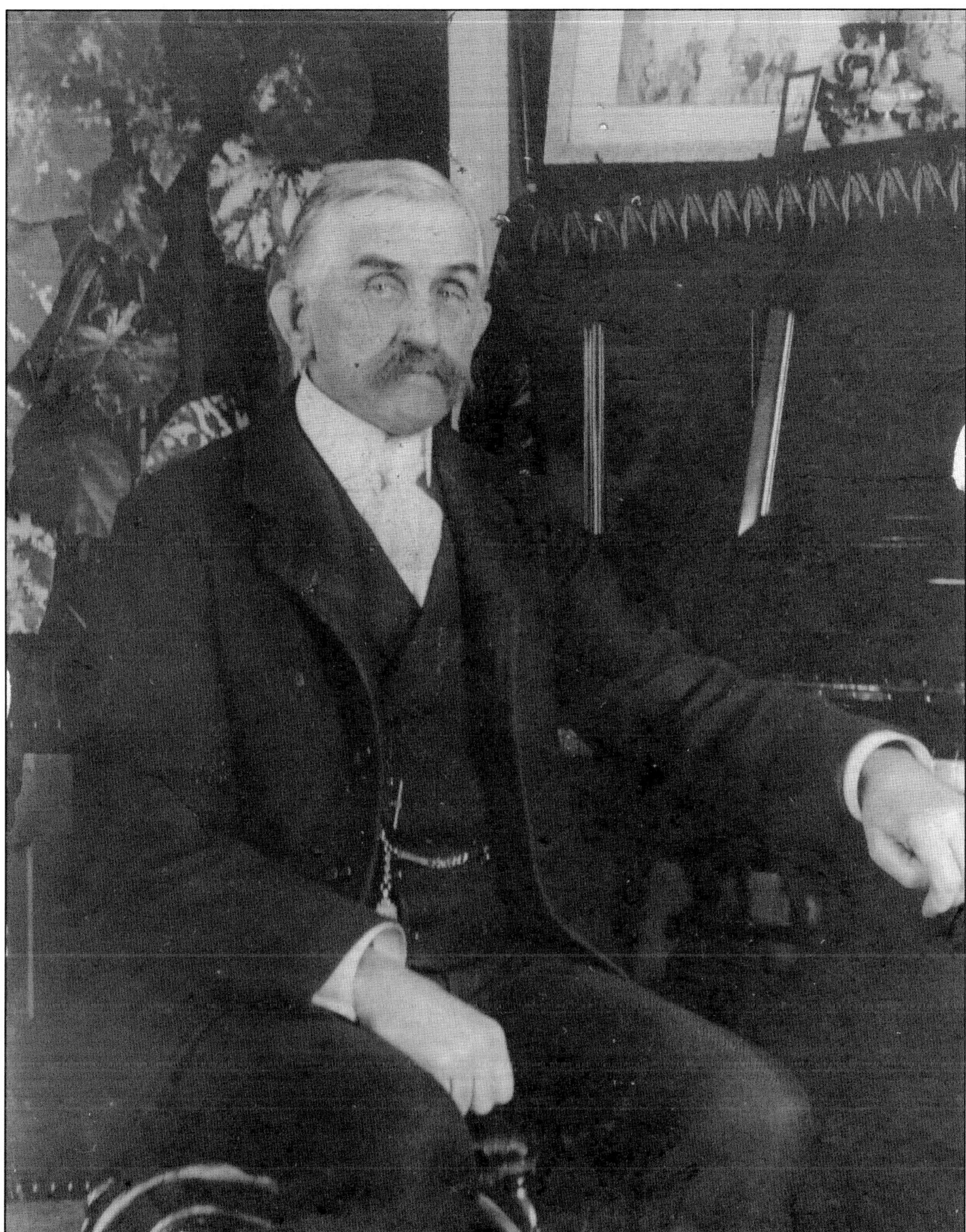

Prof. Enos Albert Blanchard served as the instructor of the Yarmouth Band. Professor Blanchard was a musician of prominence who found himself in the position of teaching the newly formed band the basic rudiments. In the early years, only one member could actually read music, but under the direction of Professor Blanchard, the band later gained a well-deserved reputation and was in great demand. After two seasons, they were invited to play at the junior declamations at Bowdoin College. Professor Blanchard left but returned 10 years later and once more became director.

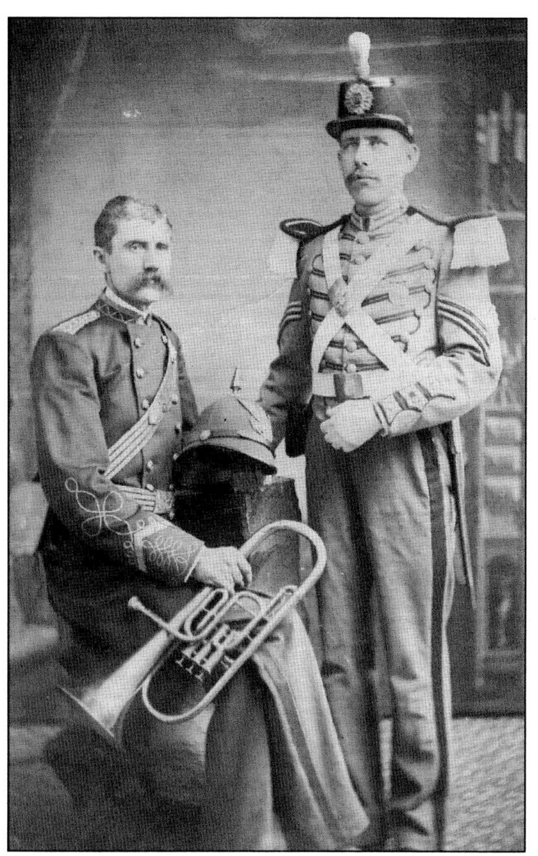

Monroe Stoddard (left) and Frank Hale are pictured in this photograph that shows the uniforms of the Yarmouth Band and the Yarmouth Rifles. According to an 1884 newspaper clipping found in the Yarmouth Rifles account book, "the company expended nearly $1,500 during the past year, the principal sum being for uniforms and the company colors." Stoddard also served as general supervisor of the cotton mill.

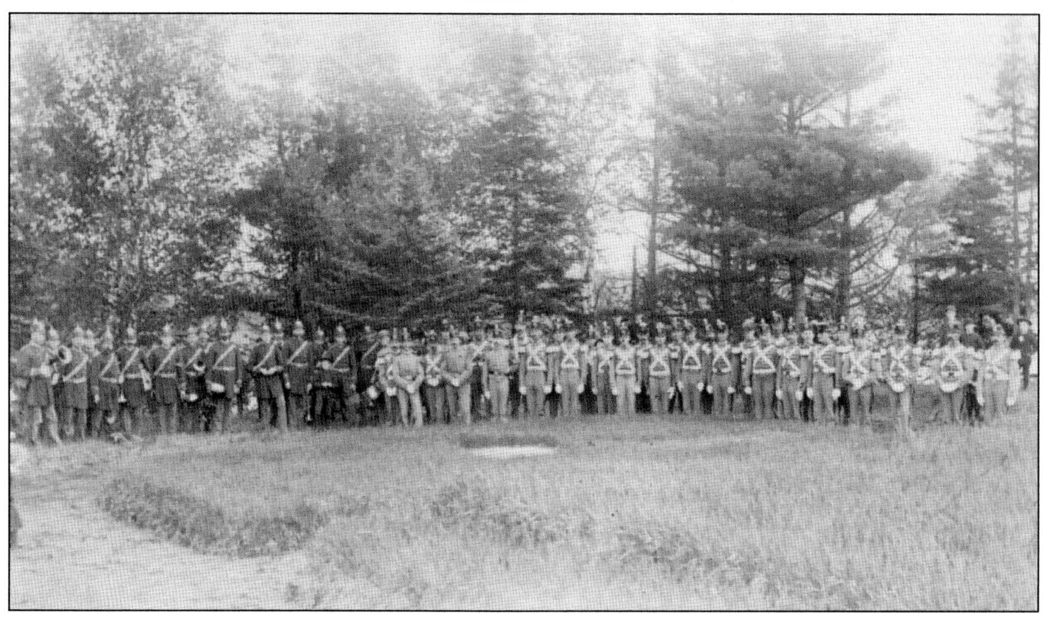

Shown together in this field, the Yarmouth Band and the Yarmouth Rifles often participated in musters, parades, and other events together. The Yarmouth Rifles, formed in 1883 and maintained until 1897, was one of the largest and best-drilled military companies in the state.

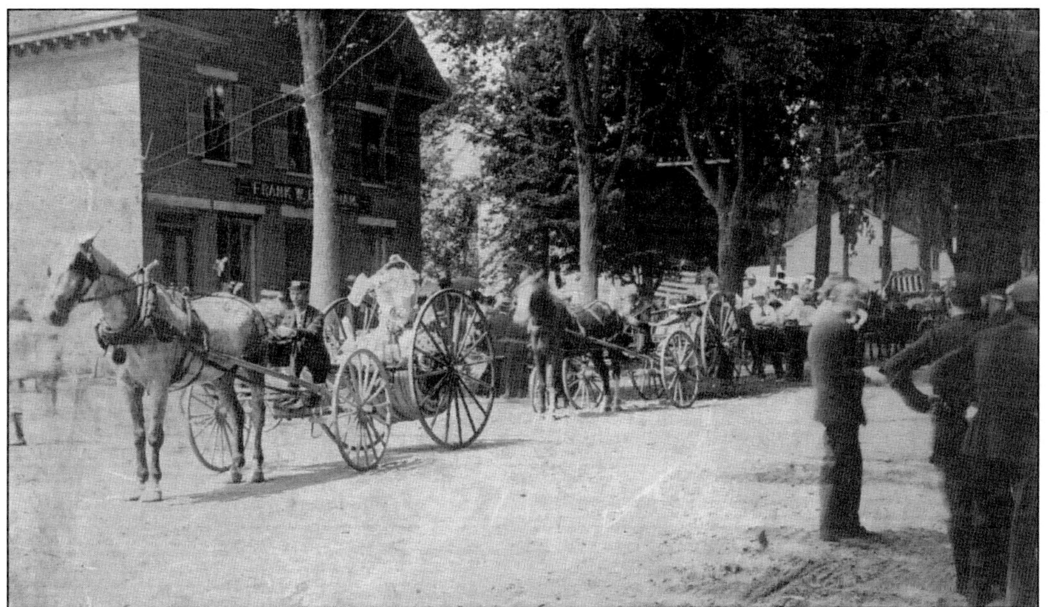

In celebration of the town's new water system, a firemen's muster was held, and companies from as far away as Waterville attended. A morning parade of firemen, bands, and military companies was followed by afternoon contests for firemen and their equipment.

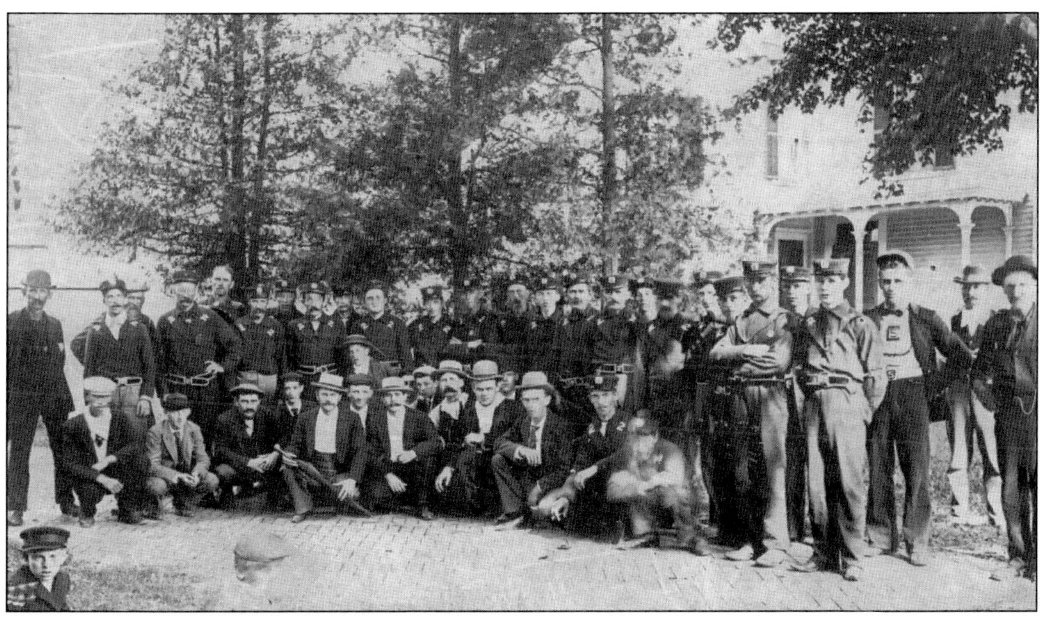

The majority of men in this photograph have No. 2 on their uniforms, indicating they were members of Hose Company No. 2. Hose Company No. 2 was located in Falls Village at the top of the hill leading down to the harbor. Members of Hose Company No. 1 were stationed at the fire barn on Center Street, built in 1904.

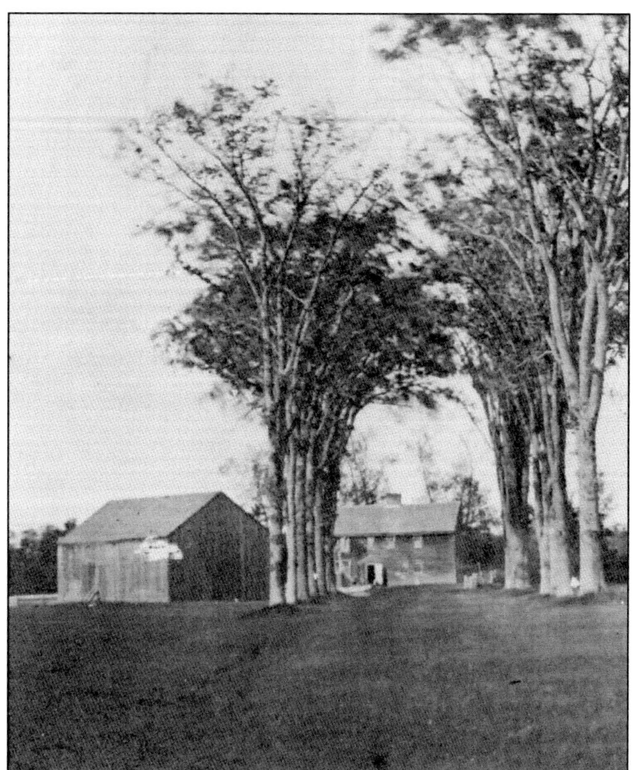

Jacob Mitchell built his garrison on the west bank of the Royal River about 1729 as one of the nine fortified houses intended to protect settlers from attacks. The rows of elms south of the house led to Gilman Road and the old Meetinghouse under the Ledge. Mitchell's family lived in the house until 1799. This photograph was taken around 1900.

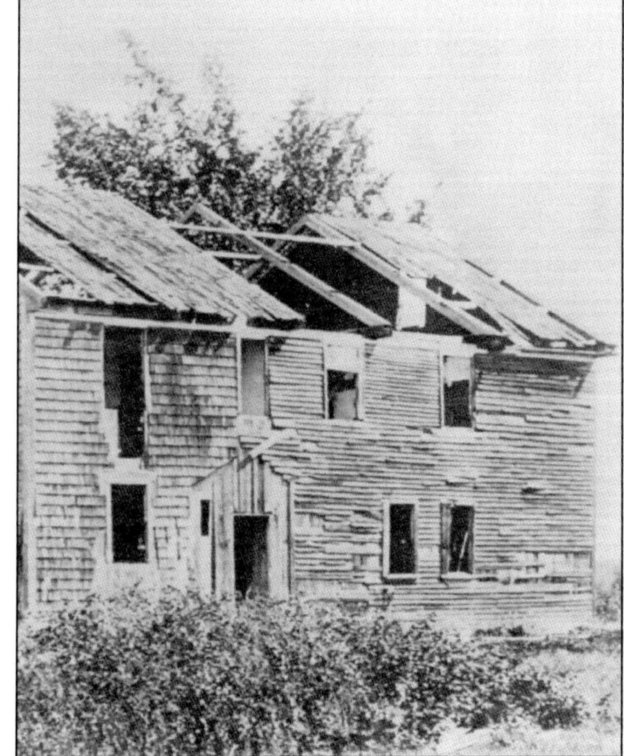

Zadoc Whitcomb purchased the Mitchell garrison, and members of the family owned the house for the next century. The house and barn were abandoned and gradually deteriorated. In 1915, the Catholic Church purchased the property for Holy Cross Cemetery.

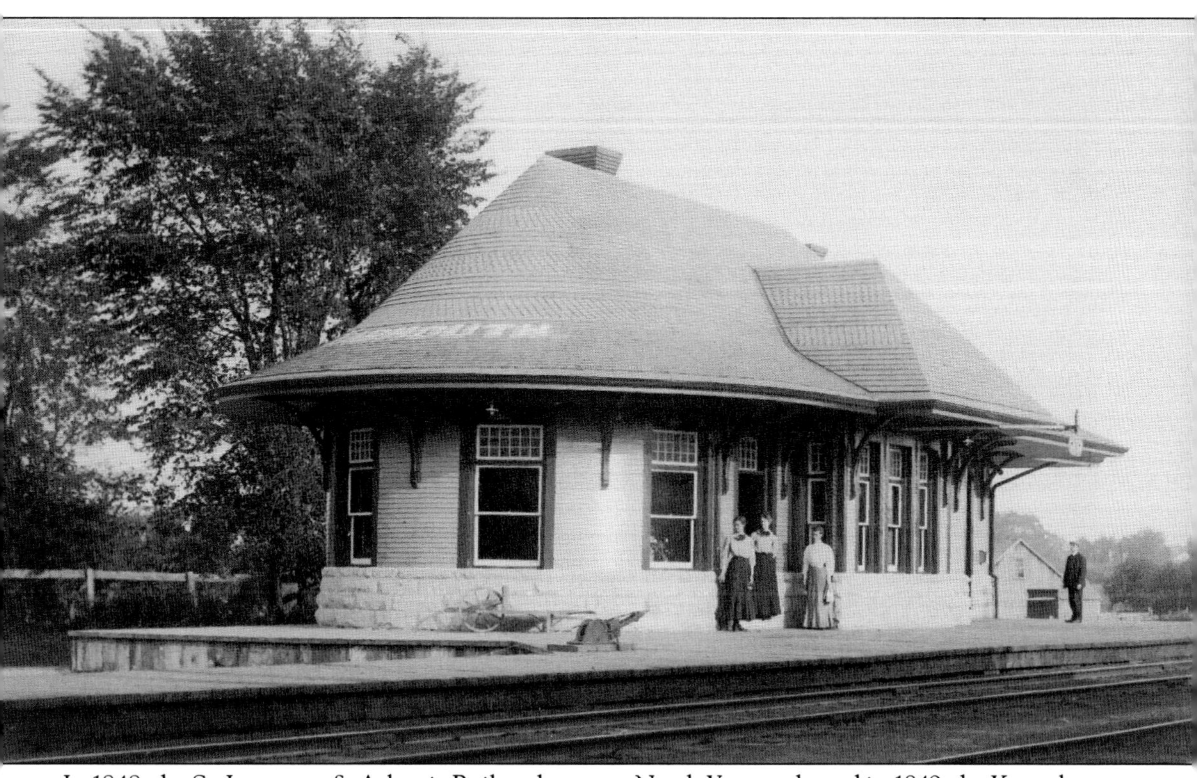

In 1848, the St. Lawrence & Atlantic Railroad came to North Yarmouth, and in 1849, the Kennebec & Portland (later Maine Central) arrived. The two intersected just outside of town at Yarmouth junction. The Maine legislature created a board of internal improvements in 1834 with the intent of focusing on an internal railroad system that would be independent of outside control.

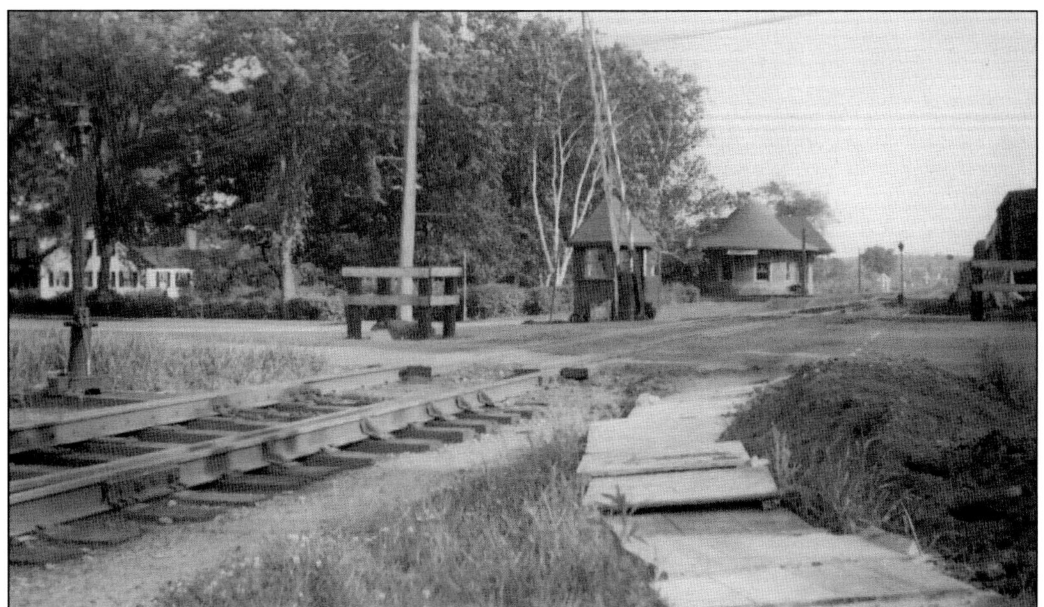

This broad gauge railroad was created to funnel interior traffic to Portland in competition with the standard-gauge railroads that brought trains into the port of Boston. The railroads allowed the shipyards and the mills to transfer goods quickly and efficiently.

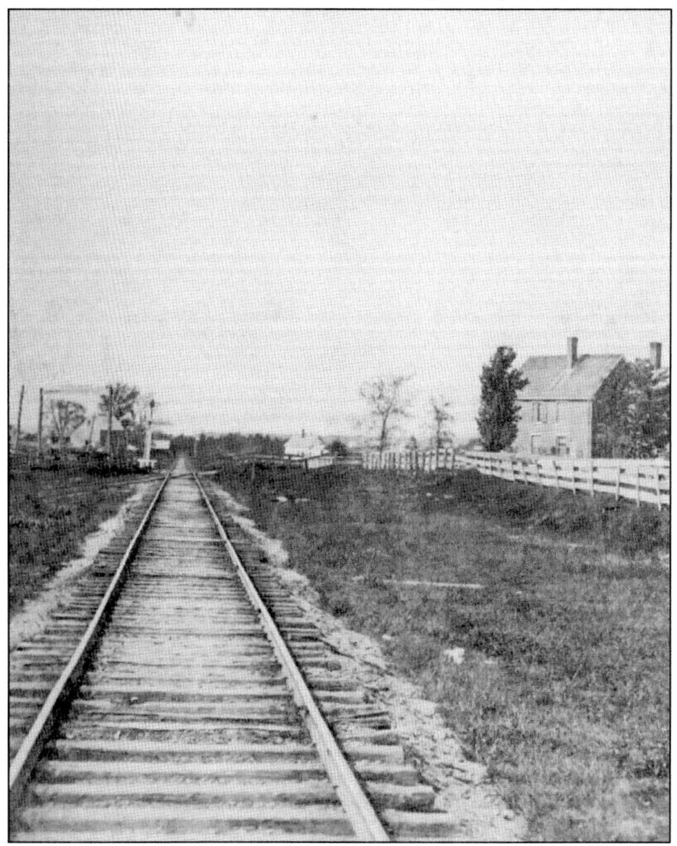

Portland businessman John Poor recognized the opportunity for the city to serve as an ice-free winter port for Canada. Poor believed rail connections with Boston would threaten Portland's seaport and advocated a separate system of Maine gauge railroads. As it tied its system into the rest of the nation, the Maine Central abandoned the broad gauge for the widely used standard gauge in 1871.

Two

Royal River and the Mills

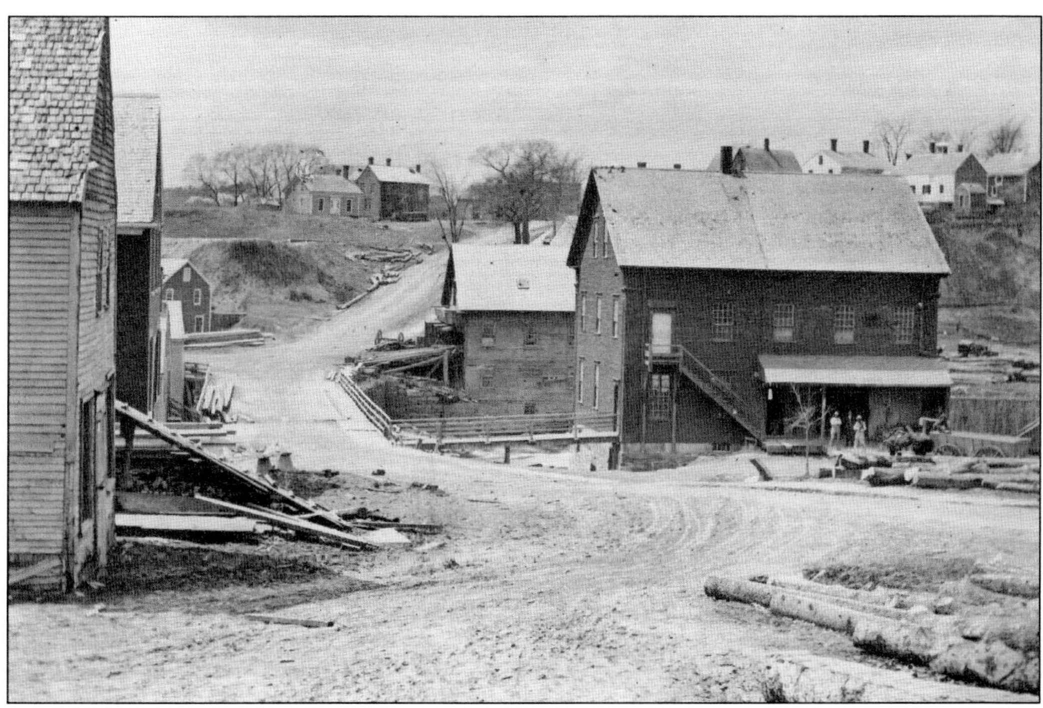

Many different mills were located on both sides of East Main Street falls. This image, looking across the East Main Street Bridge toward Main Street, shows a gristmill on the east bank. Other mills that operated in this area included a fulling mill, an iron foundry, a tannery, a blacksmith shop, and an electric power plant. Some of the men who "went to sea" remained at home during the winter and attended navigation classes taught at night in the mill.

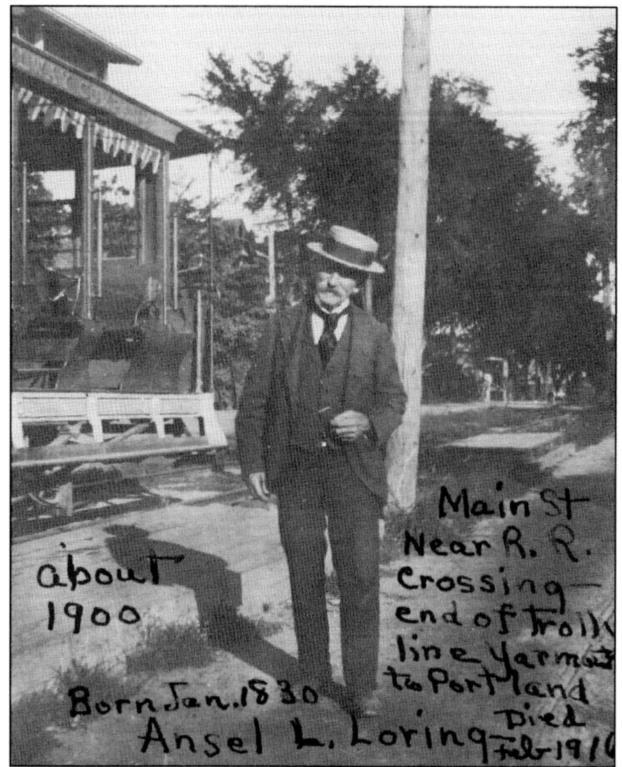

Ansel Lothrop Loring was an entrepreneur and part owner of the gristmill across the falls from Craig's sawmill. Loring left Maine in 1849 at age 19 on the bark *Glen* to sail to California, where he spent three years prospecting and mining gold. Following his return to Yarmouth, Loring operated a mill at the fourth falls until it burned in 1870. He rebuilt his flour and plaster mill at the lower falls, which he operated until 1885.

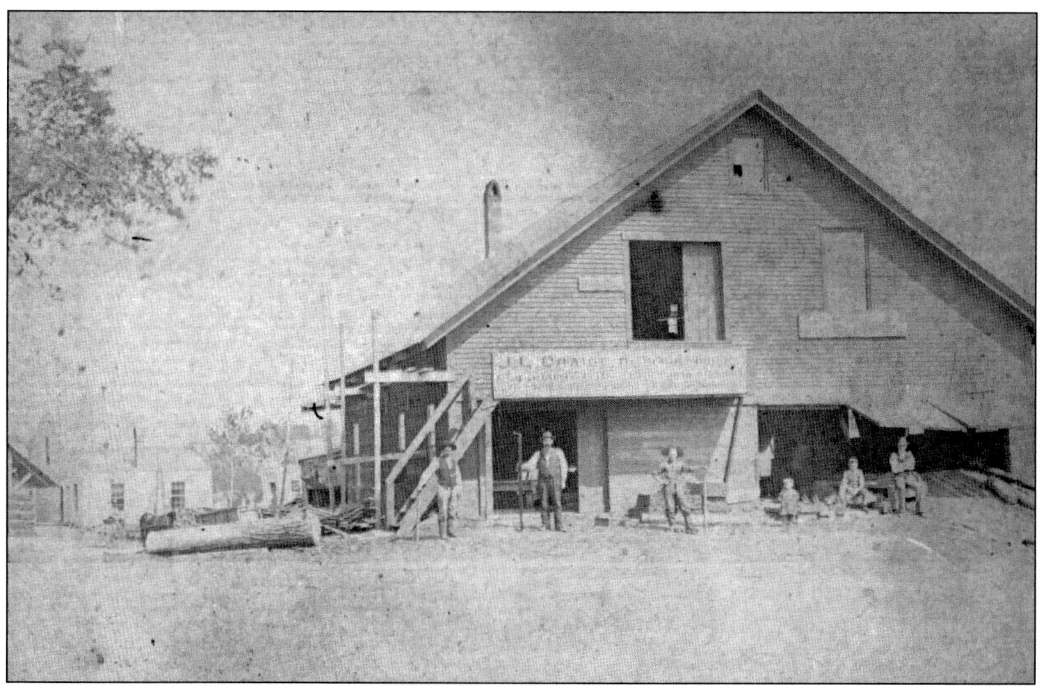

Craig's sawmill was located at the first falls. From the time of the first settlement, a sawmill was an essential business to support the growth of the town. Oxen were used to bring logs from the inland area to the mill. The first falls is located on Lafayette Street across from the harbor.

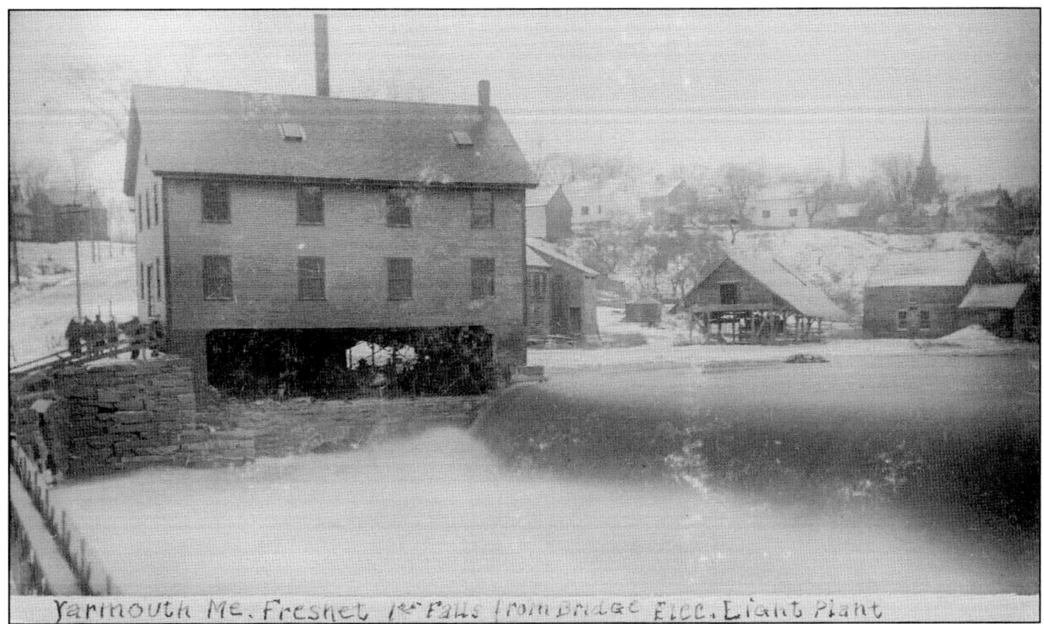

This c. 1896 photograph is of a freshet at the Yarmouth electric light plant, located at the first falls. Theresa Merrill, a local schoolteacher, wrote in her diary that a freshet seriously damaged the side foundations of the electric light plant and that water rushed through the basement. According to Merrill, the scene was one of desolation and ruin.

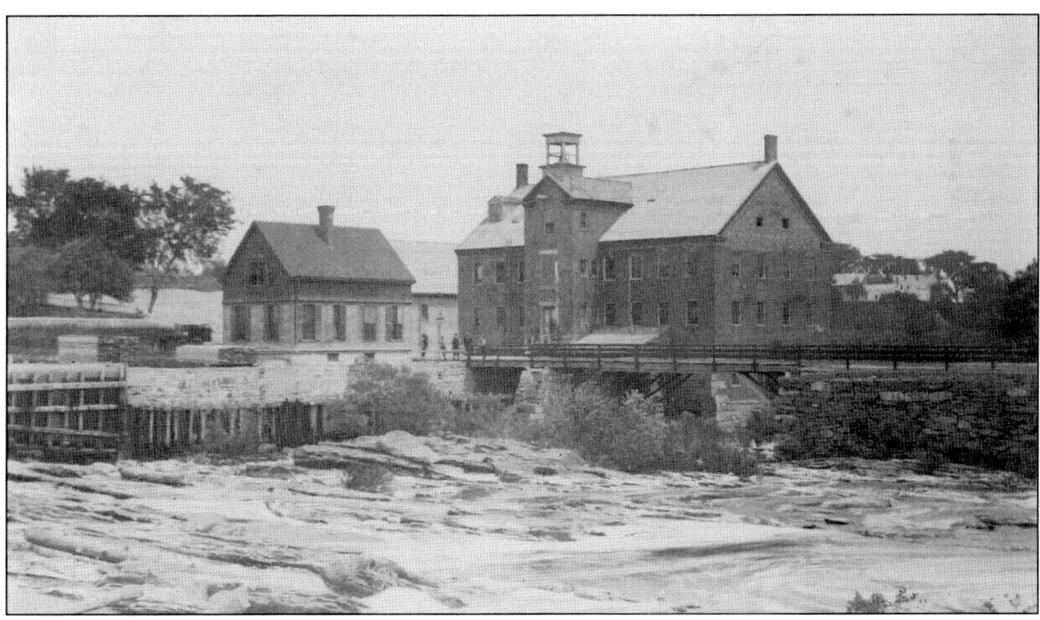

This is one of the earlier photographs taken of the cotton mill on Bridge Street. The building across from the cotton mill was the location of a paper mill that began operation in 1816 when William Hawes and George and Henry Cox constructed their mill on Bridge Street. It lasted in various forms until about 1840.

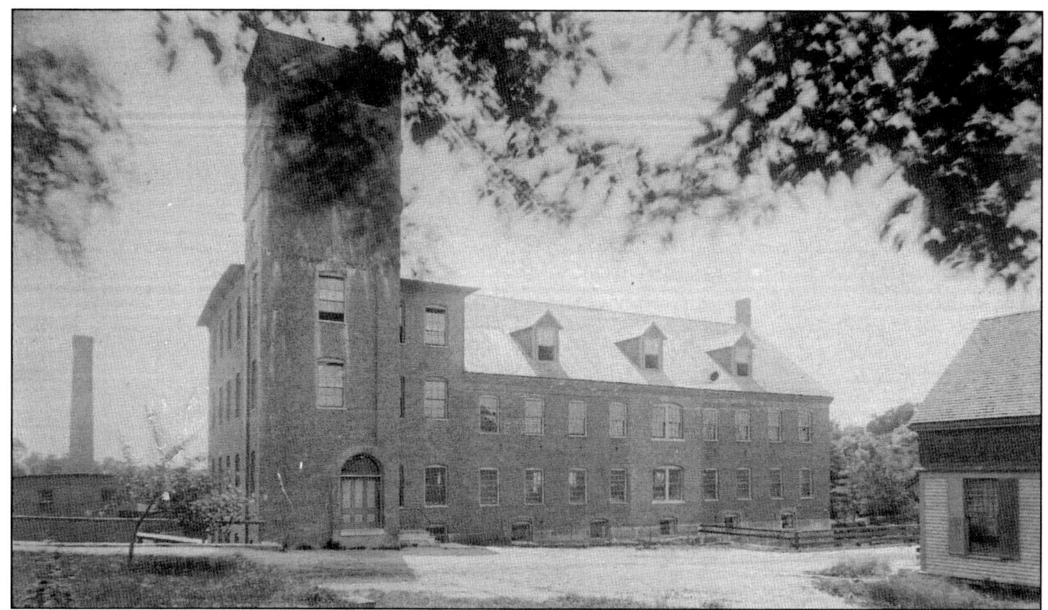

This photograph, taken prior to 1890, is a view of the cotton mill from the street. In 1855, the Royal River Manufacturing Company was established. Barnabus Freeman, a Yarmouth attorney, took it over in 1871, and together with Lorenzo L. Shaw called it Freeman, Shaw and Company until 1888, when Freeman retired. L.L. Shaw ran the factory until his death in 1907.

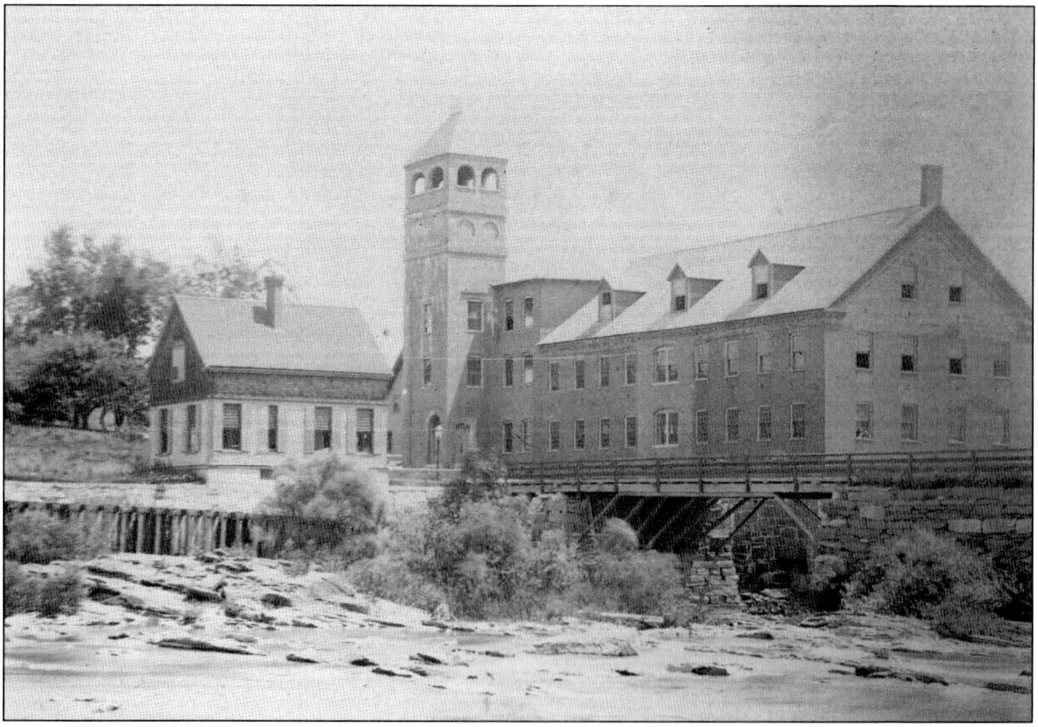

This view of the cotton mill was taken from across the Royal River with the mill's offices in the building at the far right. This photograph was taken after construction on the mill tower was completed in 1890.

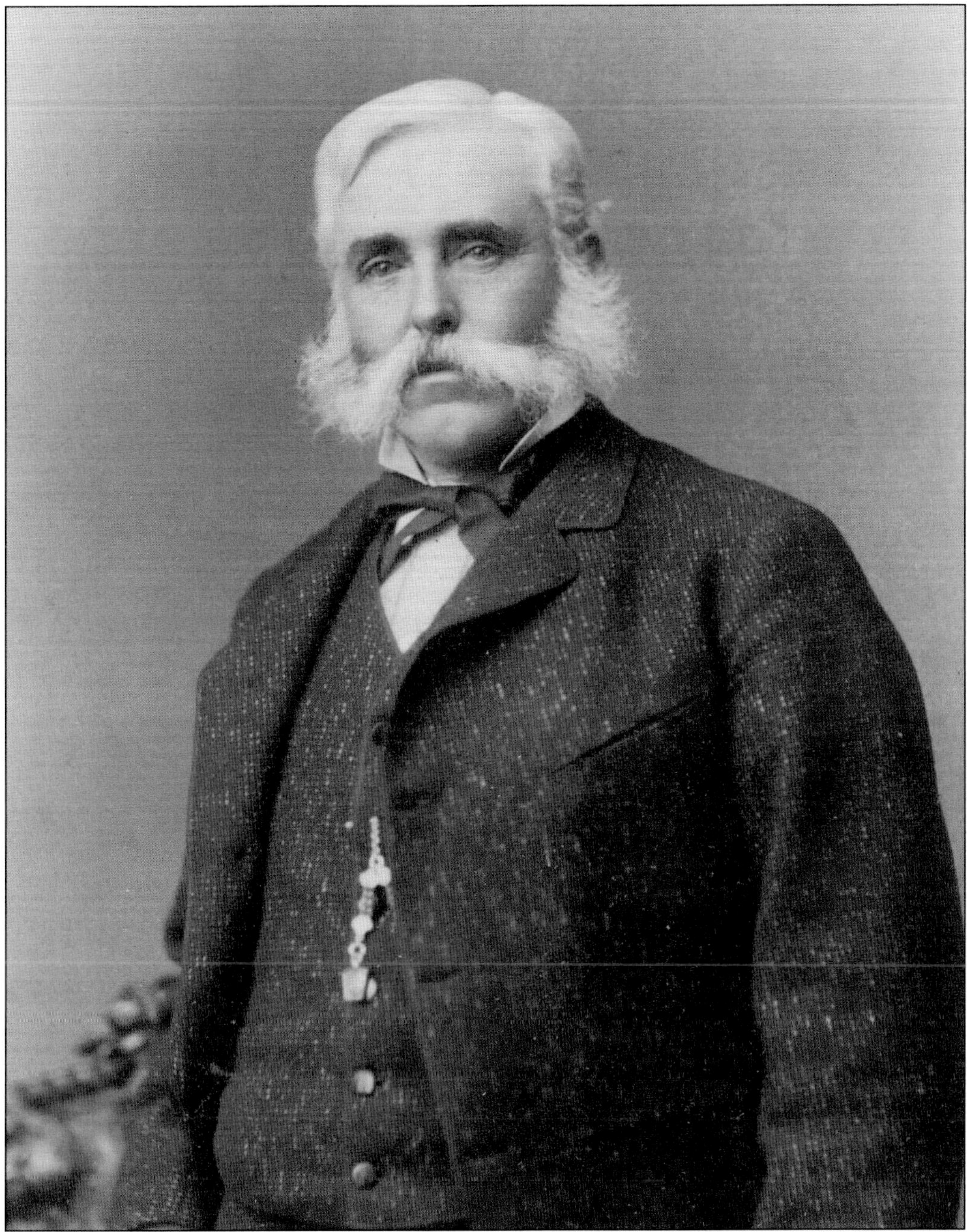

In 1871, Lorenzo L. Shaw was the joint manager, along with Barnabus Freeman, of the Royal River Manufacturing Company. While L.L. Shaw never took a salary, he used the income from the mill to pay for his personal needs and those of his family.

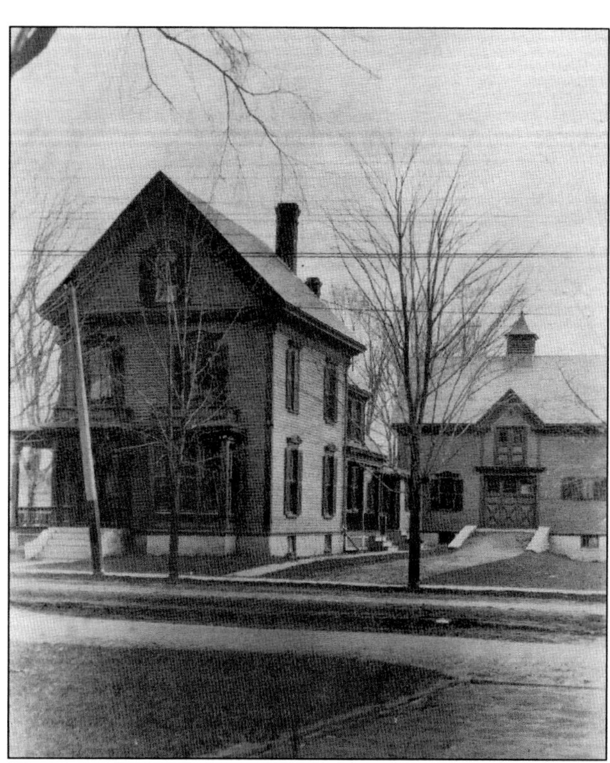

Shown is the home of L.L. Shaw on the corner of Main Street and Bridge Street. Shaw had this house built on the location of the former Old Sloop site.

The Portland Photo and View Company produced this image of the inside of Royal River Manufacturing Company in 1889.

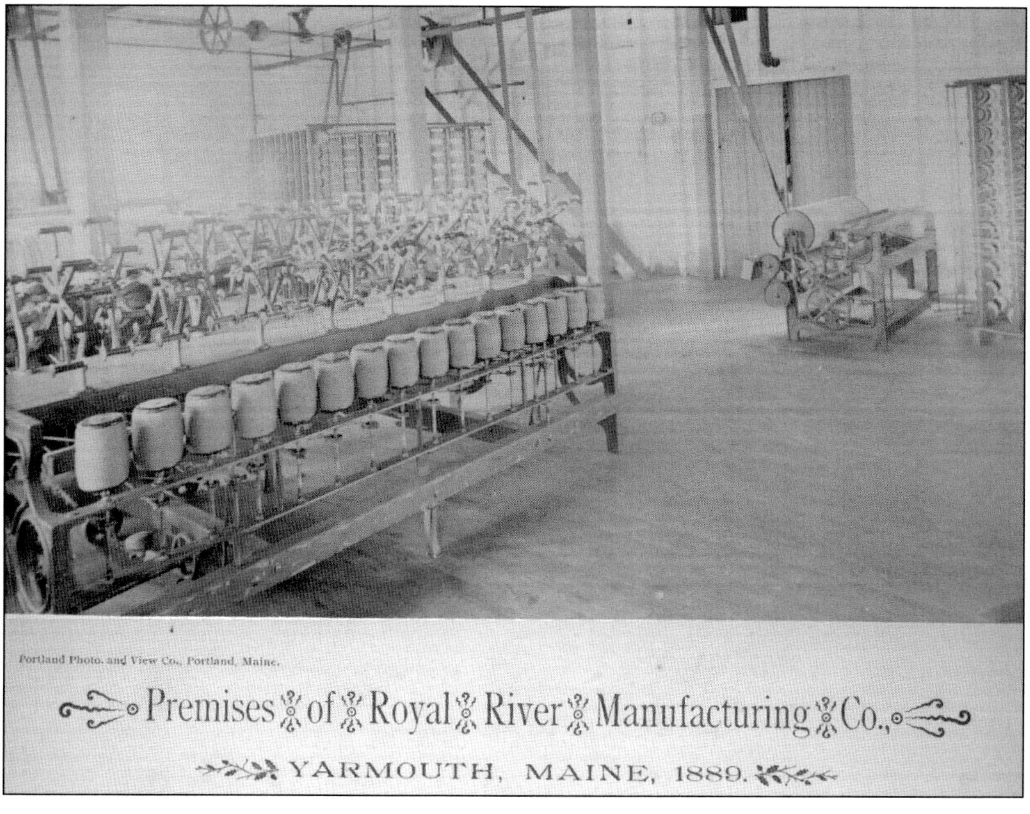

Portland Photo. and View Co., Portland, Maine.

Premises of Royal River Manufacturing Co.,

YARMOUTH, MAINE, 1889.

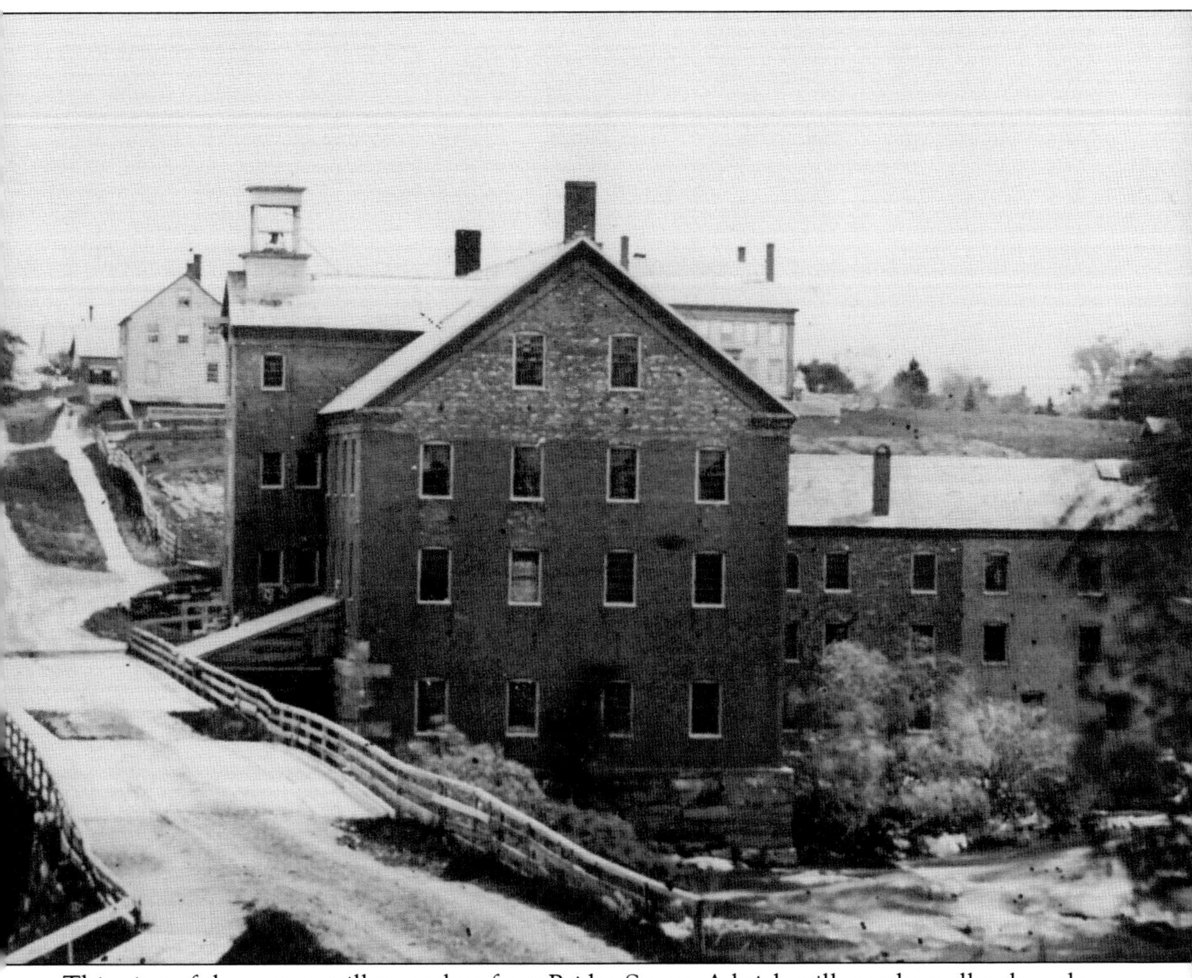

This view of the cotton mill was taken from Bridge Street. A brick mill, much smaller than the one in this photograph, was destroyed by fire in 1855 but was immediately rebuilt. The mill was under the management of F.O. and H.J. Libby until Barnabus Freeman took over in 1869.

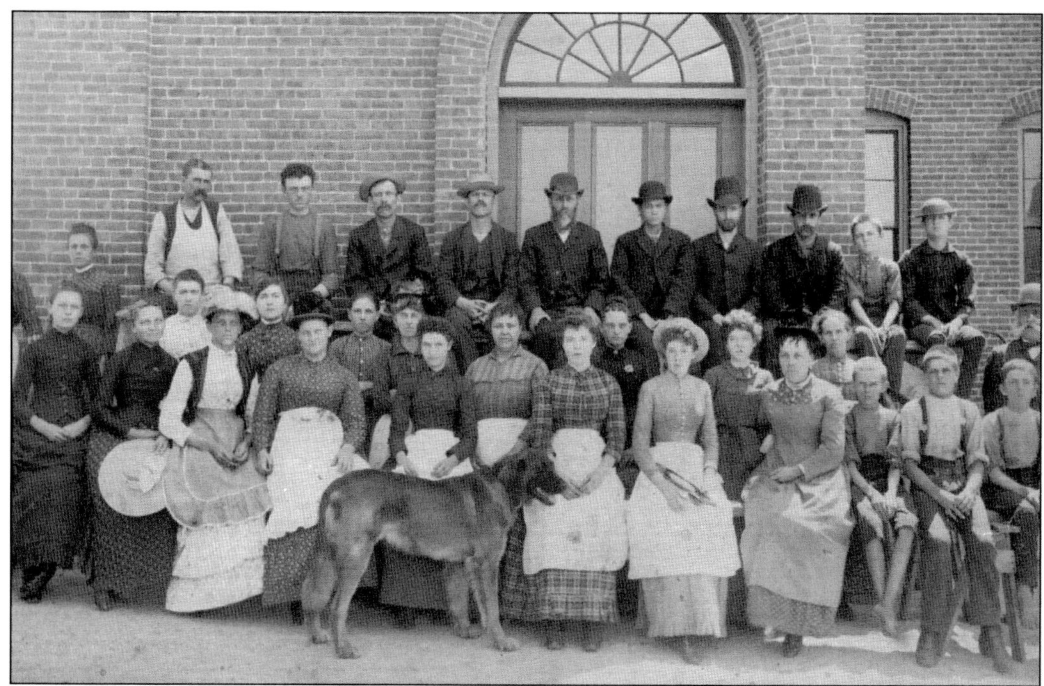

In this c. 1887 photograph of the workers at the Royal River Manufacturing Company, L.L. Shaw is standing at the far right. The Royal River Manufacturing Company employed 60 people: 40 women, 10 men, and 10 children. Half of the employees were French Canadians from Prince Edward Island. Weavers could earn $1.40 to $1.50 a day.

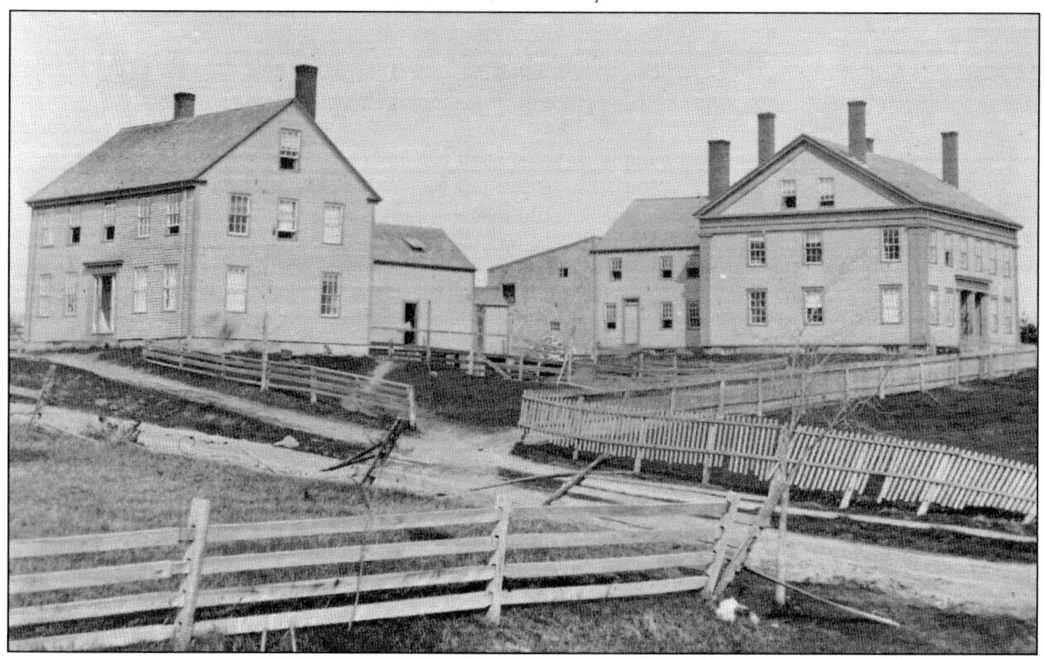

Shown are the boardinghouses for the mill workers. If an employee chose to live in these boardinghouses at the top of the hill, he or she would pay $2 to $3 a week for a room and meals. An employee's day started at 6:00 a.m. and ended at 6:00 p.m., with a 45-minute break for lunch.

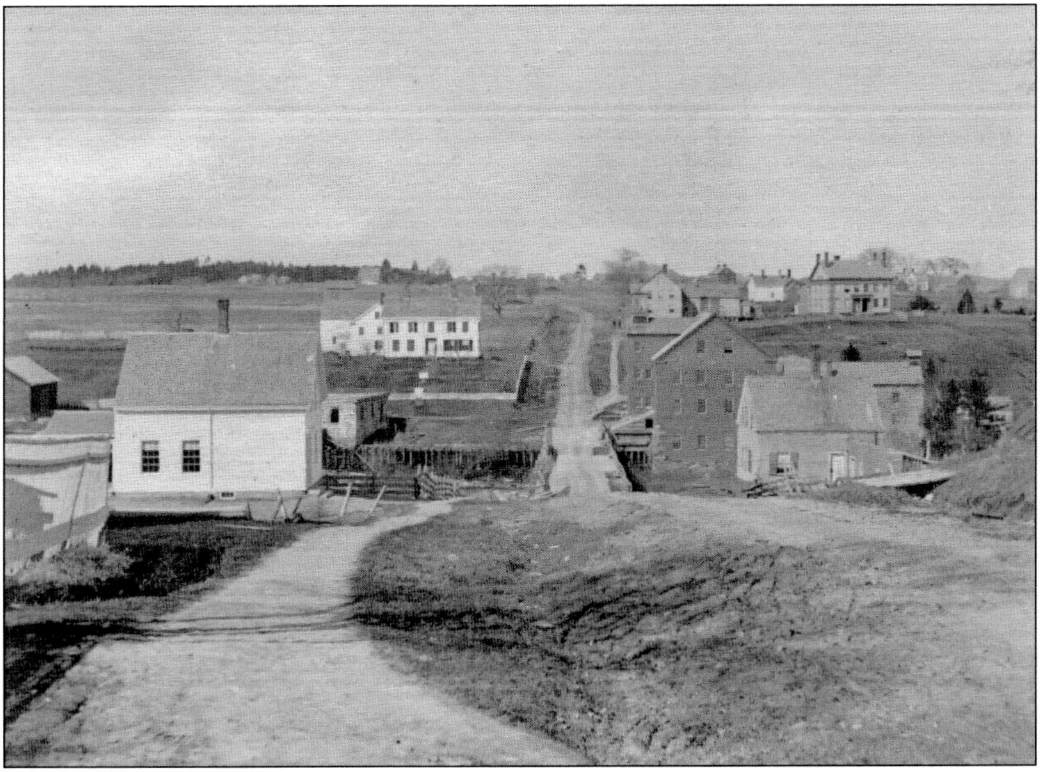

This is another view of the cotton mill from Bridge Street. The site of the former paper mill is on the left, and the boardinghouses are in the distance. Also shown is Capt. George Loring's house on the upper left side of the road. The house still stands today.

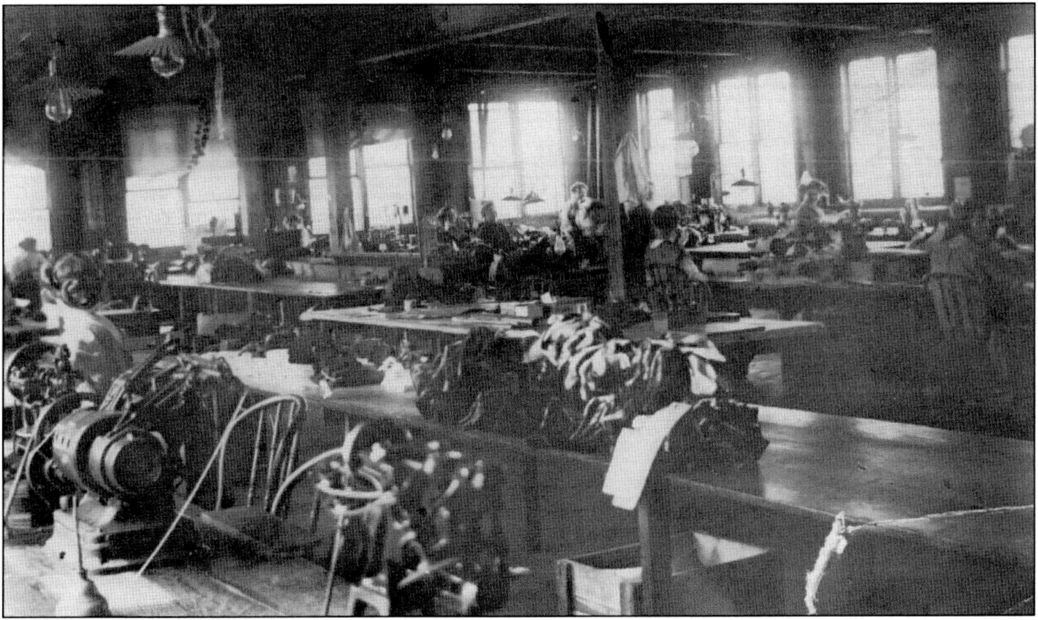

Shown is a view of the inside of the Royal River Manufacturing Company. The workers are all women. The mill produced seamless grain bags as well as both course and fine spinning yarn.

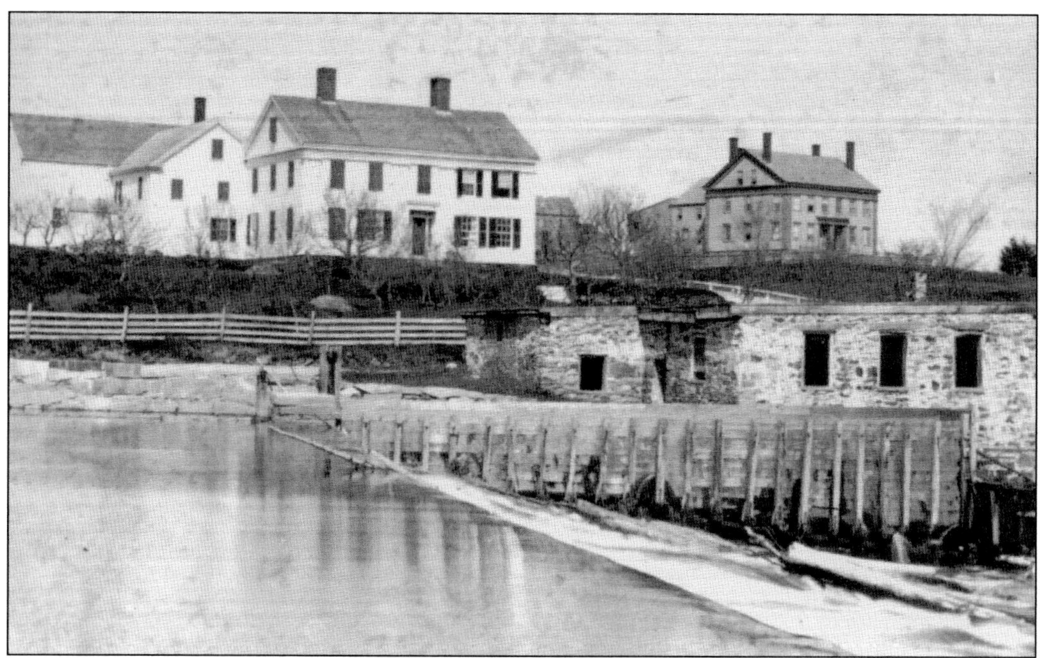

William Hawes and George and Henry Cox built a rag cotton paper mill on the second falls in 1816. It failed after five years and was purchased by William and Calvin Stockbridge, who successfully operated it for 20 years before it shut down. In this photograph are the remains of the Stockbridge Paper Company.

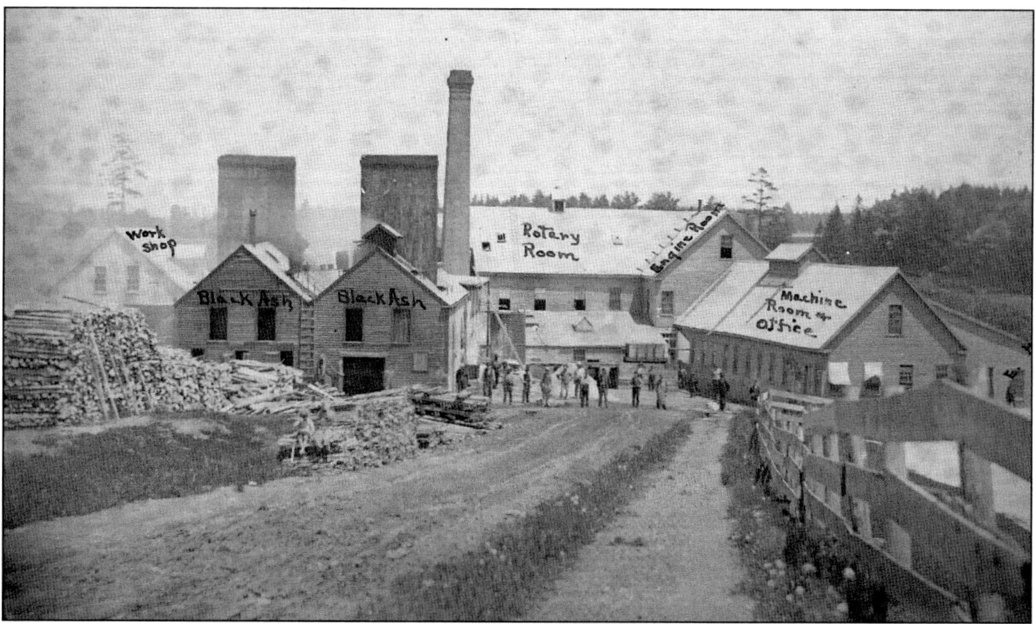

The Yarmouth Paper Company was built at the third falls in 1864. The mill began as a small wooden building until it caught fire and was replaced with brick buildings. Taking advantage of the power of the river, the Yarmouth Paper Company was the first soda pulp mill of its kind in New England. The mill produced high-quality pulp that could be used in the production of books and magazines.

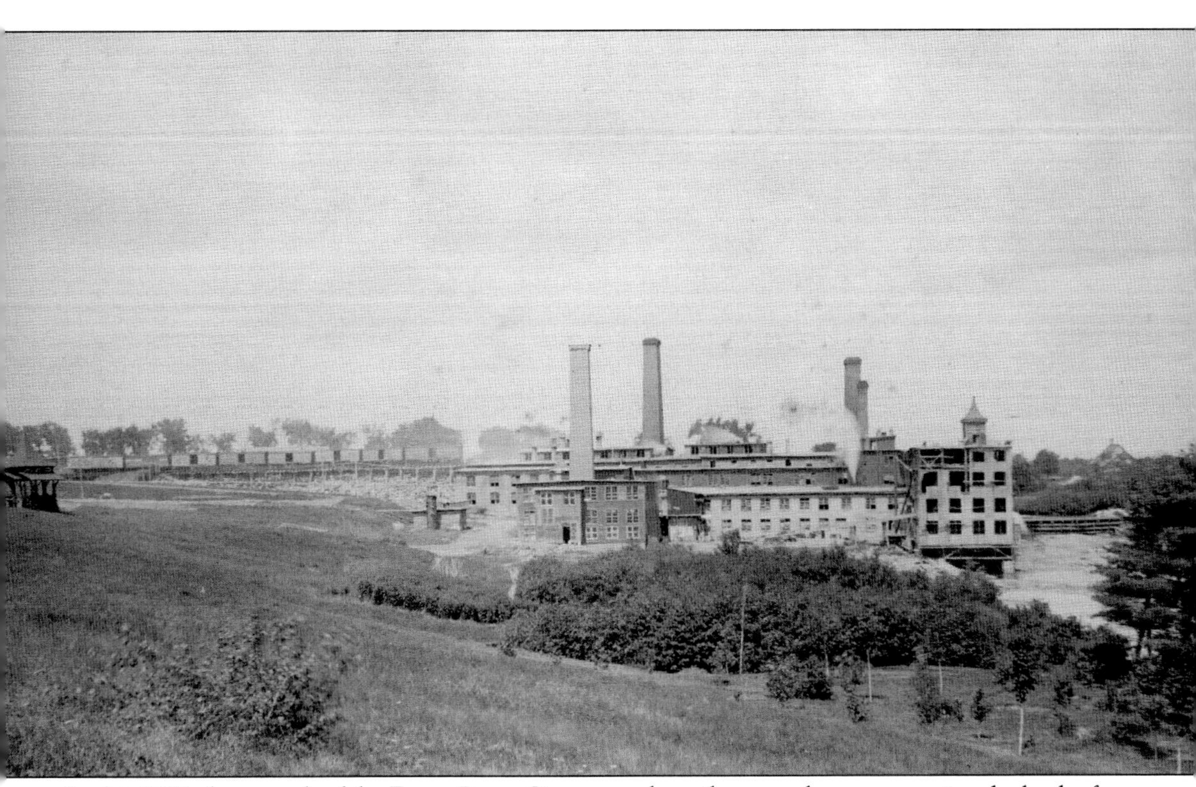

In this 1889 photograph of the Forest Paper Company, the railway can be seen entering the back of the plant. The Yarmouth Paper Company was purchased by S.D. Warren and George Hammond in 1874, who renamed it the Forest Paper Company. The soda pulp fiber was shipped out to other manufacturers to be made into various grades of paper.

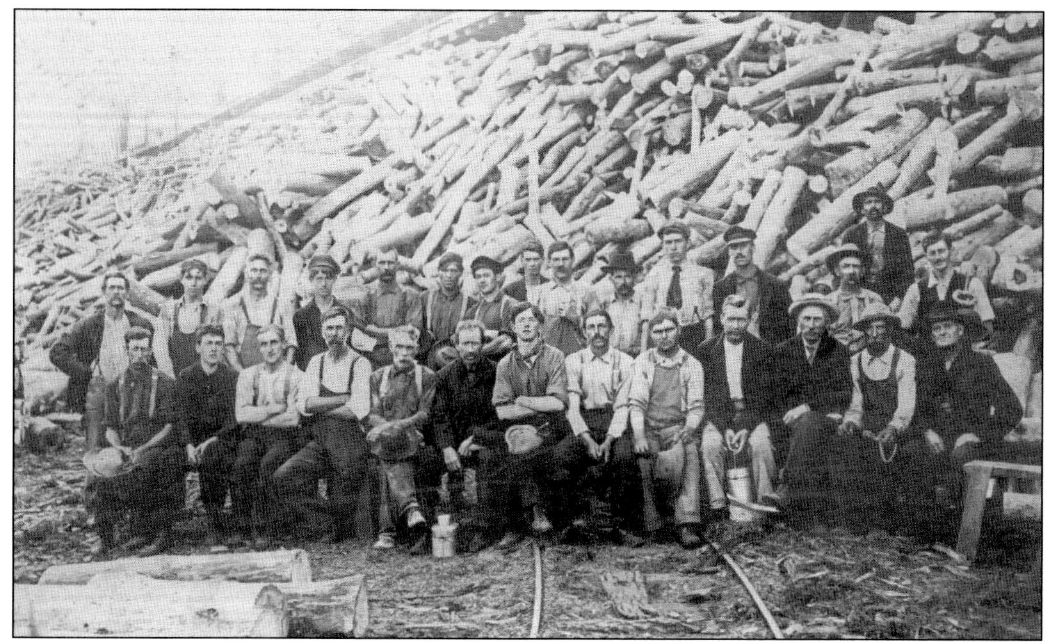

Mill employees are shown here sitting in front of the immense pile of poplar logs that were used to make soda pulp. Spur tracks transported the wood and other materials in and out of the plant.

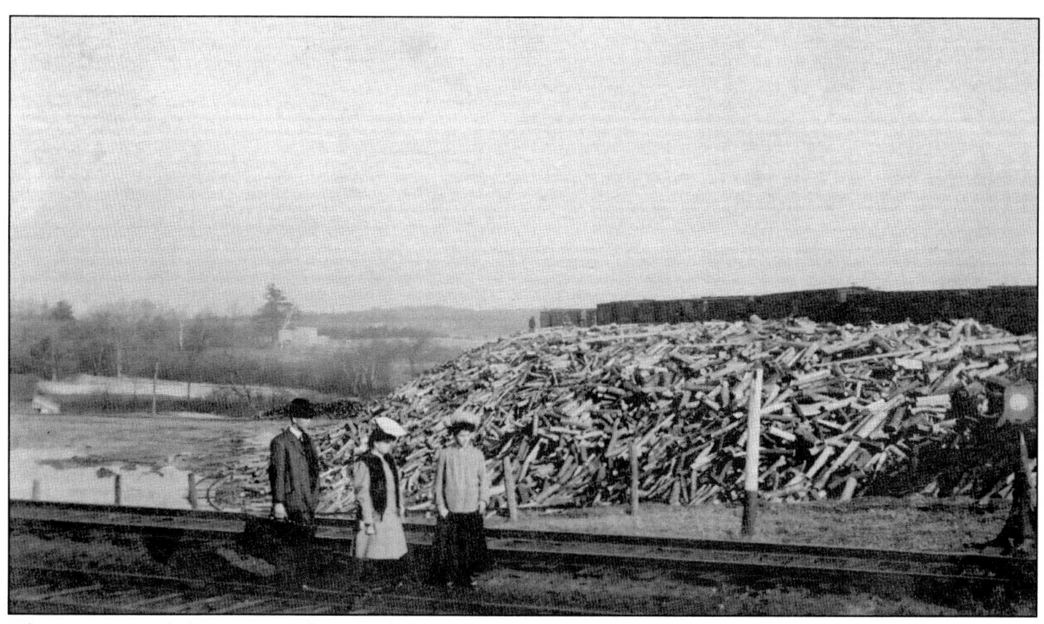

Three young adults are standing in front of a pile of pulpwood in the Forest Paper Company yard. This photograph was taken next to the Grand Trunk Railroad tracks in 1905. The pulpwood extended all the way to the fourth falls.

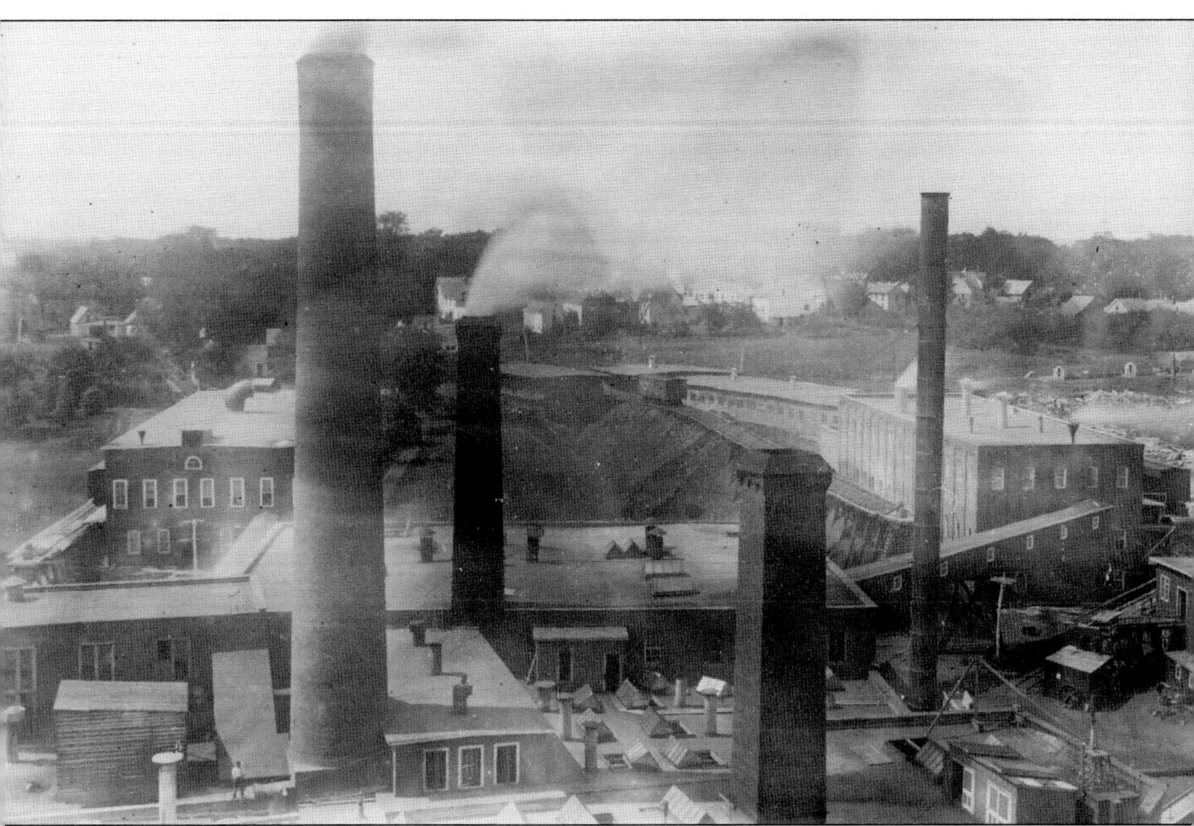

This photograph shows the smoke that was emitted from the chimneys of the Forest Paper Company. The pulp that was produced was shipped in its natural state or pressed into huge rolls for books or magazine paper.

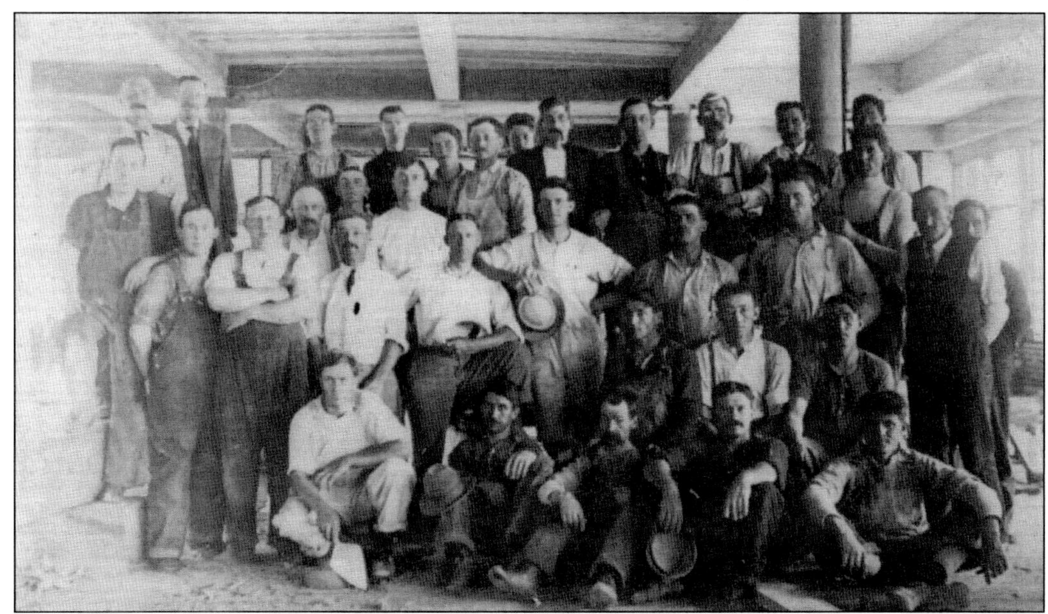

Workers from the Forest Paper Company are shown in this c. 1900 photograph. At the height of production, the mill employed 275 people. The Forest Paper Company closed in 1923. When the mill closed, the town declined due to the loss of employment.

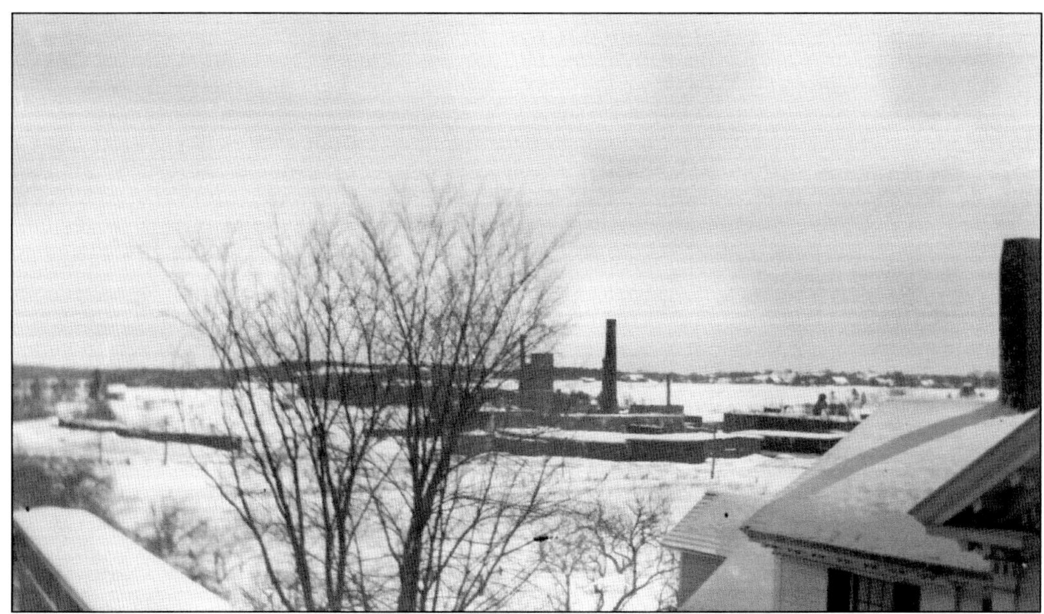

This photograph of the Forest Paper Company was taken from a roof on the corner of Portland and Main Streets. From this vantage point, it is apparent how the company dominated the town center.

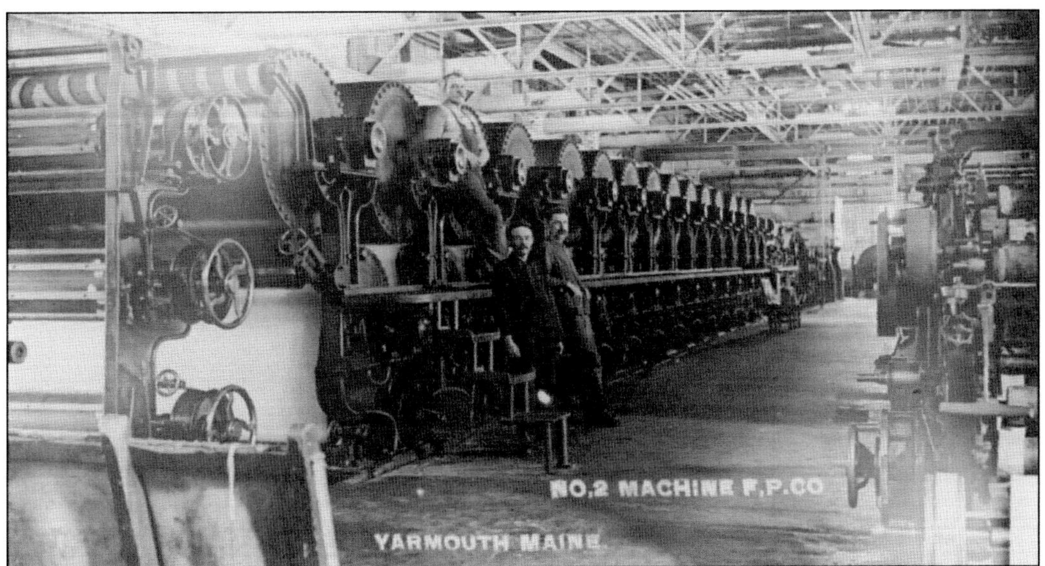

Shown in this photograph is the interior of the Forest Paper Company at the No. 2 machine. Daniel Frye stands above while Bert Kenney and Cliff Bennett lean against the machines. Daniel Frye was the president of the Yarmouth chapter of the International Brotherhood of Pulp, Sulphite, and Paper Mill Workers. The workers in Yarmouth decided to form a union on August 20, 1916. On September 22, Local No. 89, the Yarmouth chapter, moved to select a committee to meet with Forest Paper Company management and demand recognition of the union. The vote was unanimous, with all 103 members in favor.

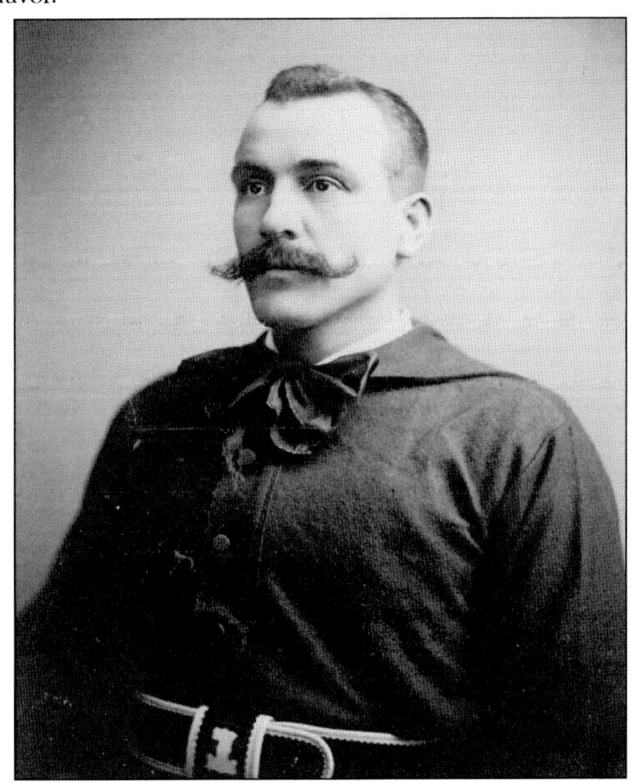

Daniel Frye, James McCray, and James E. Brady were the officers of the Yarmouth union. On September 23, the union called for a strike. On September 29, Local No. 89 held a dance to raise money for the union, at which they raised $39.25. On September 30, the union sent a committee to meet with Frederick Gore, the company manager, to discuss a blacklist of employees not to be rehired after the strike. Many paper company workers left Yarmouth after the 1916 strike ended.

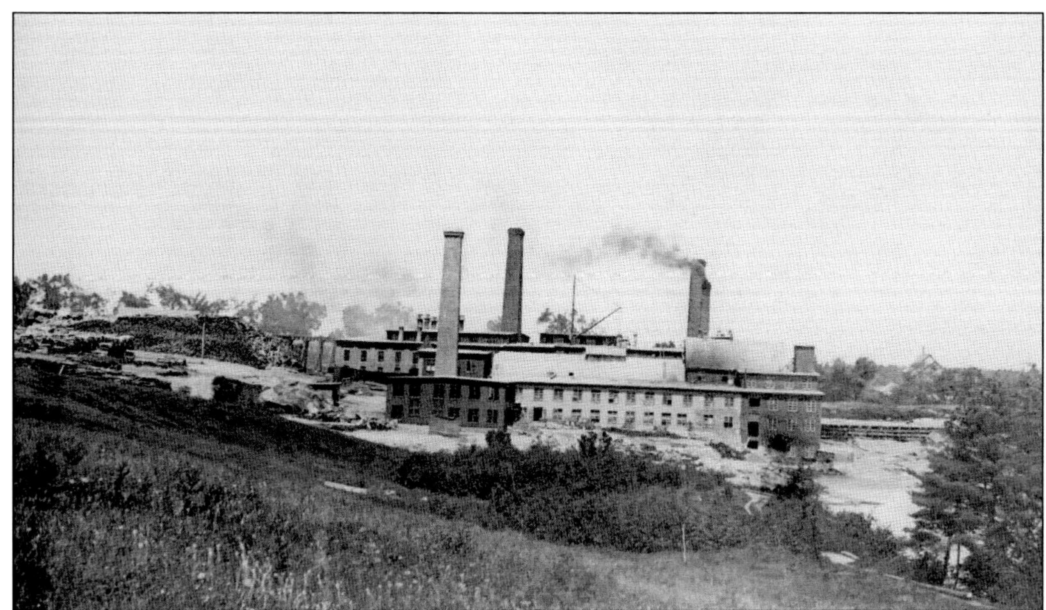

The Forest Paper Company used the English soda ash process to make pulp. Part of this process used caustic soda to break down the wood fibers. The remnants of this process were dried and burned, creating large amounts of black soda ash. In addition, hypochlorite of lime was used to bleach the pulp and create a whiter mix.

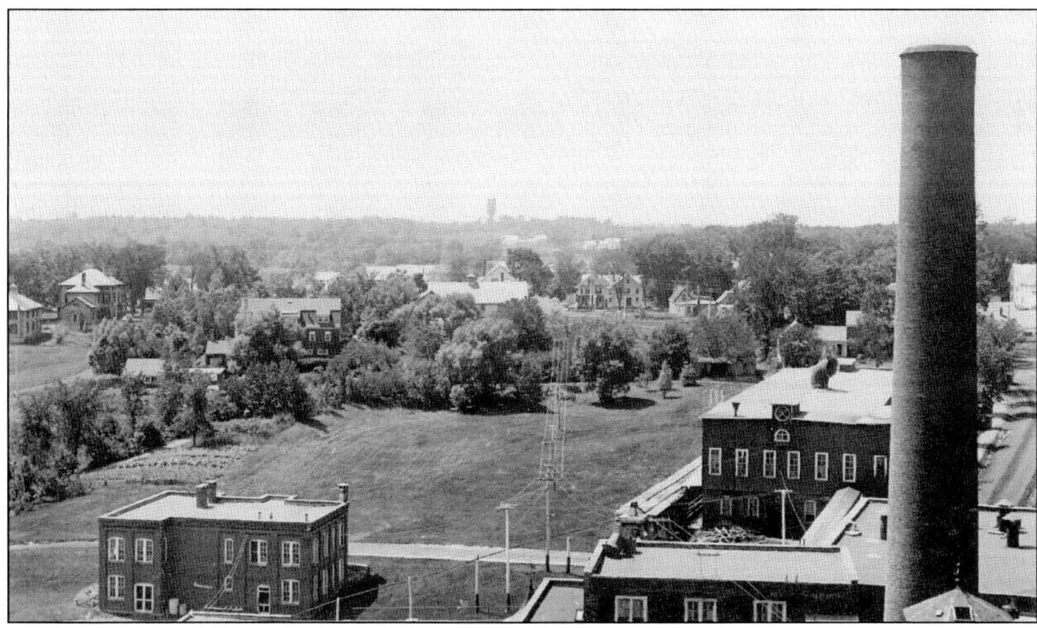

With the rapid growth of the mill, the amount of water diverted for power decreased the flow at the second falls, which had a direct effect on the Royal River Manufacturing Company. In addition, the black ash was dumped into the river. As the river clogged and the quality of the water decreased, the cotton mill complained. The Forest Paper Company paid Royal River Manufacturing Company $750 in 1907 and $450 in 1908 as a penalty for pollution of the river.

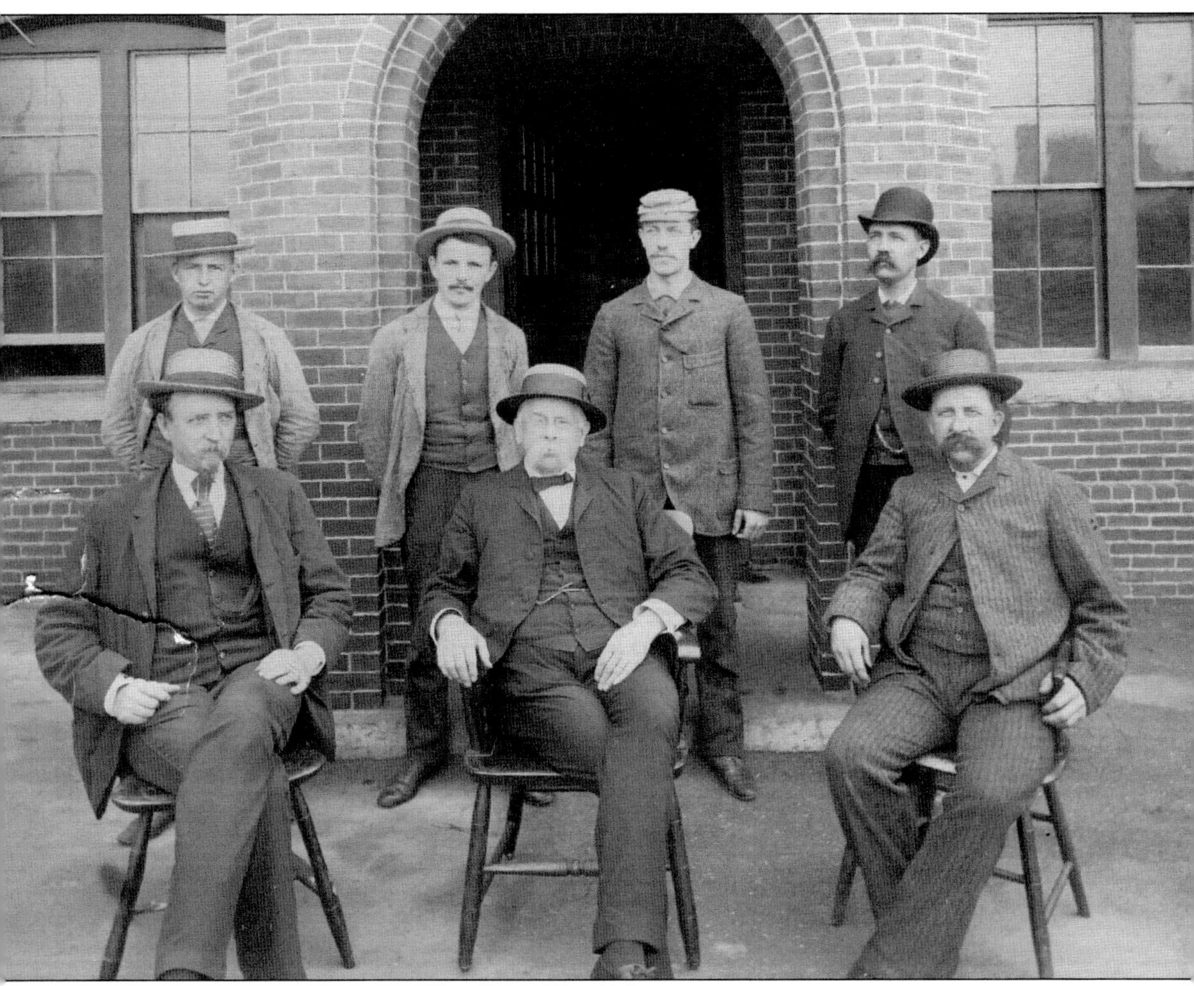

Officers of the Forest Paper Company are, from left to right, (sitting) Edward H. Wilson, cashier; George W. Hammond, agent; and William Merrill, superintendent; (standing) Frederick E. Gore, chemist; Raoul Girouard, electrician; Alexander H. Twombley, draftsman; and Frederick A. True, paymaster.

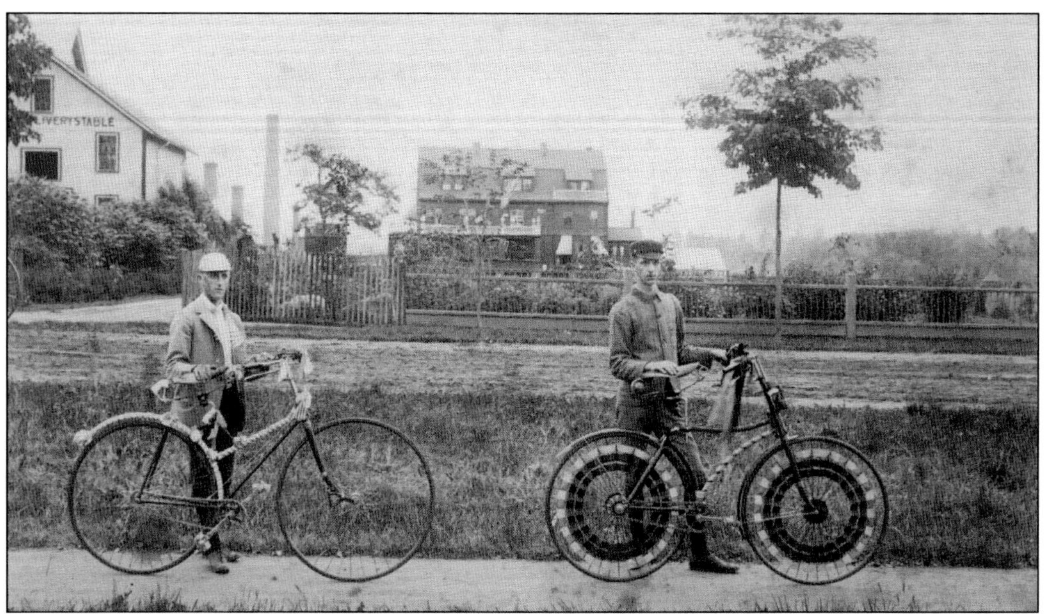

Two men pose in front of Camp Hammond during a Fourth of July celebration. Camp Hammond was built in 1889–1890 for George Hammond, manager of Forest Paper Company. It was constructed with a single exterior wall of heavy planks over timbers. This shingle-style residence was designed to be slow burning, with no hidden spaces or hollow walls.

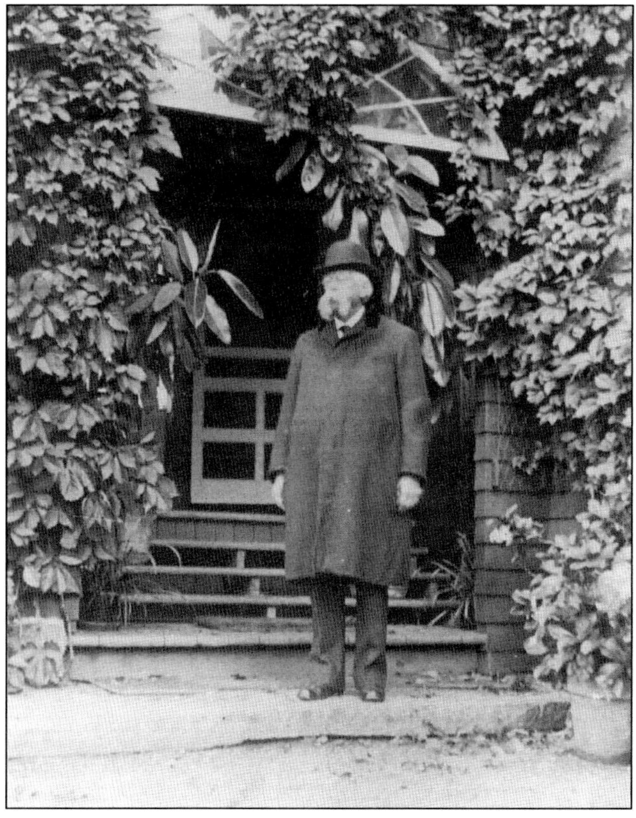

George W. Hammond is shown standing in front of Camp Hammond. Frederick Law Olmstead, who designed Central Park in New York City as well as the landscaping for the Chicago World's Fair in 1893, designed the landscape for the exterior.

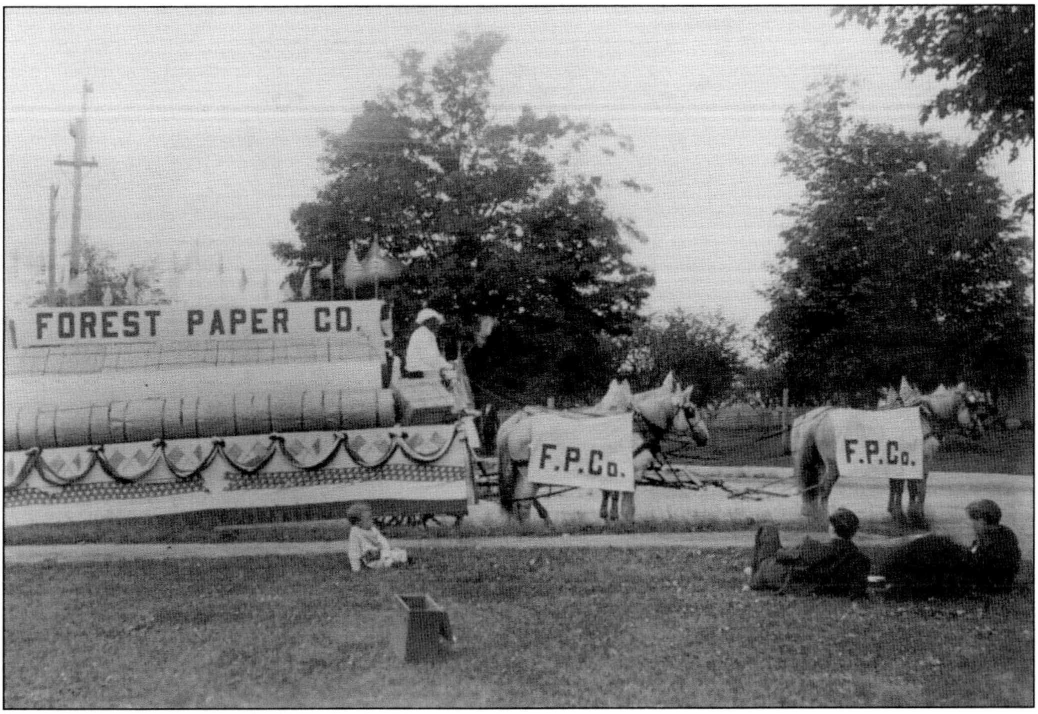

Because of its international success, the Forest Paper Company was able to expand its production over the course of its existence. What started as a small wooden mill building became an industrial complex, sprawling over 10 acres with 10 brick buildings.

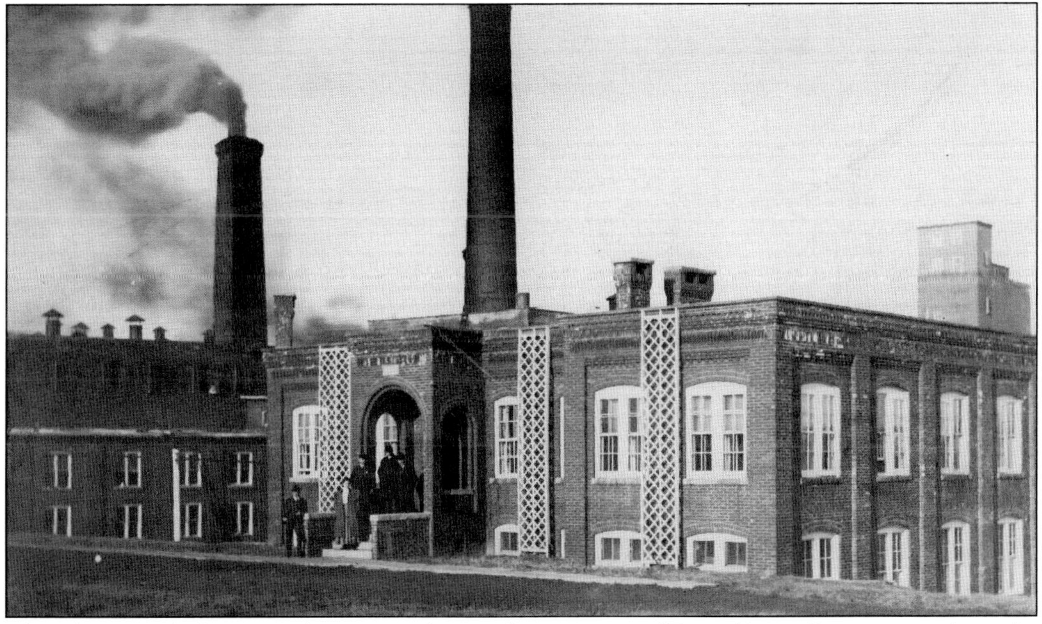

This photograph shows employees standing at the entrance of Forest Paper Company, with smoke billowing from the stacks in the background. Most of the improvements to the company were due to the persistence of George W. Hammond, who committed himself to keeping up with the rapidly changing times.

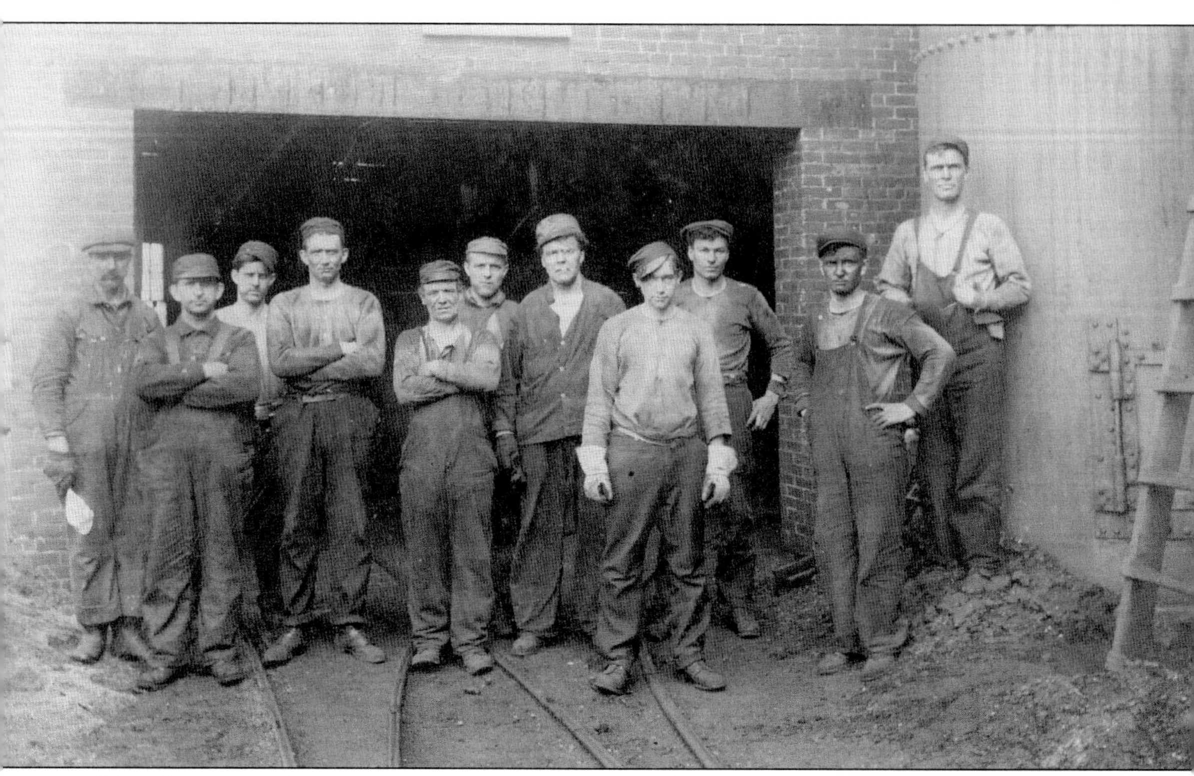

This photograph shows paper company employees standing at the entrance, under a sign that reads, "For the car." Spur tracks were laid to transport wood and other materials, water management systems were introduced, and for a time, Forest Paper Company was the largest soda pulp mill in the nation.

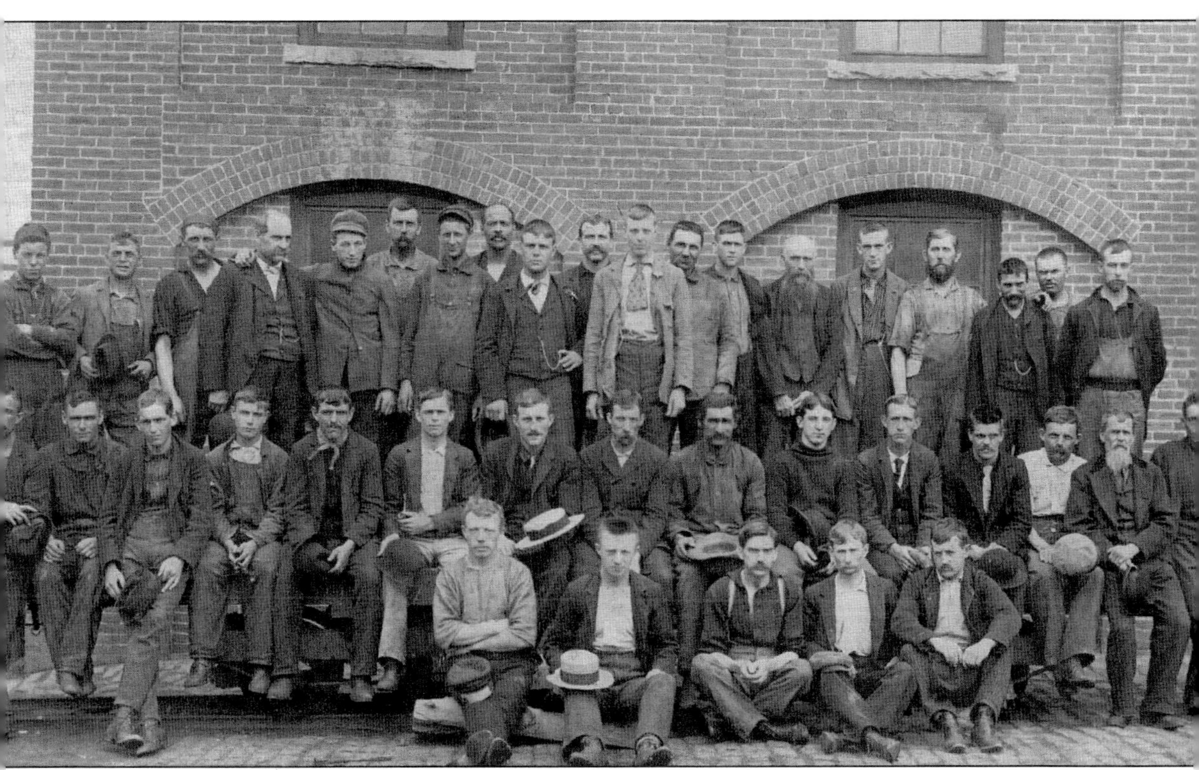

Officers and employees of the Forest Paper Company are shown together in this photograph. In the upper left corner of the photograph, one employee is shown with his arm around an officer. All but two of the men have removed their hats for the occasion.

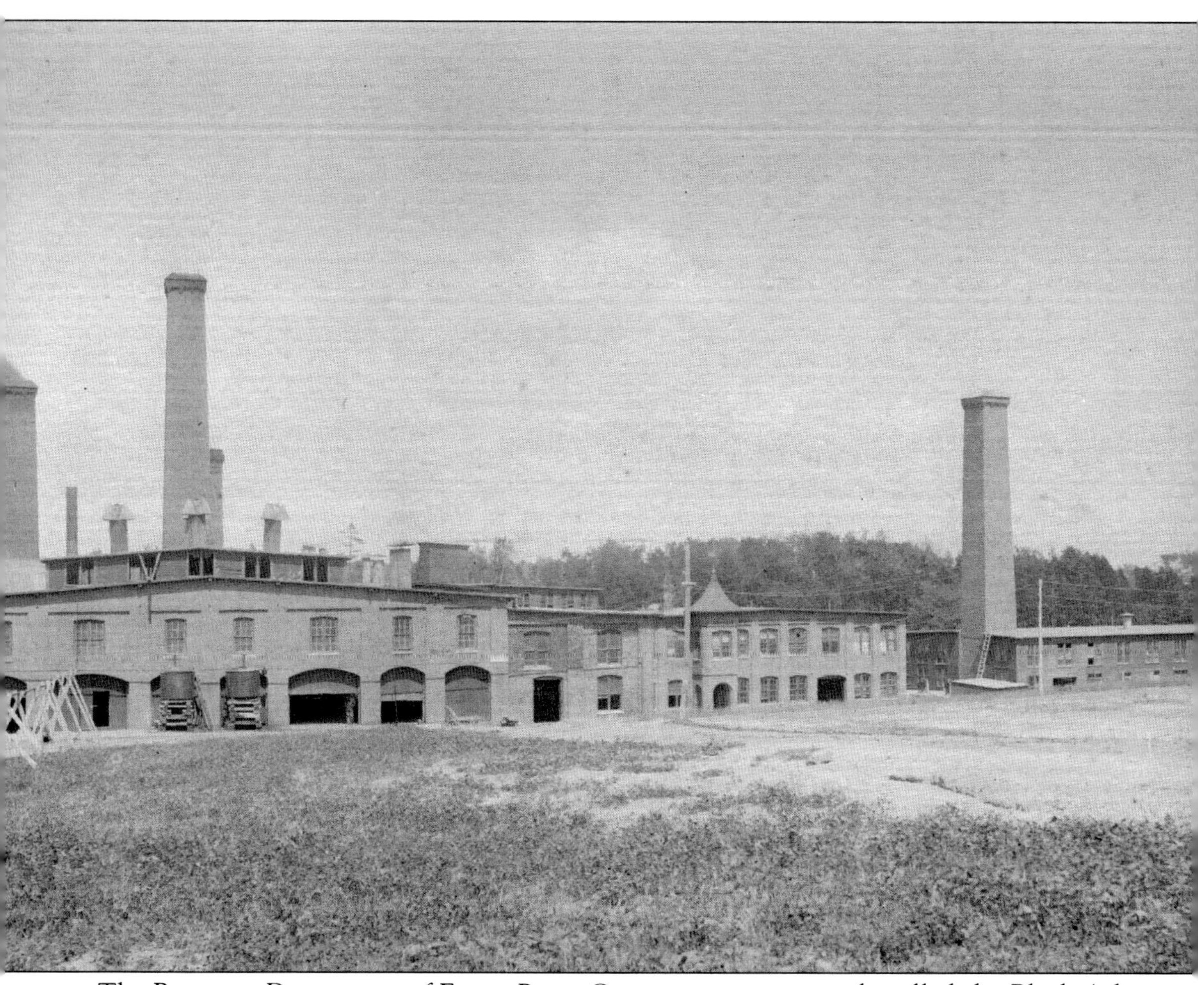

The Recovery Department of Forest Paper Company was commonly called the Black Ash Department. The Forest Paper Company sluiced the ash through troughs to Brickyard Hollow, where a pipe had been laid to drain water out to the river and a dam had been built at the head of the gully. Brickyard Hollow, the space on Main Street between Falls Village and Yarmouthville, was quite extensive, with a deep valley and a stream running through the area.

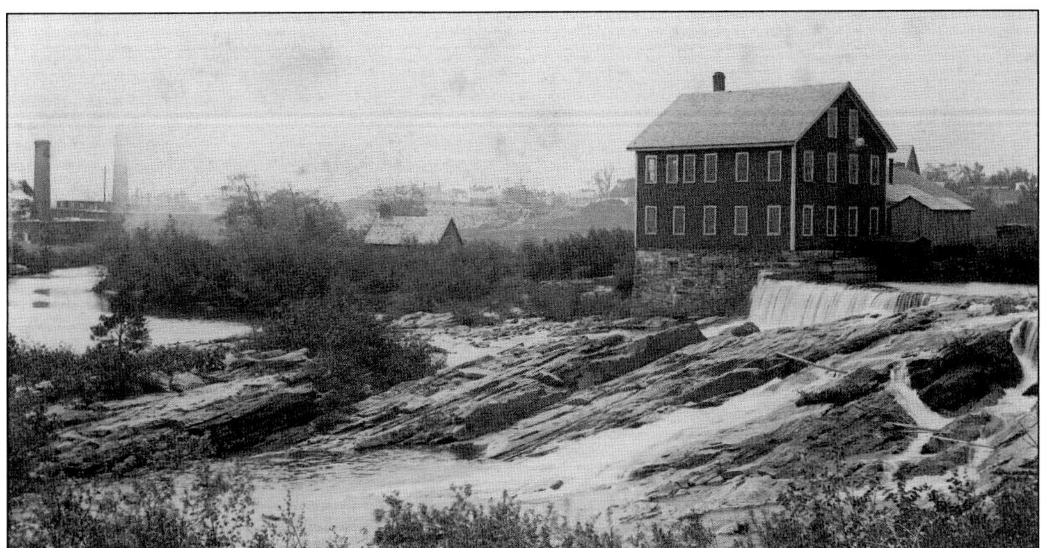

On the fourth falls, Charles Weston opened a machine shop in 1876. His shop made leather-working machinery, turbine waterwheels, balancing presses, and more. Weston's products were sent to England, Germany, Australia, Denmark, and Canada. After the plant was discontinued in 1892, Forest Paper Company purchased the water rights.

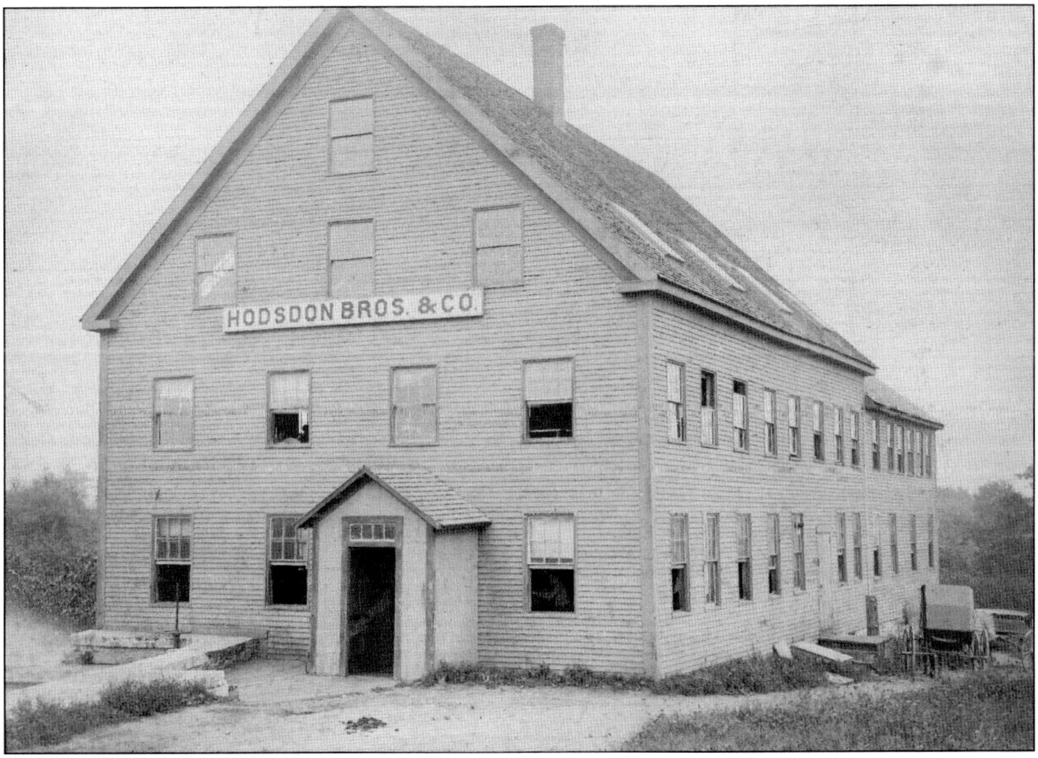

Joseph Hodsdon came to Yarmouth in 1880 and took over the Farris tannery on the fourth falls. The shop produced shoes in that building until it burned. Hodsdon rebuilt his company, and in 1896, it became the Hodsdon Shoe Company, which manufactured women's shoes and boots. During this period, Hodsdon also served as a state senator in Augusta.

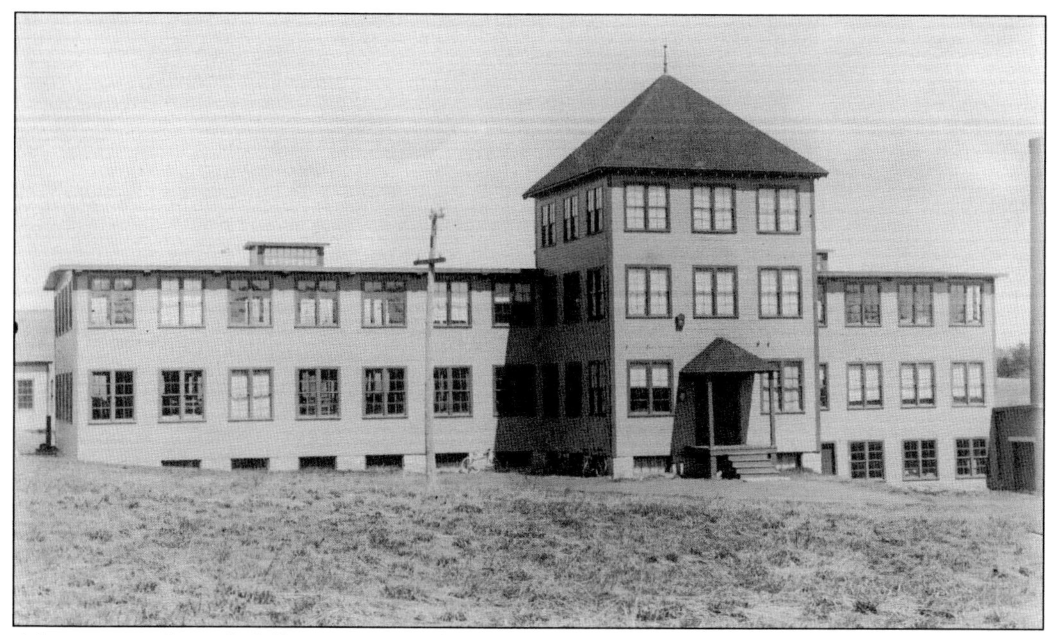

After passing through different owners, this building was purchased by the Forest Paper Company. In 1923, the Sportocasin Company leased the building and began making a soft, pliable moccasin-like shoe. The company was later purchased by the Morrison and Bennett Shoe Company and reorganized as the Abbott Company. That company manufactured the ski shoes used on Comdr. Richard Byrd's first Antarctic expedition.

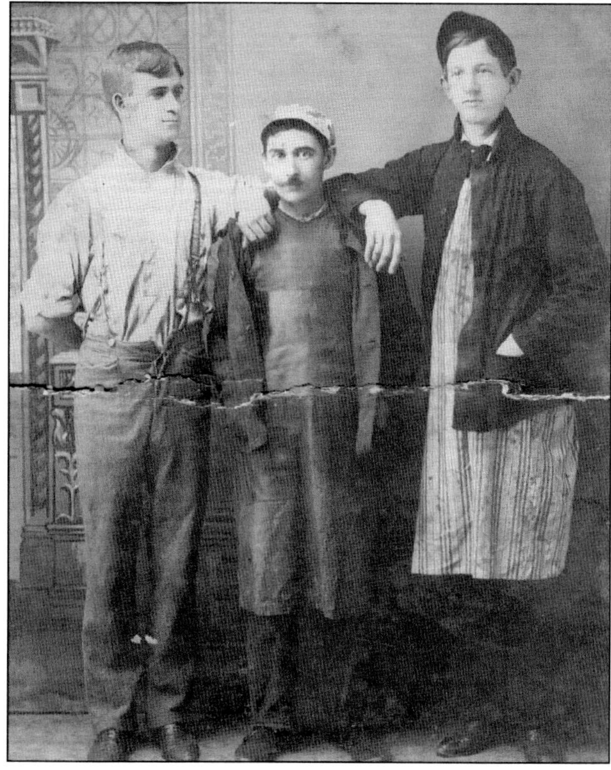

Mill workers pose at the Hodsdon Shoe Company in 1898. From left to right are Arthur Bennett, Arthur "Skinny" Skillings, and Ed "Chicken" Leighton.

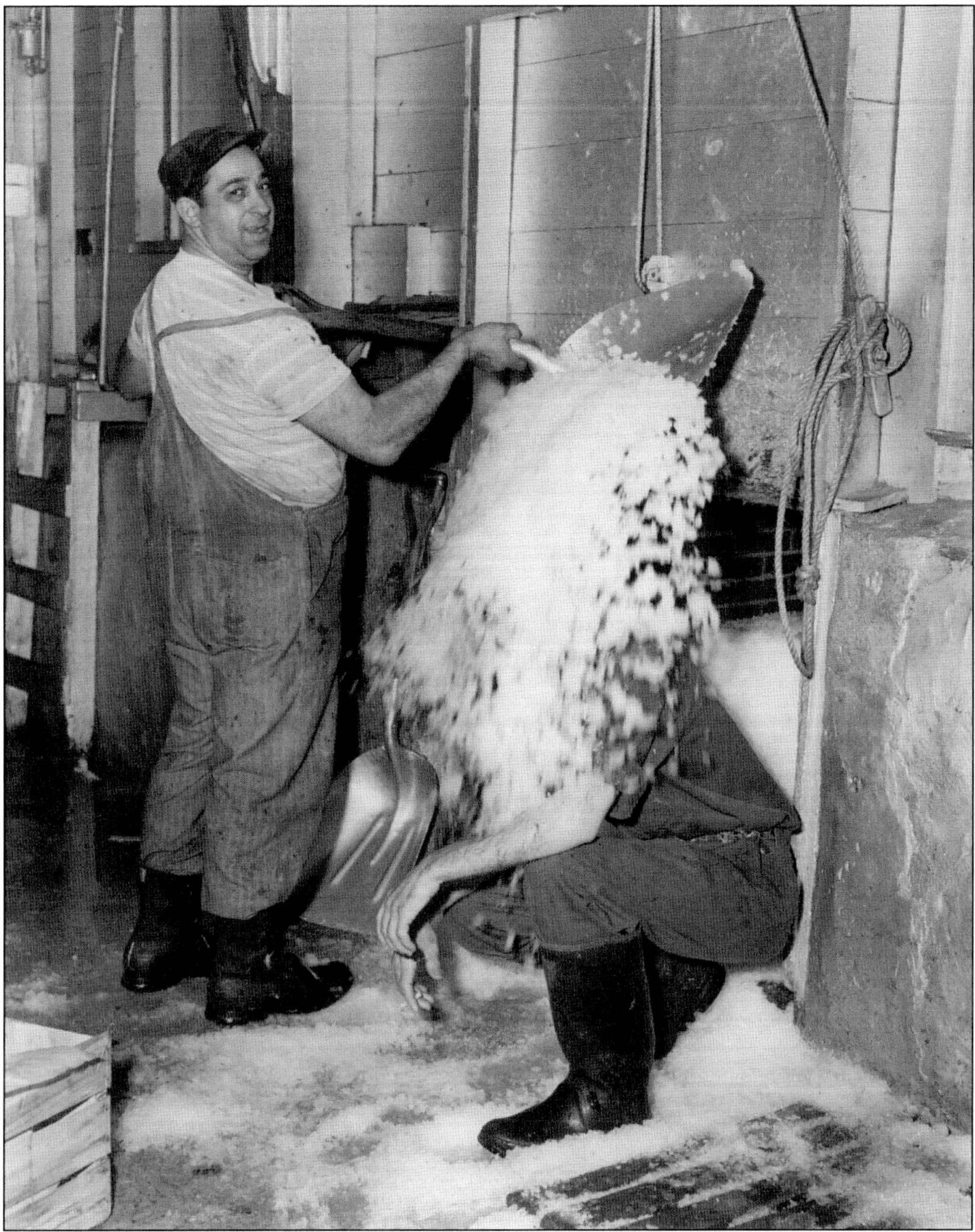

Glick Brothers Poultry Processing Plant started in 1940 on the fourth falls. In 1952, it was the largest business in Yarmouth, employing 60 people. The Glick brothers bought birds from Maine farmers and were able to process 1,800 birds per hour. The business closed in 1965. This 1953 photograph is of Bill Sidman and Robin Clukey.

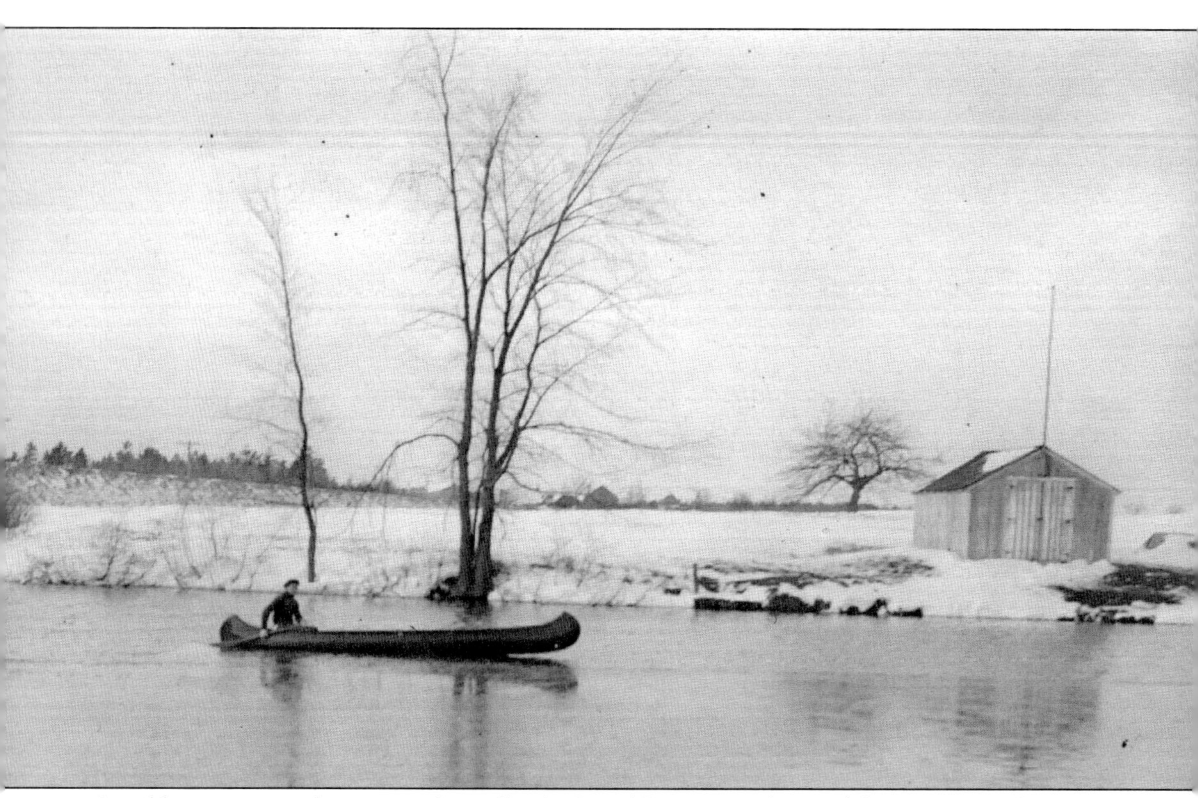

In addition to providing power for mills, the Royal River was also used for recreational purposes, such as canoeing. Today, there is a kayak and canoe carry-in spot located at the fourth falls along East Elm Street. In the winter, ice-skaters can be seen above the fourth falls when the river freezes over.

Three

SHIPBUILDING

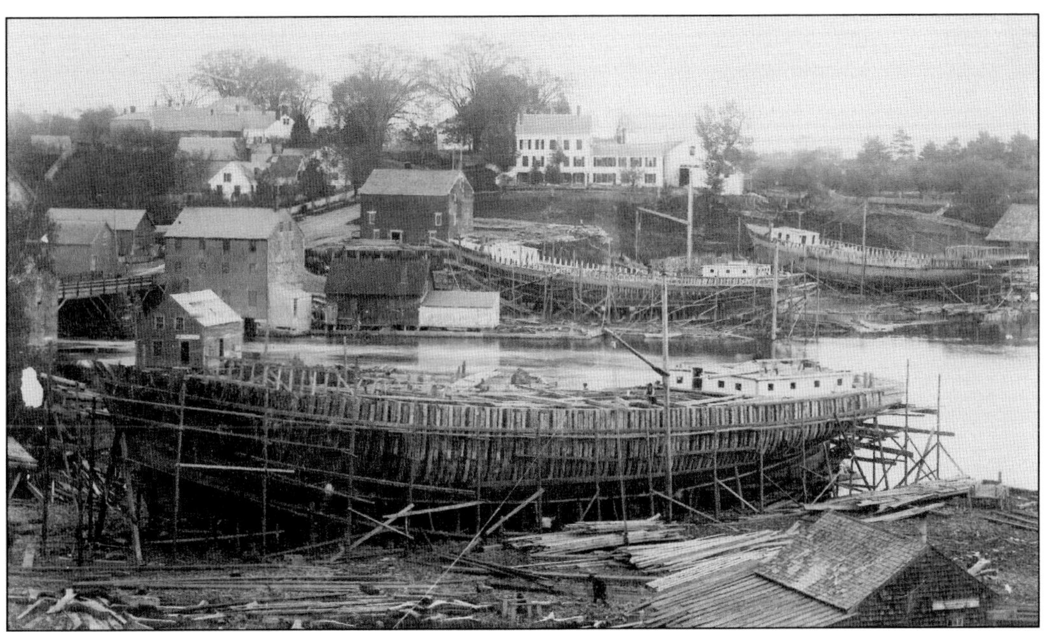

The Hutchins & Stubbs shipyard is on the left, and Giles Loring's yard is on the right in this 1883 photograph. The vessels, in varying phases of construction, are the *Aphile* and *Amelia* on the left, and *Ethel* M. *Davis* on the far right.

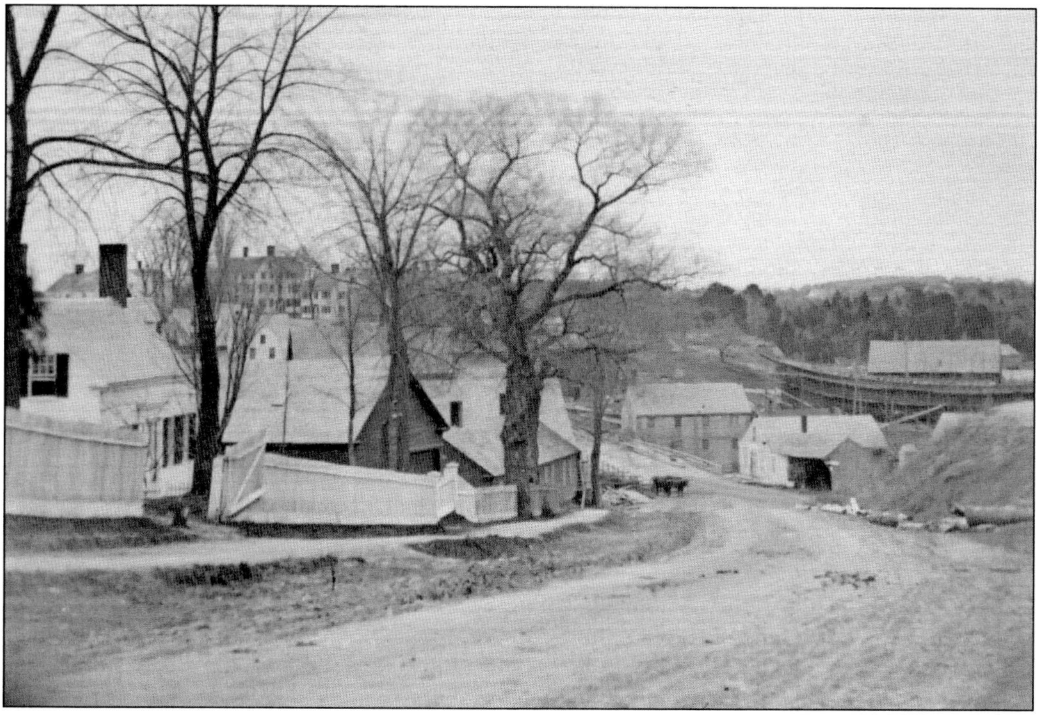

Pleasant Street was the home of many in the shipbuilding industry, including Capt. William Gooding and his brother Henry Gooding, who was considered the "second-best caulker in the state."

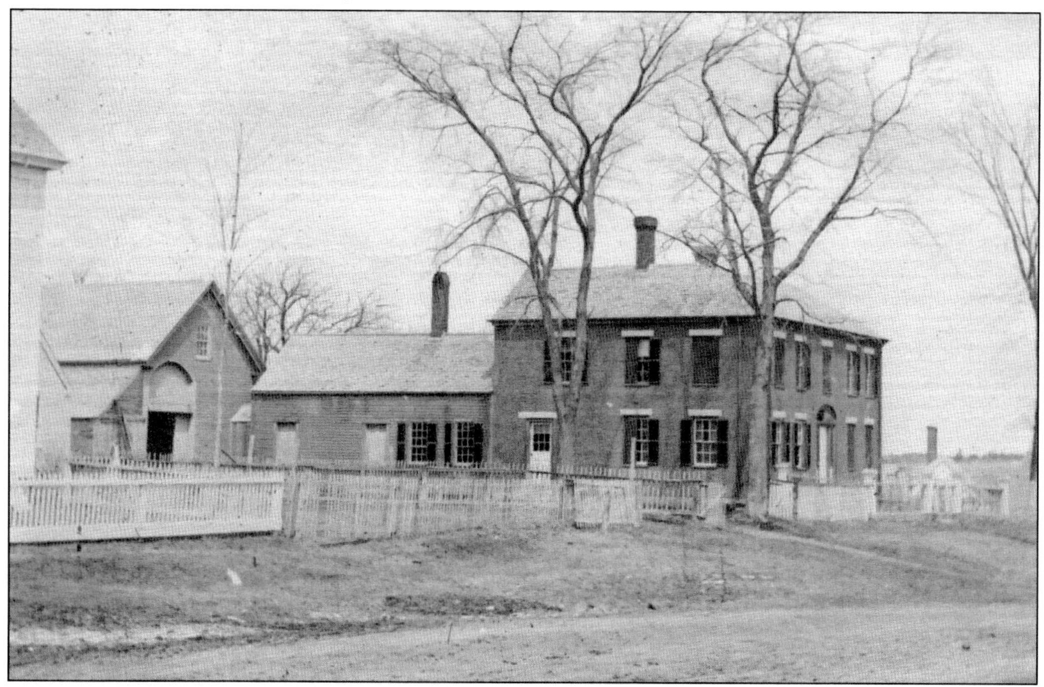

Lyman Walker lived in this house on Pleasant Street. Without the trees that cover the landscape today, Walker had a direct view of his shipyard located at the bottom of the street, between Blanchard Bros. shipyard and Hutchins & Stubbs.

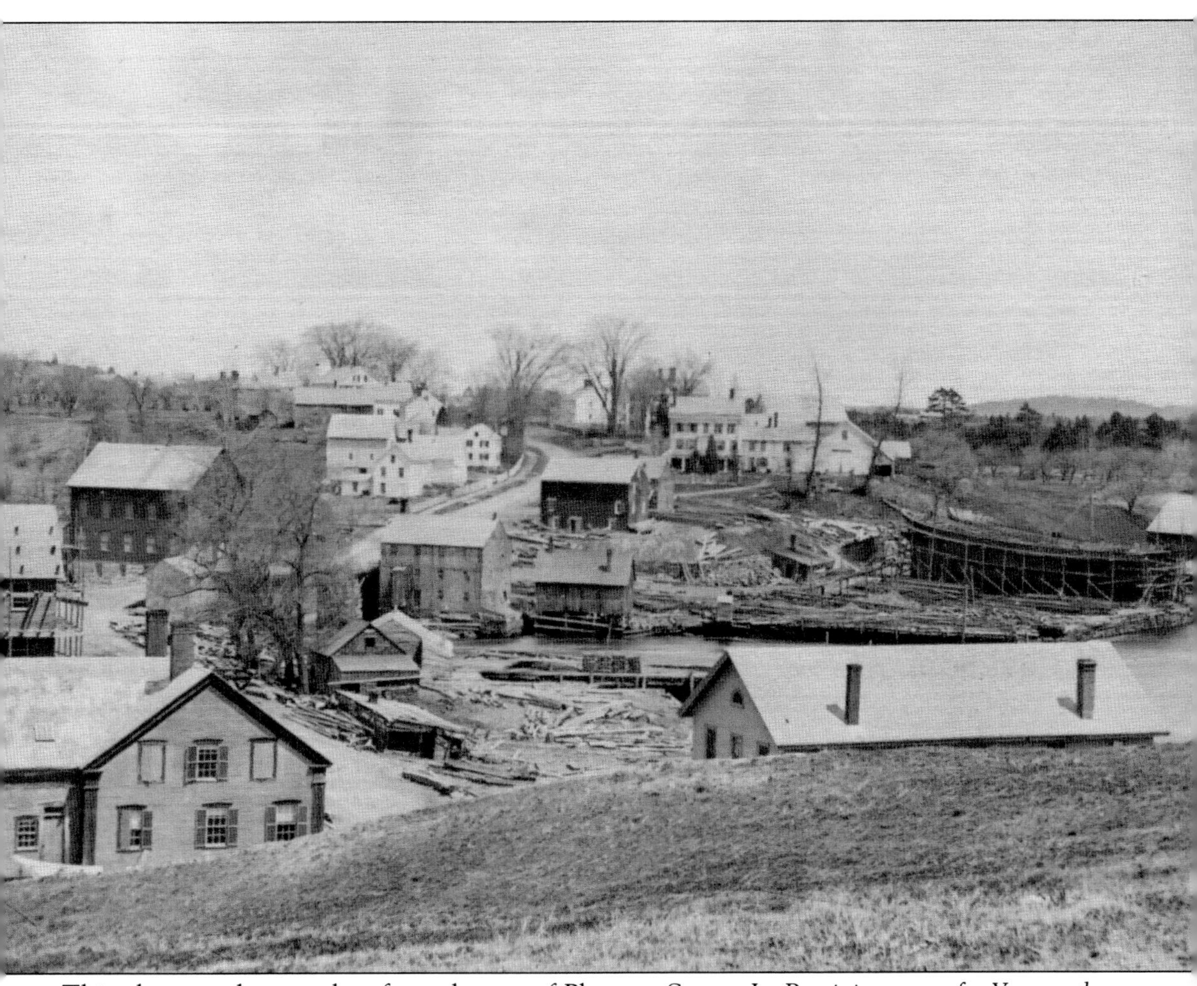

This photograph was taken from the top of Pleasant Street. In *Reminiscences of a Yarmouth Schoolboy*, E.C. Plummer wrote a description of the harbor. He notes that, in place of the steel structure that spanned the river at that time, there was a wide wooden bridge. At the east end was the gristmill. Near the shipyards, there were blacksmith shops, where bolts were cut and broad bar iron was turned into massive mast caps, chain plates, and other ship fittings.

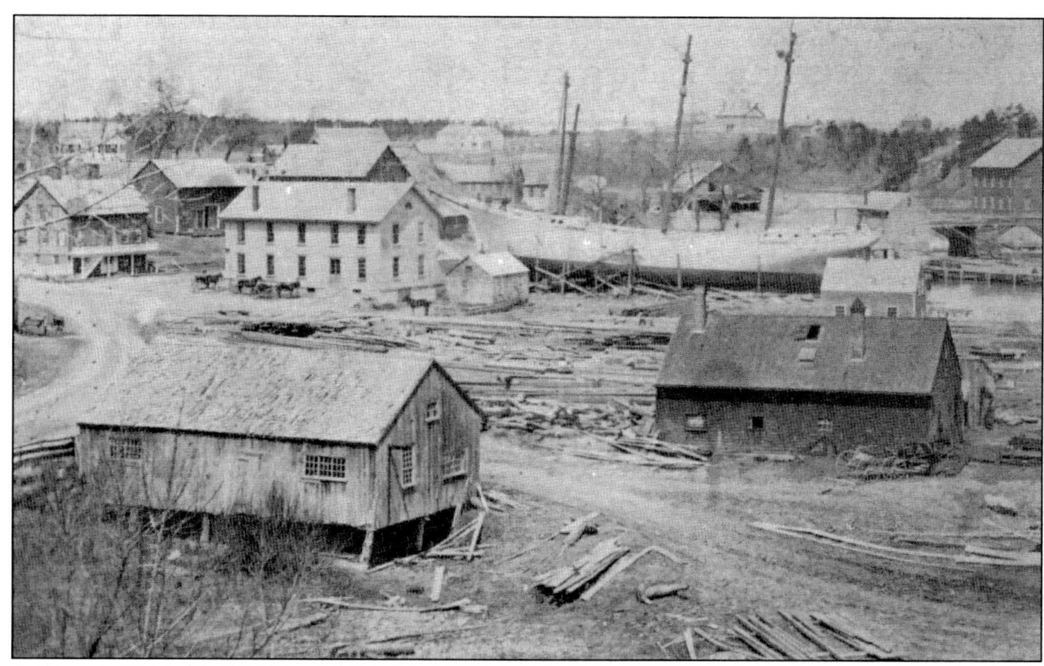

A factory for tackle blocks and deadeyes, both required in the rigging of ships, was located near the harbor. On one side, there was an unpainted, three-story building, in which the basement was used for the storage and turning of treenails. Ship joiners occupied the second floor while the third story was used as a boardinghouse.

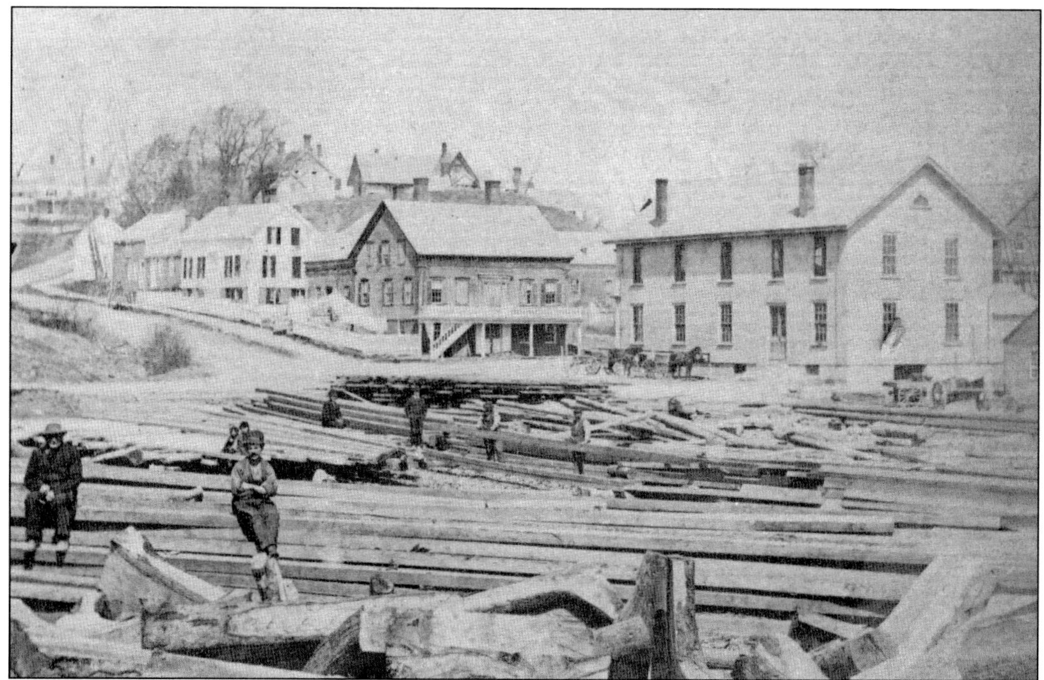

This photograph was taken at the bottom of Pleasant Street as it merged into the harbor area. Men are shown sitting on planks with pieces of wood to be used for knees in the foreground. In the background, men are carrying one long plank with carts used for hauling lumber behind them.

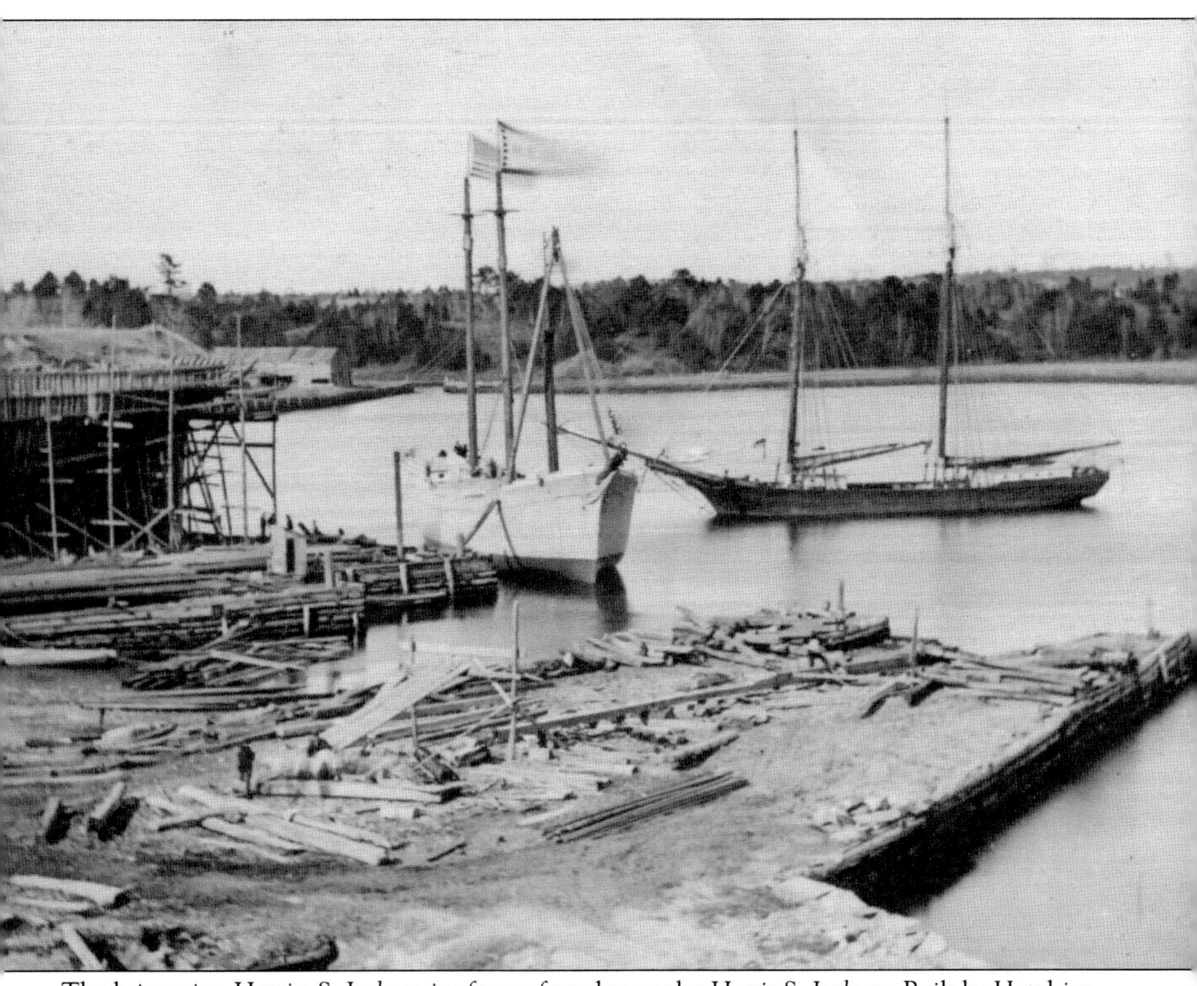

The brigantine *Harriet S. Jackson* is often referred to as the *Hattie S. Jackson*. Built by Hutchins & Stubbs in 1874, it is one of 12 vessels that were either being built or launched in that year, the most ever in Yarmouth yards.

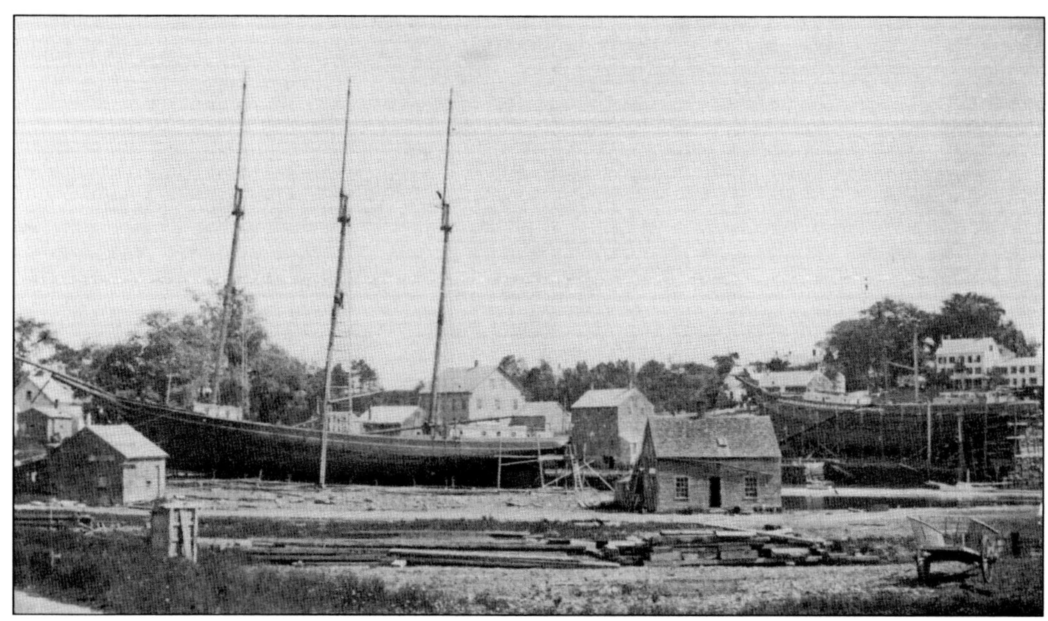

Shown in this photograph is the schooner *Mattie J. Alles*, built in 1883 by Hutchins & Stubbs yard. Hutchins & Stubbs vessels were noted for their craftsmanship and beauty of line.

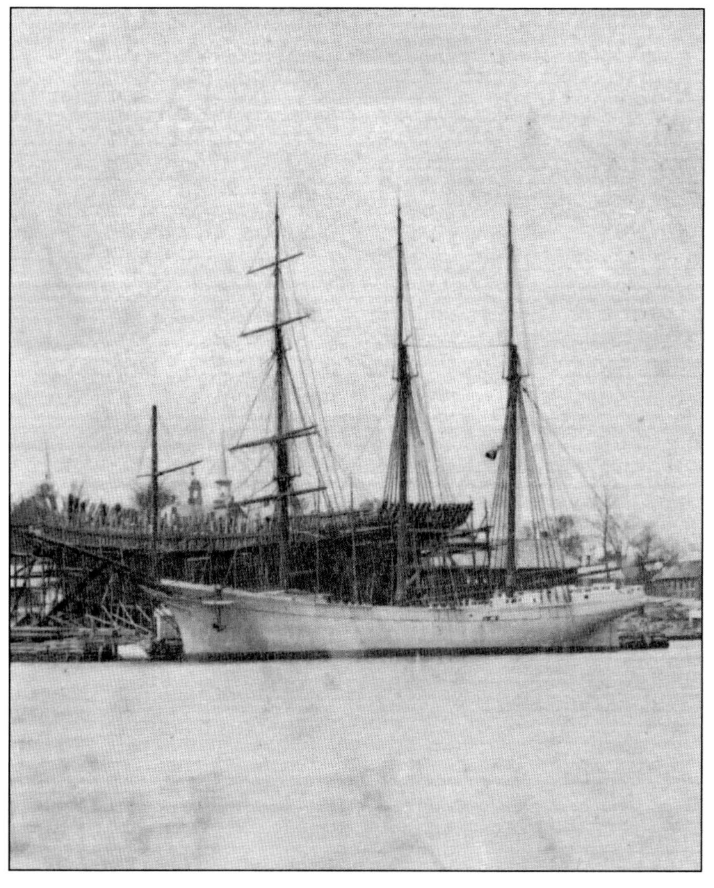

This 1874 photograph of the *C.F. Sargent* and the *Harriet S. Jackson* was taken at the Blanchard Bros. shipyard. Joseph Seabury and his son Joseph Albert Seabury built both vessels. Although Union Wharf is known as the site of the Blanchard yards, the firm began its business in the Seabury yards on the eastern side of the river. Capt. Sylvanus Blanchard bought shares in Union Wharf and, in 1857, established the Blanchard Bros. shipyard. Joseph Seabury and J.A. Seabury continued to build for the Blanchards.

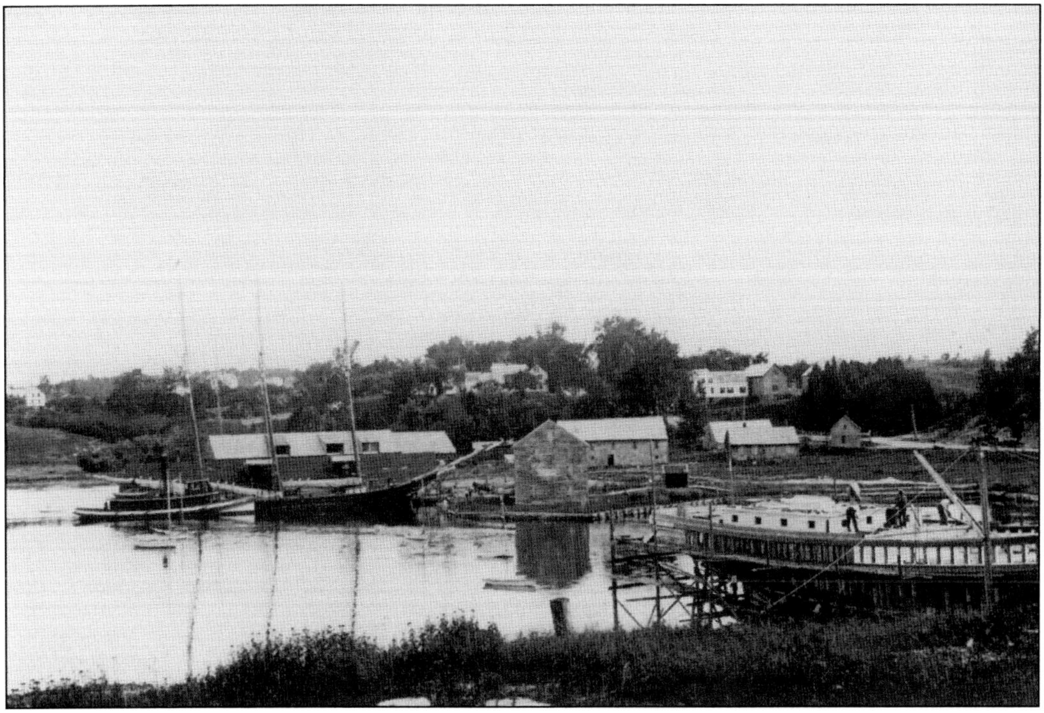

The Giles Loring yard was located on the east side of the harbor. Loring started in the Pratt shipyard when he was 30 years old. After establishing his own shipyard, Loring expanded into the Jeremiah Baker yard to become the major yard on that side of the harbor. Loring built 34 vessels, primarily barks and brigs.

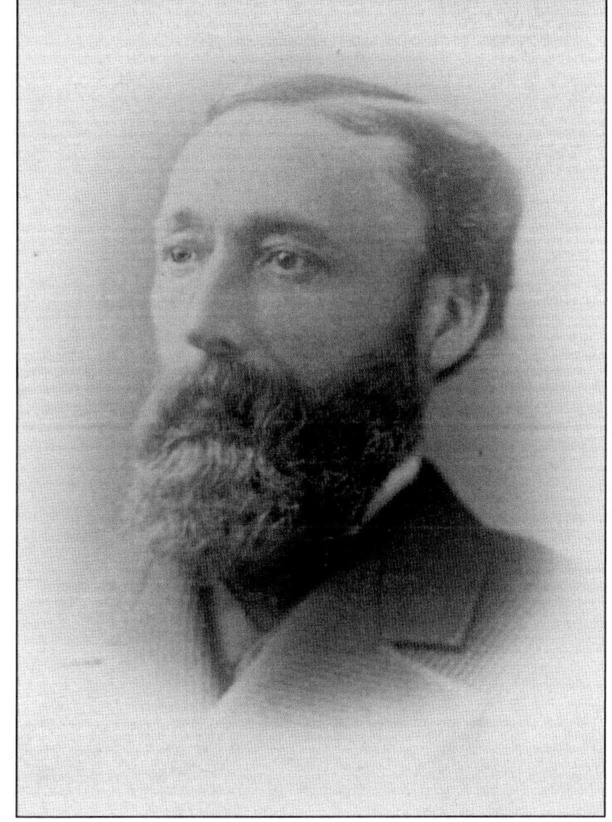

The firm of Hutchins & Stubbs, composed of Henry Hutchins and Edward J. Stubbs (pictured, began building about 1851 and continued until 1884. The yard was located between the western end of the bridge and Union Wharf. The largest vessel built in the yard was the bark *George A. Wright*, built in 1877 for Capt. Benjamin Webster.

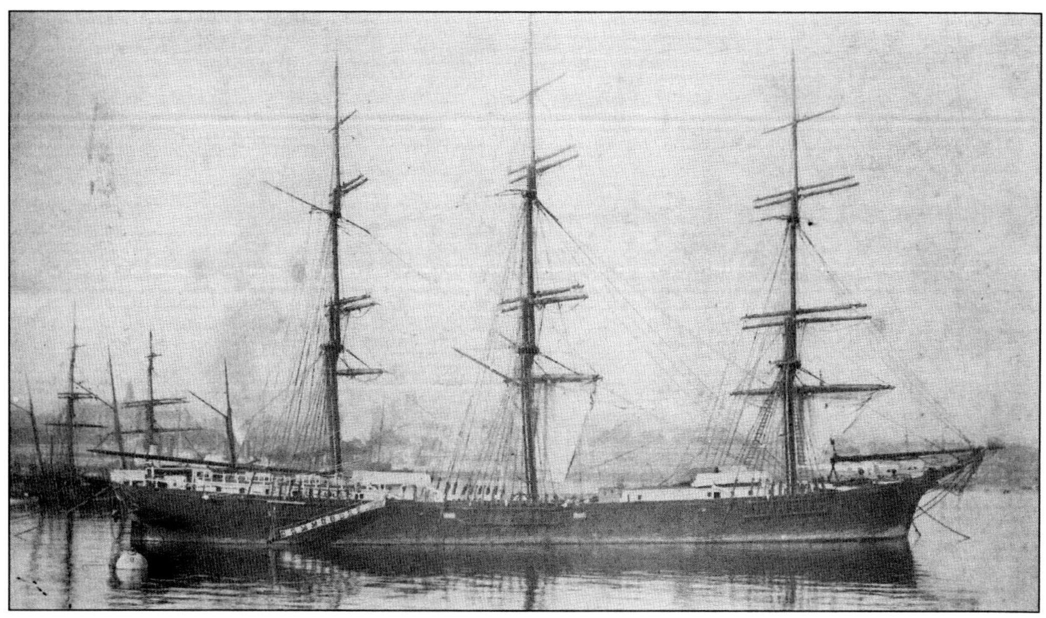

The Blanchard Bros. had a reputation for expert workmen and the latest improvements in rig and equipment. The *Commodore*, launched in June 1879, was the last vessel this firm produced. Although somewhat smaller than the *Admiral*, the *Commodore* was one of the largest vessels built in Yarmouth, at 1,979 tons.

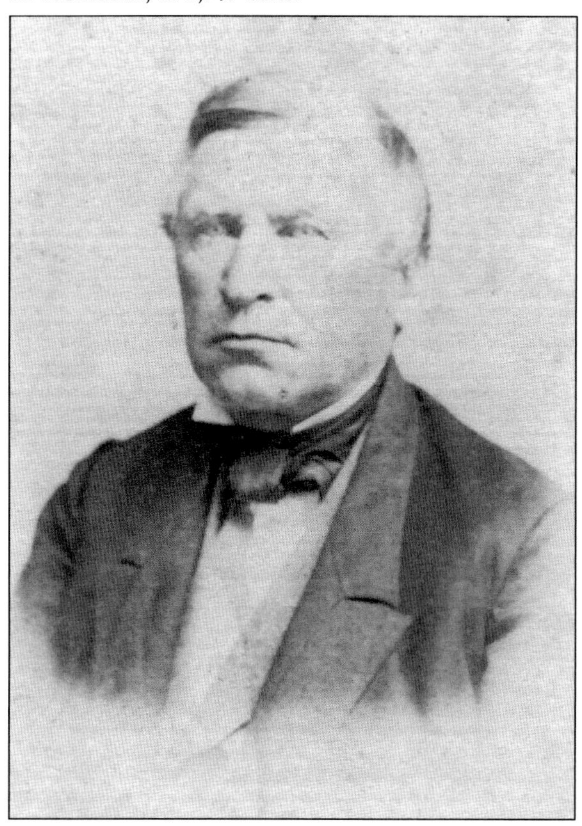

Capt. Paul Blanchard was one of the wealthiest men in Yarmouth. Along with his brothers Perez and Sylvanus, he owned Blanchard Bros. shipyard. Before retiring from the sea and joining his brothers in the business, Captain Blanchard sailed on many long-distance voyages.

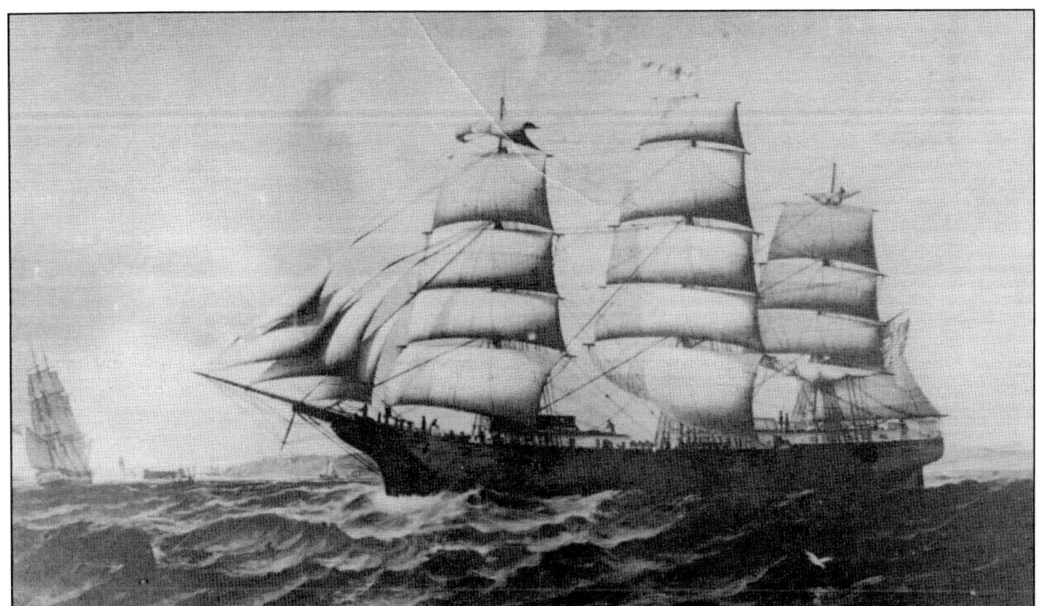

The *Lafayette*, seen here, was captured and sunk in 1862 after an encounter with Rafael Semmes and the Confederate ship *Alabama*. Alfred T. Small of Yarmouth was the captain when the ship was overtaken near Seal Island in the Bay of Fundy. Captain Small was ordered to remove his crew, and the ship was set on fire. As the *Lafayette* had been sailing on an English account, the English government paid full indemnity, amounting to $140,000, to Captain Small and the owners in 1875.

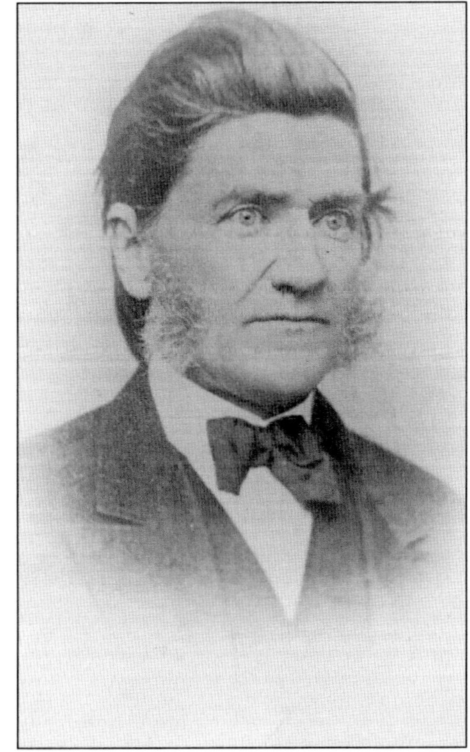

Before Ferdinand Ingraham achieved financial success with the Blanchard Bros. shipyard, he traveled twice to California to seek his fortune in the gold rush. During Ingraham's second trip, he became severely ill and returned to Yarmouth with the assistance of an Odd Fellow brother.

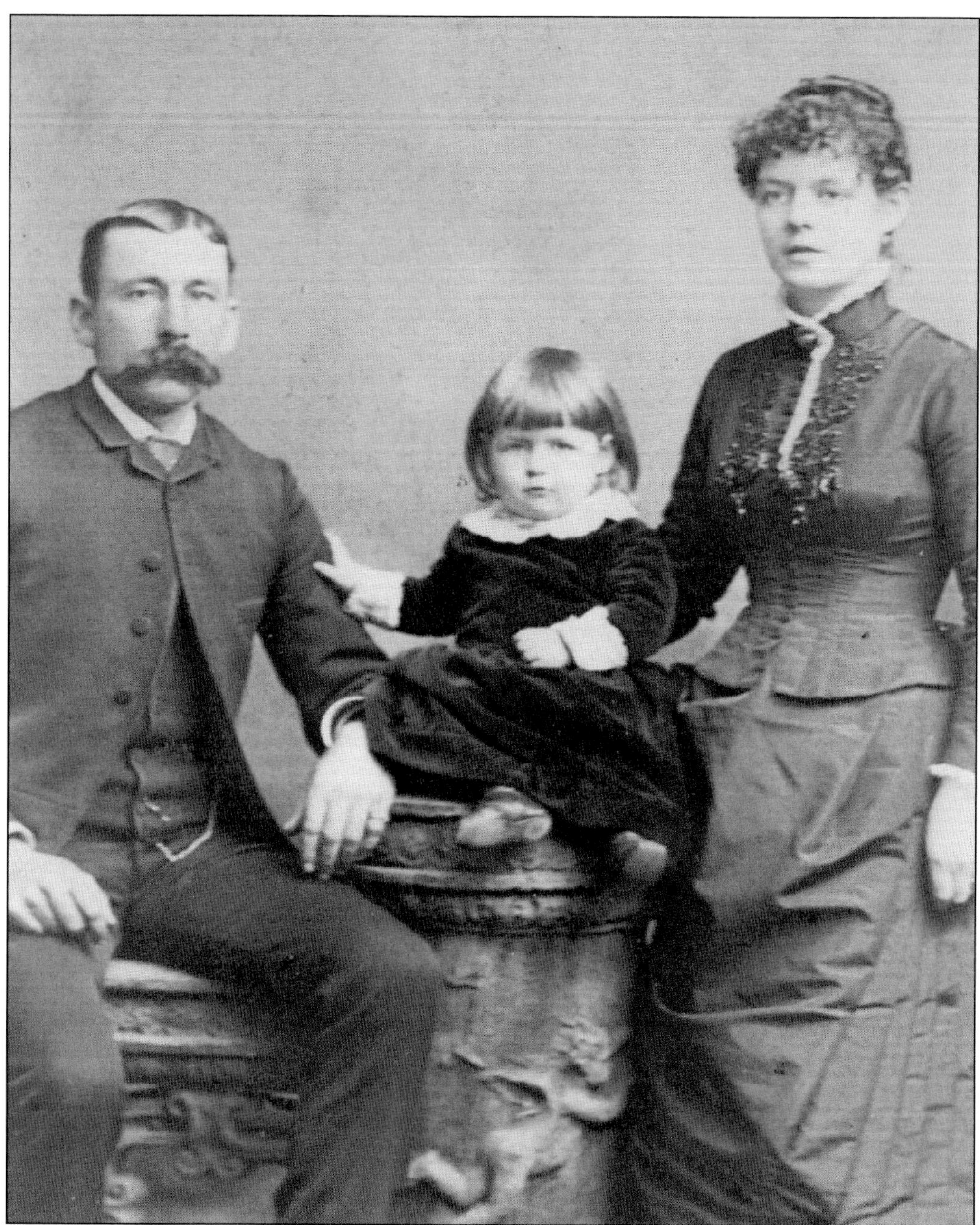

Capt. William Gooding met his wife, Marion, in Australia during one of his voyages. They were married, and she moved to Yarmouth. Gooding was the captain of the *Tewskbury L. Swett* when it was wrecked in the Caroline Islands. Marion Gooding refused to believe that her husband was not going to return and turned down insurance claims. Nineteen months later, Captain Gooding returned with an incredible story of a hurricane and being stranded on an island with dangerous "natives." The story was published and has continued to be a part of Yarmouth lore; however, the logbook, located in the Yarmouth Historical Society archives, indicates that Captain Gooding may have exaggerated the details. It is a fact that he was stranded and did return. Of this venture, he was quoted as saying, "That was the voyage I didn't survive."

Many Yarmouth sea captains, including Charles Chandler Oakes, traveled as far away as China and South America. Oakes was the captain of the *Governor Goodwin* and later the *P.N. Blanchard.* Captain Oakes made the transition from sail to steam in the 1890s.

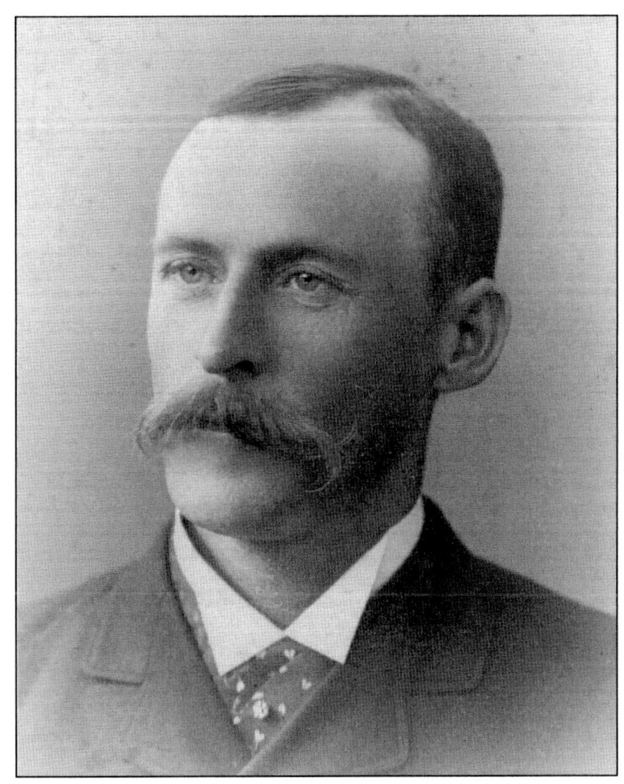

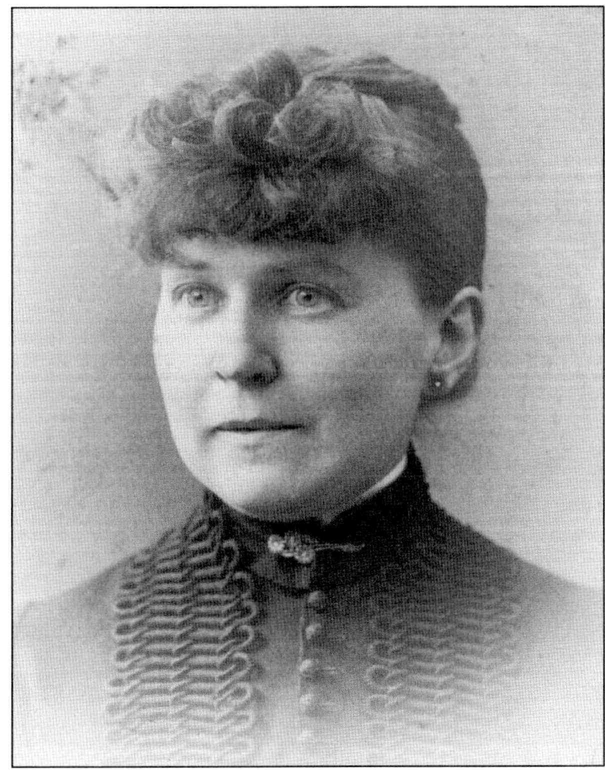

In 1888, Abbie Buxton married Charles Oakes and accompanied her husband aboard the *Governor Goodwin.* Her first voyage departed from New York and sailed to Shanghai, China. In the book, *The Old Sea Chest,* the couple wrote of the journey from Talcahuano, Chile, around Cape Horn, as well as their other travels.

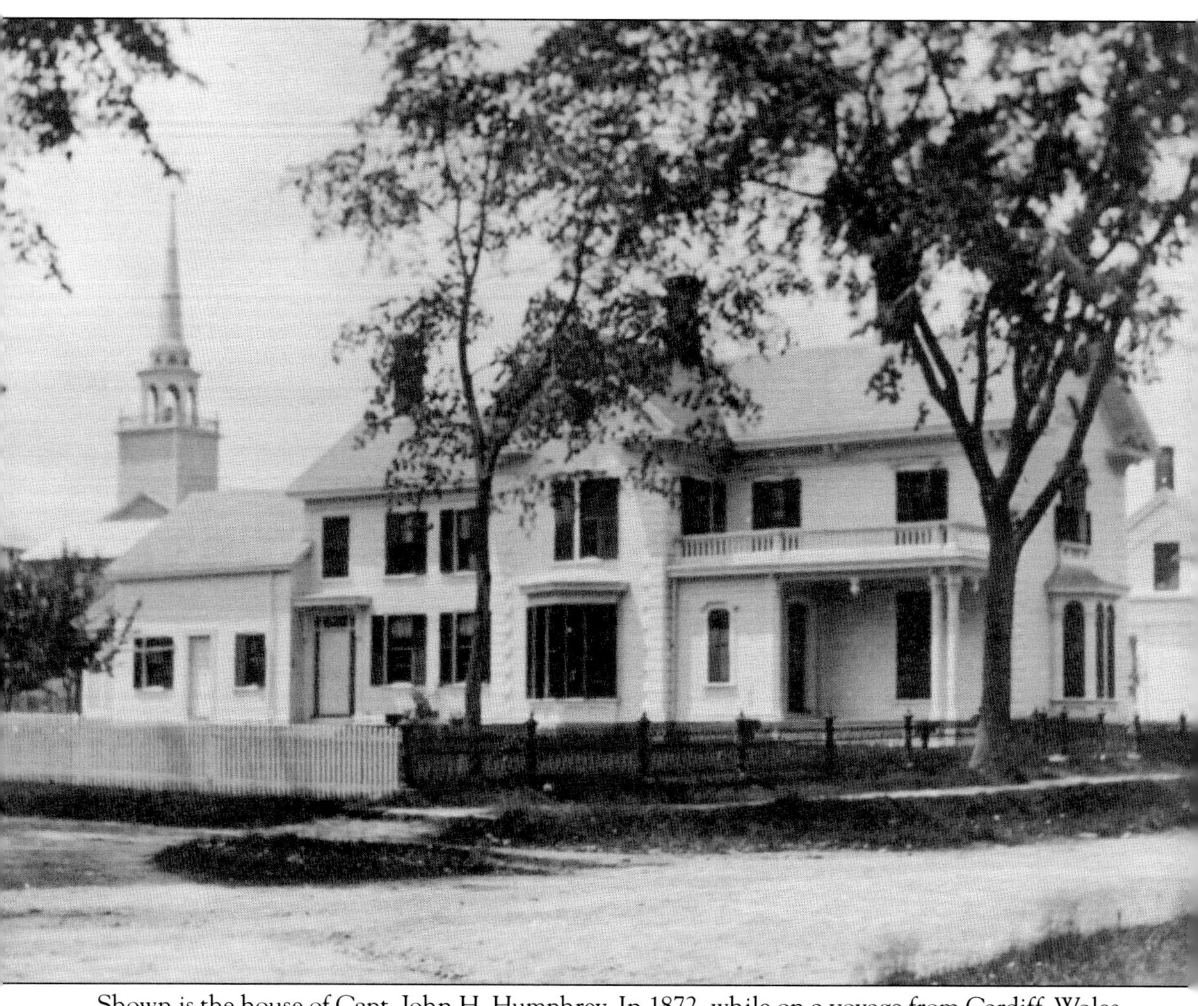

Shown is the house of Capt. John H. Humphrey. In 1872, while on a voyage from Cardiff, Wales, on board the ship *Alice Venard*, Captain Humphrey rescued the crew from the Spanish bark *Mathilda* that was on fire in the Bay of Biscay. It was later discovered that the *Mathilda*, formerly the bark *Sunrise,* was built in 1853 in the same yard as the *Alice Venard*.

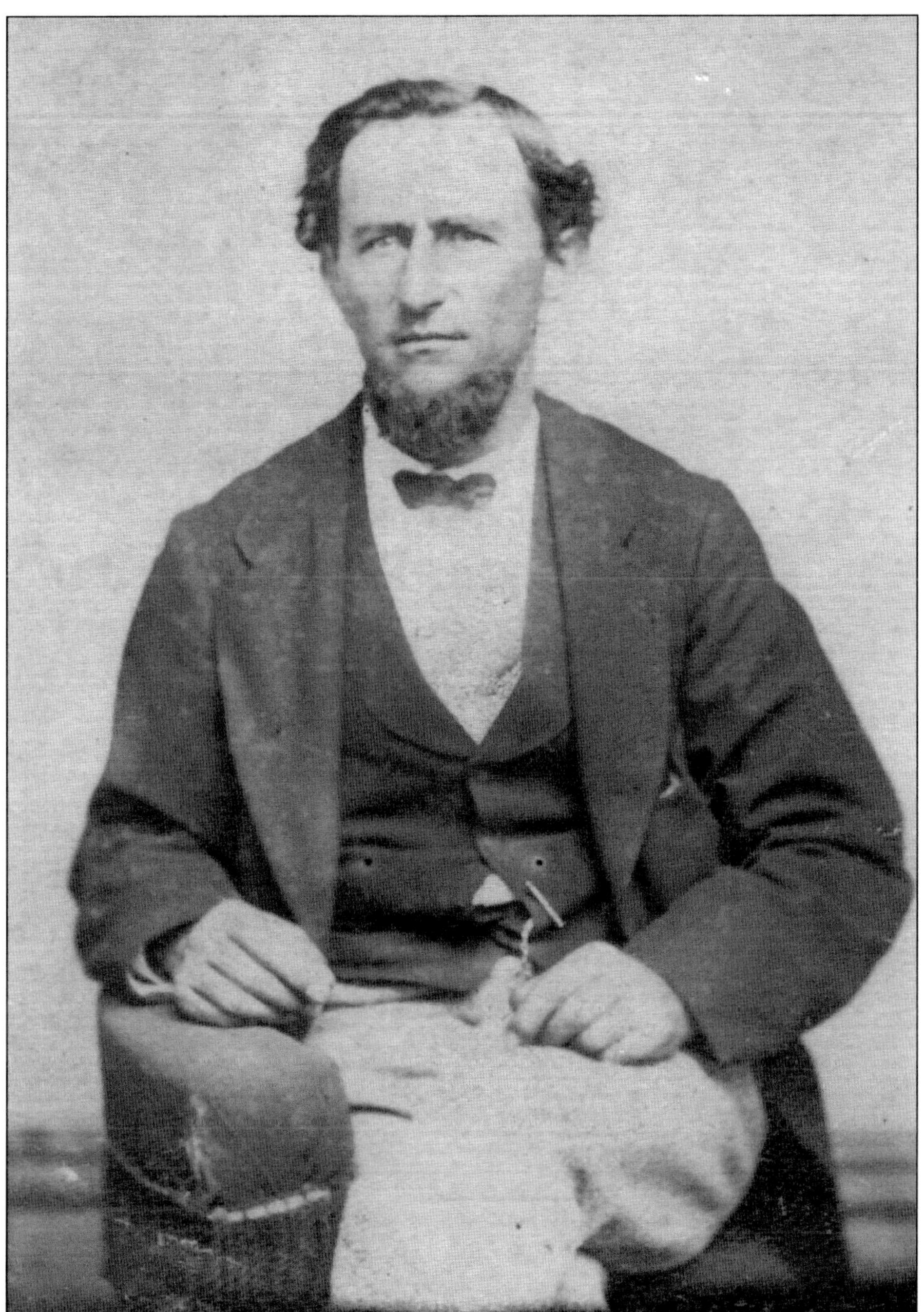

Capt. Anthony Vianello was the captain of the ill-fated ship *Star*, built in 1861, whose story remains a mystery. According to a newspaper account, the *Star* was headed to Europe with a load of guano when it was abandoned. The crew took to the boats, with one commanded by the captain and seven men and the second with the first mate and eleven men. In rough seas, the boats capsized, and all but one man drowned. The lone survivor, George Gould, appeared at the agent's office in Boston. Gould told the story and was eventually paid. It was rumored that the ship was disreputable, and a suspicion of mutiny surrounded the disappearance.

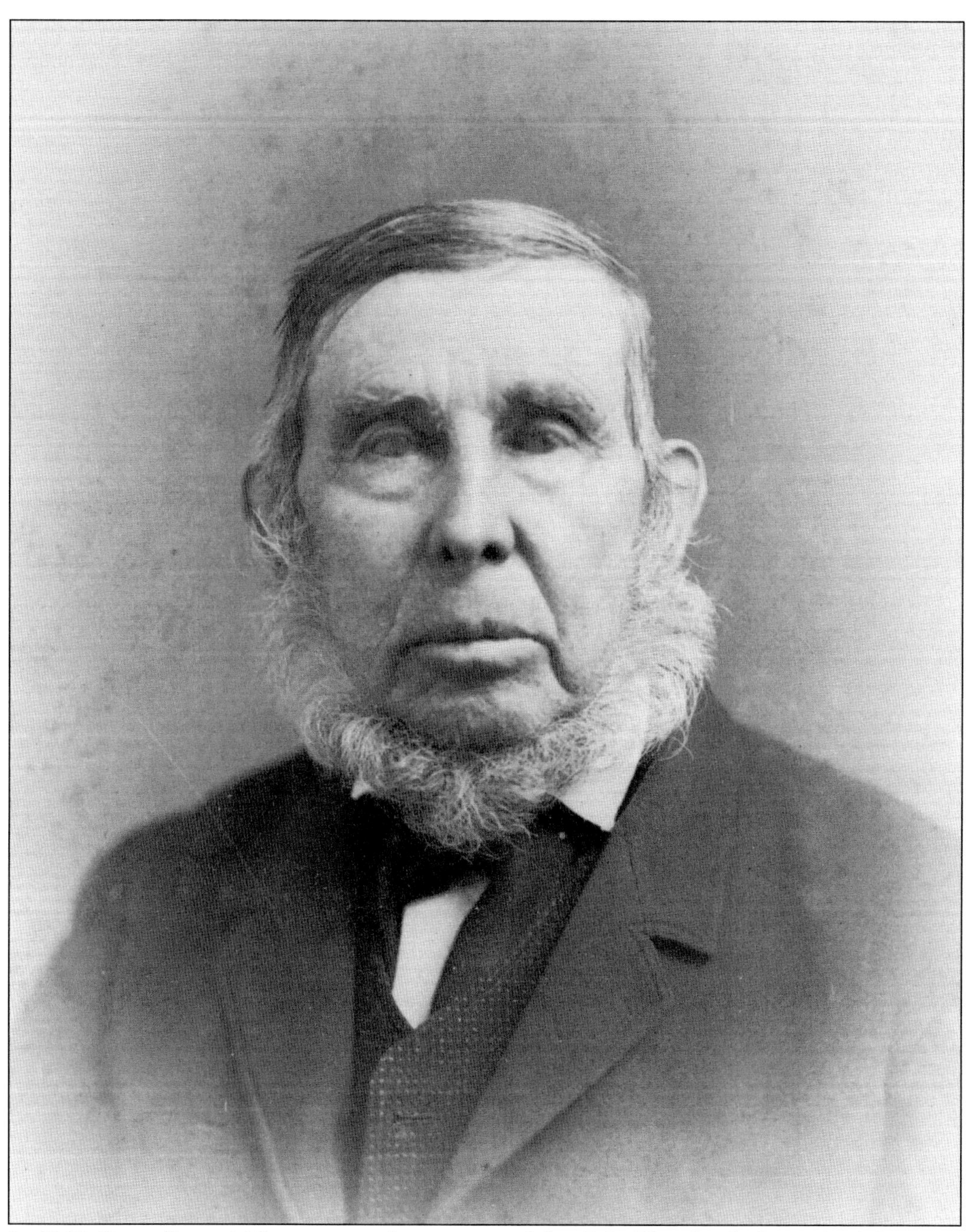

In 1867, Capt. Samuel Thomas was the captain of the *P.G. Blanchard* when 13 of the crew, including the chief mate, died of scurvy. The ship was on a voyage from Aden to Callao. Captain Thomas eventually made it to Callao with assistance from other vessels. A story told about him by a young crewmember alludes to the fact that the only time the captain spoke to him was to ask the boy whether his mother kept a cow. Captain Thomas, a bachelor, shared a house with his four sisters.

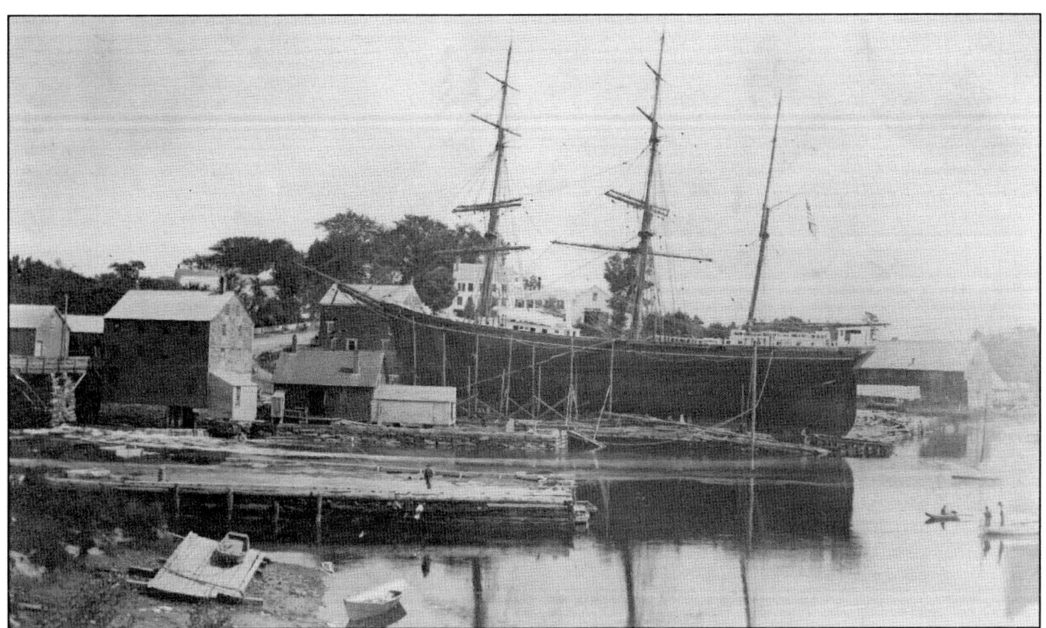

The *Onaway*, built by Giles Loring, was the last square-rigged vessel constructed in Yarmouth yards. A model of the *Onaway* was displayed at the 1893 World's Fair in Chicago.

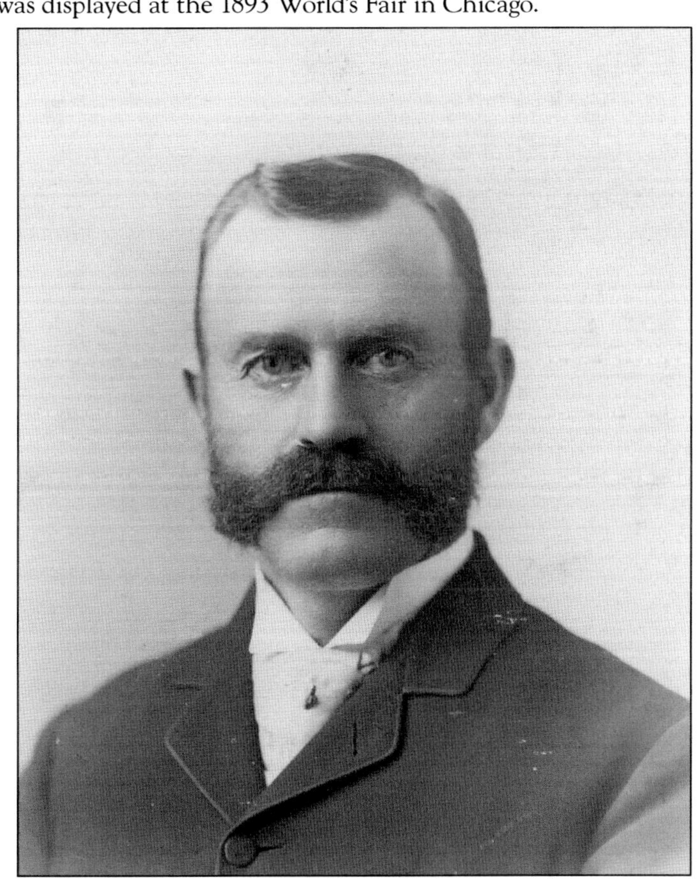

Capt. Frank Oakes was at the helm of the *S.C. Blanchard* when the ship encountered northwest gales around Cape Horn. A ship was spotted that could help the crew, and so they set off rockets as a distress signal. All on board were safely taken off, including the captain's wife. The second officer of the rescuing ship, the British *County of Lancaster,* later told the officers of the *S.C. Blanchard* that, the night the officer spotted them, he had flipped a coin to decide which of two courses he should take. The *S.C. Blanchard* was built in Yarmouth at the Blanchard Bros. shipyard and registered 1,904 tons. It was carrying wheat at the time of the incident.

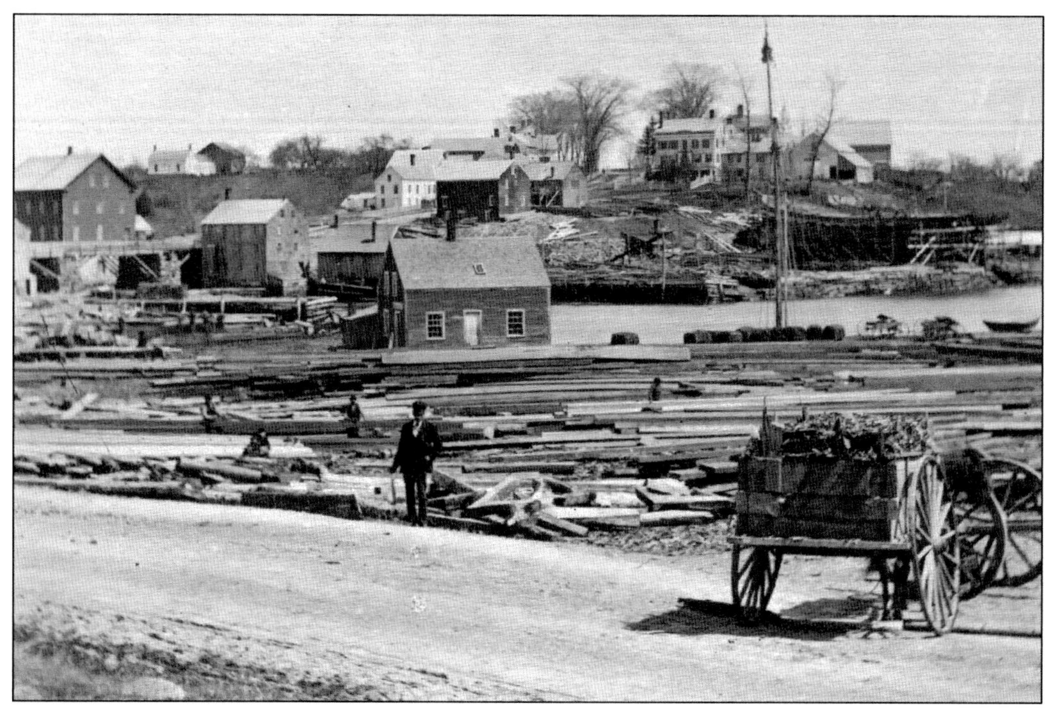

This photograph shows what the harbor looked like with piles of lumber stacked in various yards. It is likely that this was taken on a Sunday morning, as there are no shipyard employees in the photograph.

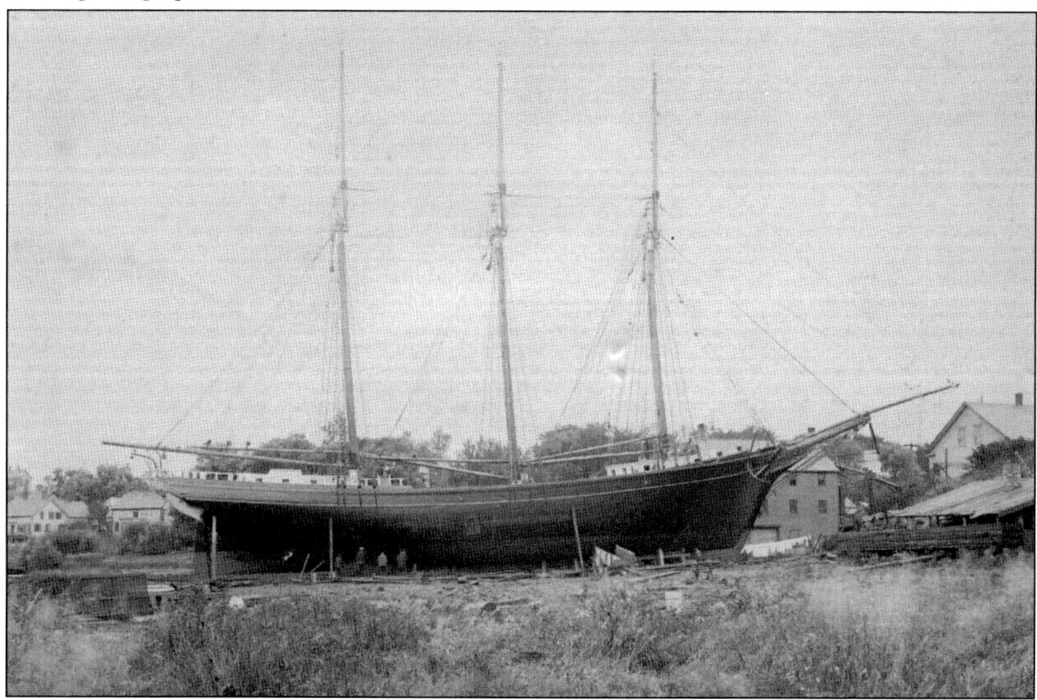

The *Damietta and Joanna* was the last vessel built in Yarmouth by Giles Loring in 1890. Loring constructed it in partnership with John M. Cobb. The three-masted schooner was 320 tons.

Four

Coming into the 20th Century

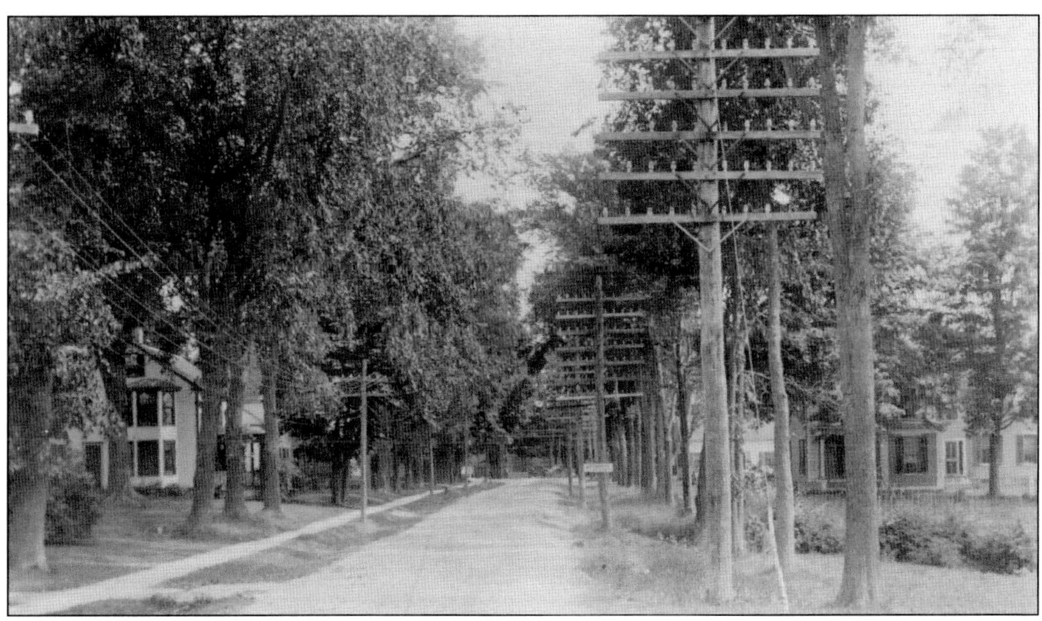

Telephone and electric wires are some of the improvements that came with the influx of money that companies such as the Forest Paper Company brought into the town. Electricity came in 1893. The Yarmouth Telephone Company was incorporated in 1895 and sold to New England Telephone in 1910. This photograph is of Portland Street around 1910.

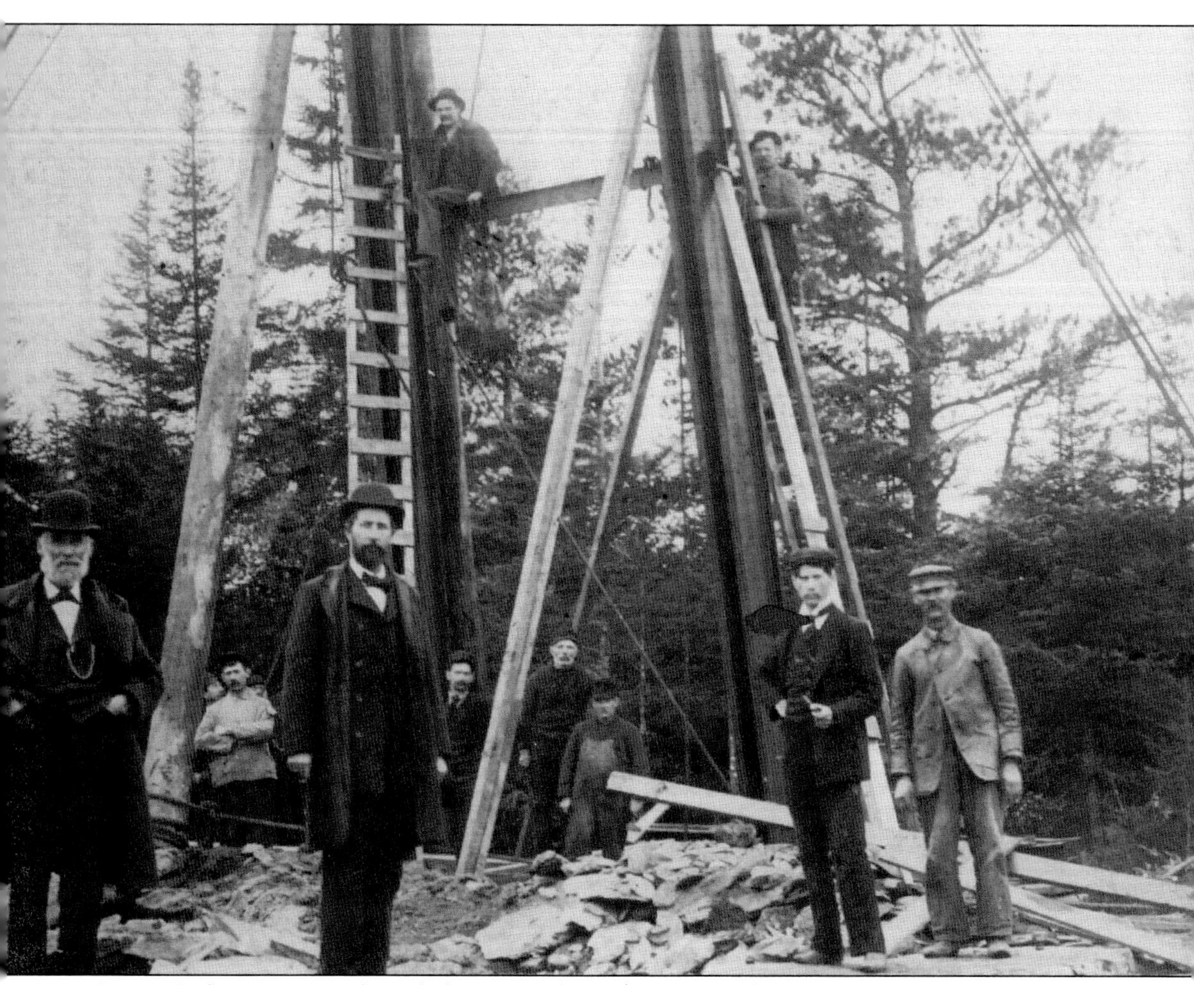

In 1895, the town voted to pledge its credit to $20,000 and issue a series of 20-year bonds to defray the expense of installing a sewer and water system. The mains were laid in the summer of 1895 by the W.A. Hayden Company. Shown in this photograph is a 30-by-50-foot elevated tank (or standpipe) for the new Yarmouth Water Company. In front of the standpipe's first two legs are, from left to right, David Lawrence, Capt. Alfred T. Small (water committee), W.H. Hayden (contractor), John Leadly (engineer), and Charles Rolfe (boss mason).

Trolley tracks are visible in this photograph of Main Street with the Merrill Memorial Library on the near left and the Masonic Hall beyond the library. The Masonic Hall was completed in 1878 and became a central gathering place for townspeople.

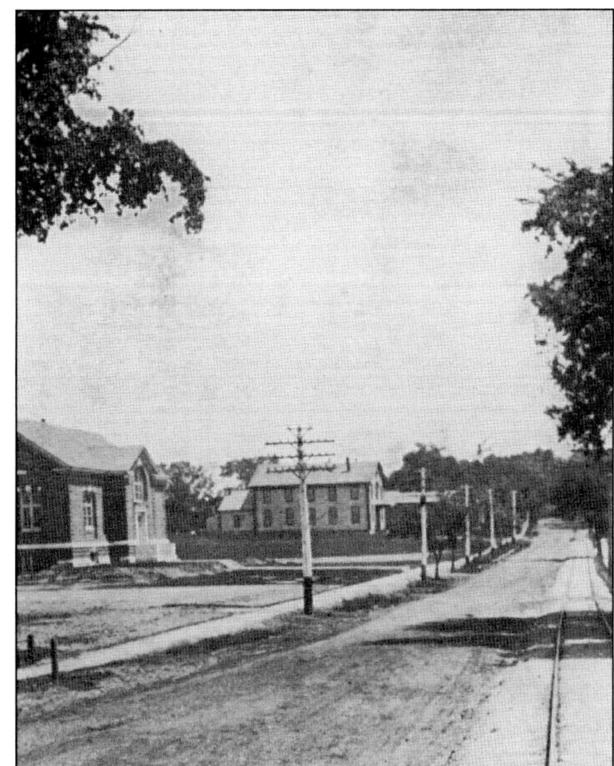

With the exception of the unpaved road and piles of logs next to the street, this view up East Main Street past the bridge is strikingly similar to that of today.

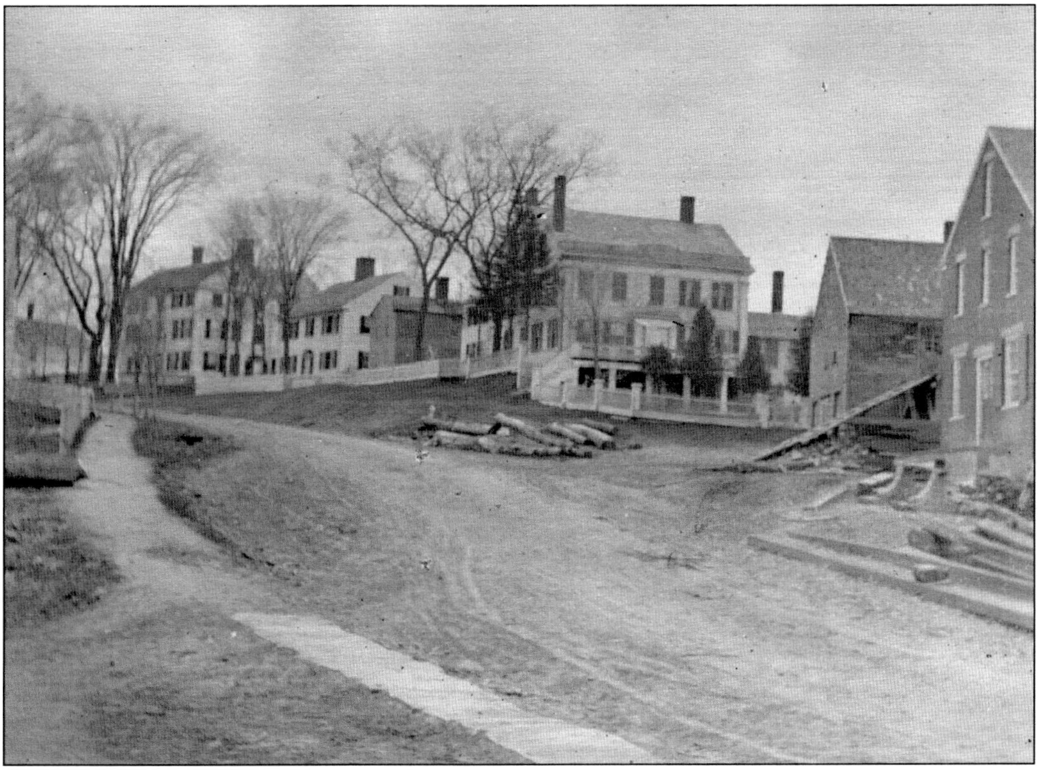

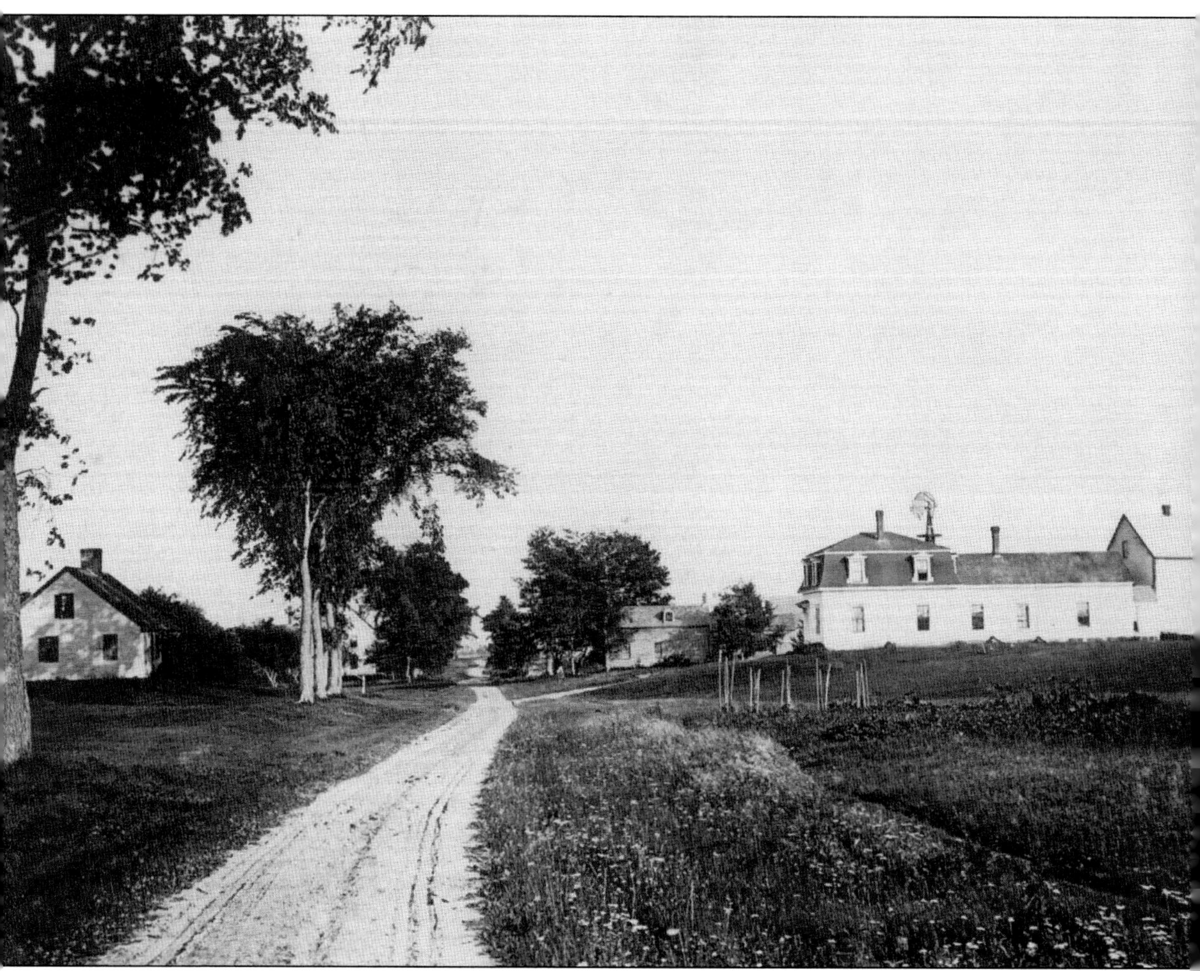

This c. 1890 photograph shows what is now Bayview Street. Samuel Gammon built the cape on the left in 1811, one of the oldest houses on the road.

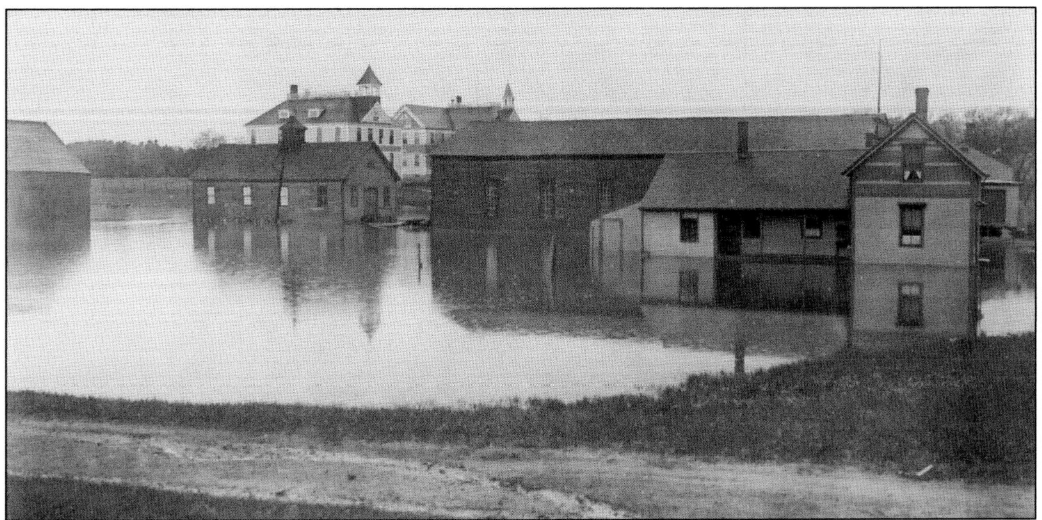

This photograph shows the trolley barn during a flooding. The trolley barn was located on Main Street where the Route 1 overpass is today. The Central Grammar School, built in 1890, and the high school, built in 1900, are visible in the background.

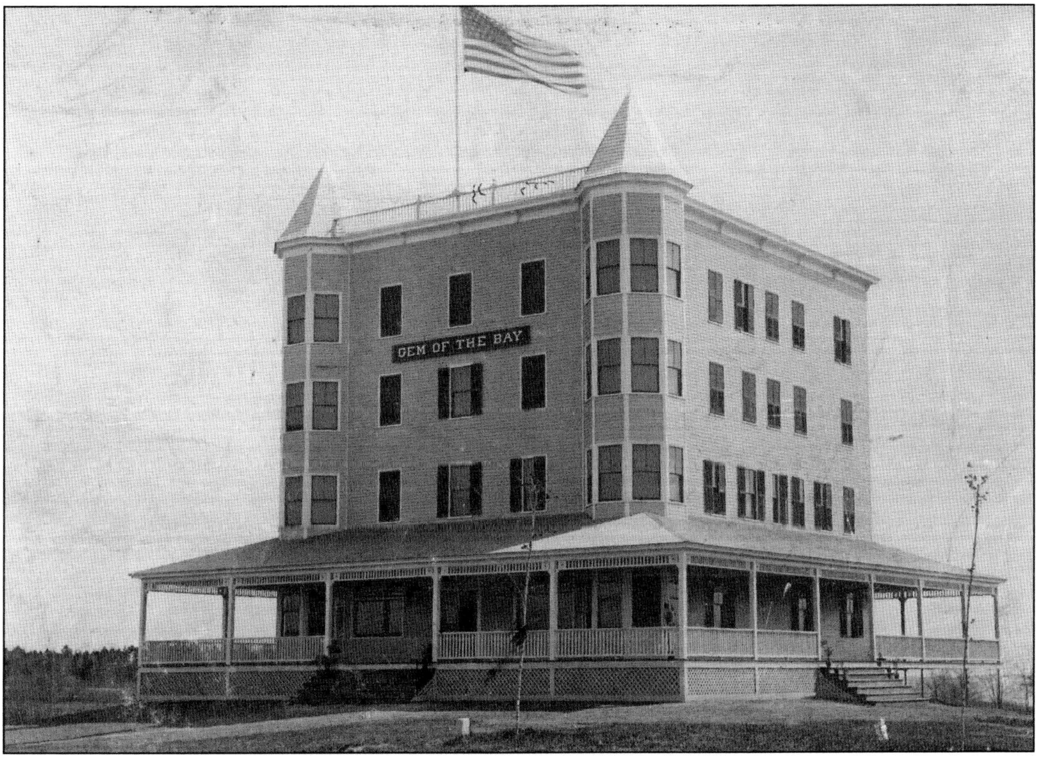

The Gem of the Bay was engulfed in a fire in October 1900. The hotel was four stories, with a piazza on all sides. A ladies' parlor, front and back offices, and a dining hall were found on the first floor, and rooms for guests and two toilet rooms were on the second floor. Each room was furnished with closets and hot and cold water. In total, there were 29 guest rooms, which were all connected to the main office via call bells. The Gem of the Bay was located at Prince's Point and was in operation for two seasons. After the fire, the owner decided the hotel was too expensive to replace.

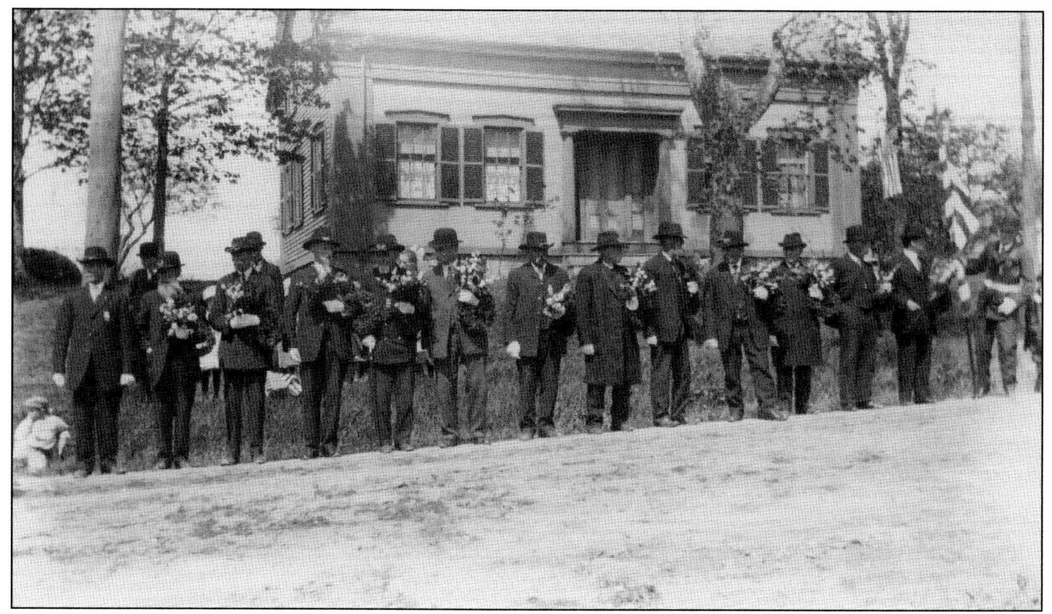

Members of the Grand Army of the Republic are shown lined up on Main Street. Some of the men in this photograph include Joe Chase, Herbert Soule, Edward Stoddard, Edward Wilson, Henry Doughty, Henry Blake, and Charles Johnson.

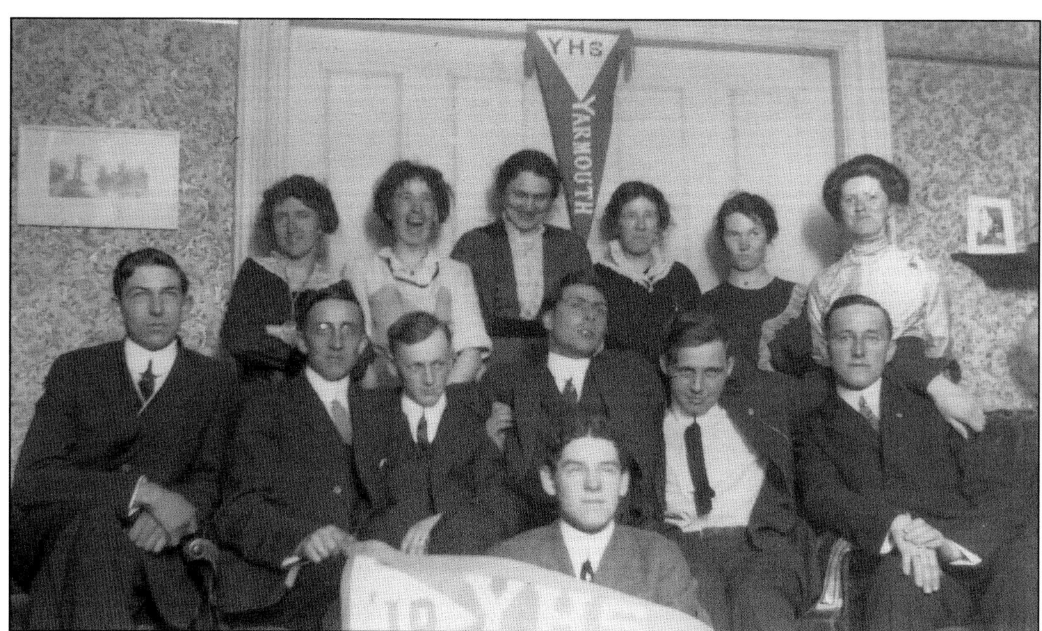

Shown here is the Yarmouth High School graduating class of 1910. In 1873, the Maine legislature passed the Free High School Act, and a public town high school was established in Yarmouth. Rather than erect its own building, the town used the funds provided by the state, along with an additional $2,000 that had been raised for the school's maintenance, to rent classroom space from North Yarmouth Academy for $365 a year.

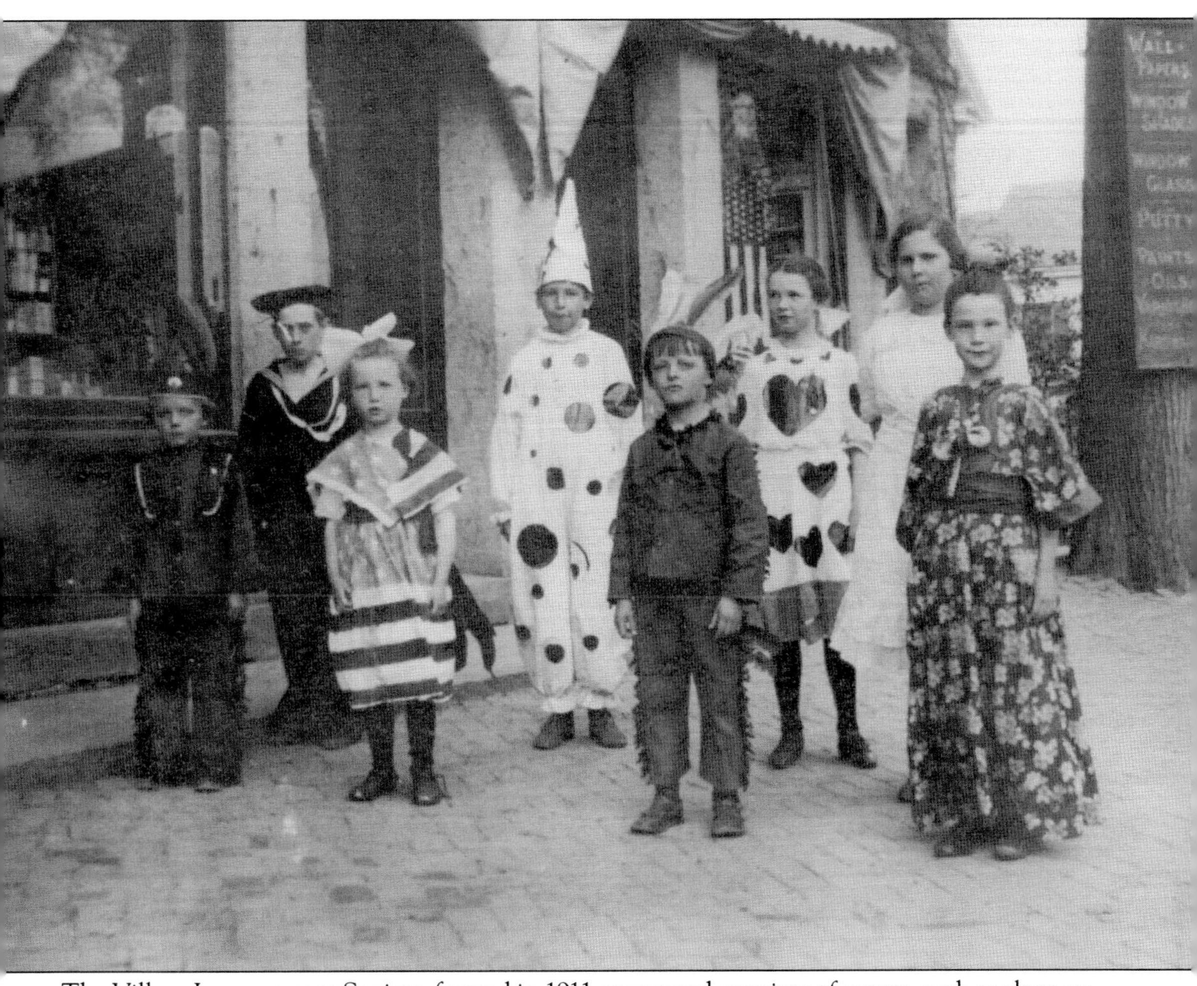

The Village Improvement Society, formed in 1911, sponsored a variety of events, such as clean-up parades, fairs, and carnivals. Shown in this photograph are children dressed for a VIS carnival. Children were urged to dress in costume in exchange for free admission.

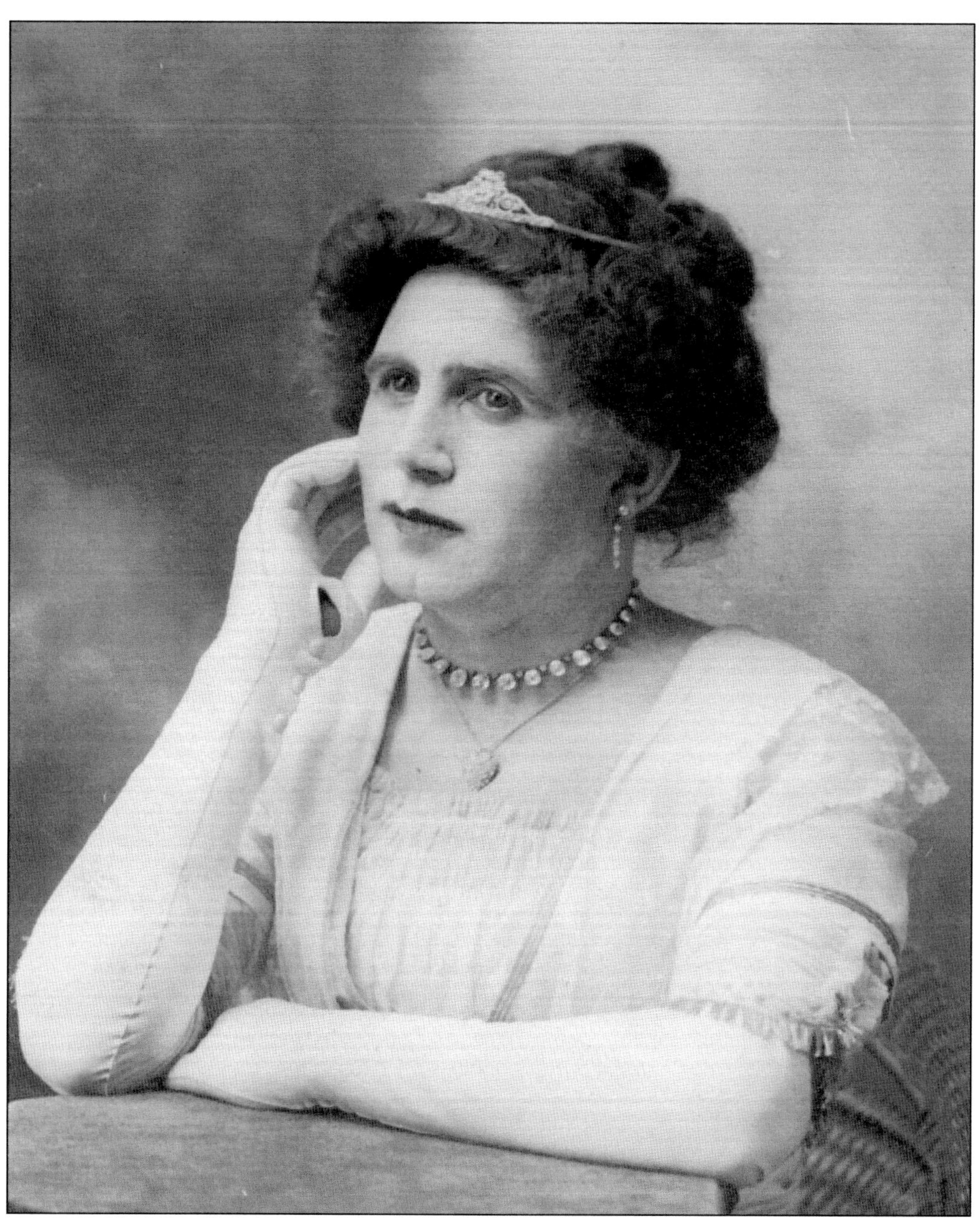

On August 14, 1912, the Village Improvement Society sponsored its second annual fair. One feature of the fair was *Fascinating Phylis*, which was a "sentimental symphony" written by Harriet Bird. James Bradley played two roles in the musical comedy, both Captain Warrington and Phylis, pictured here.

In the early years of the organization, membership to the Village Improvement Society was open to women, while men, like Chester Curtis (pictured), were allowed associate memberships. The primary concern of this women's group was cleaning up and improving the community.

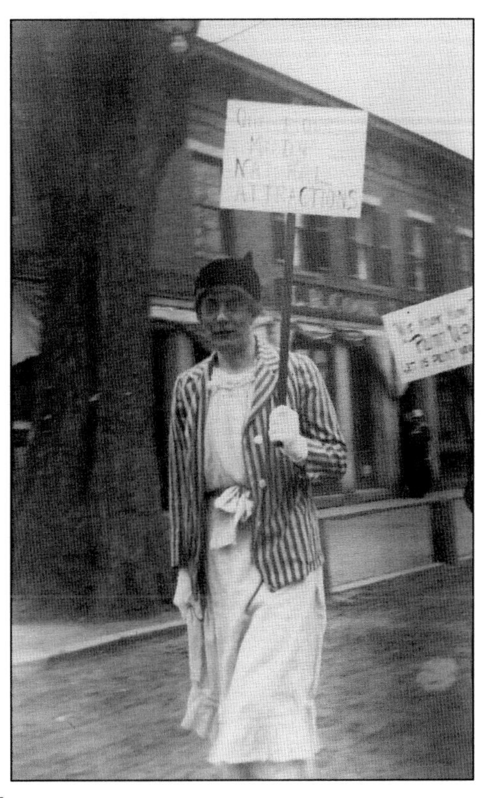

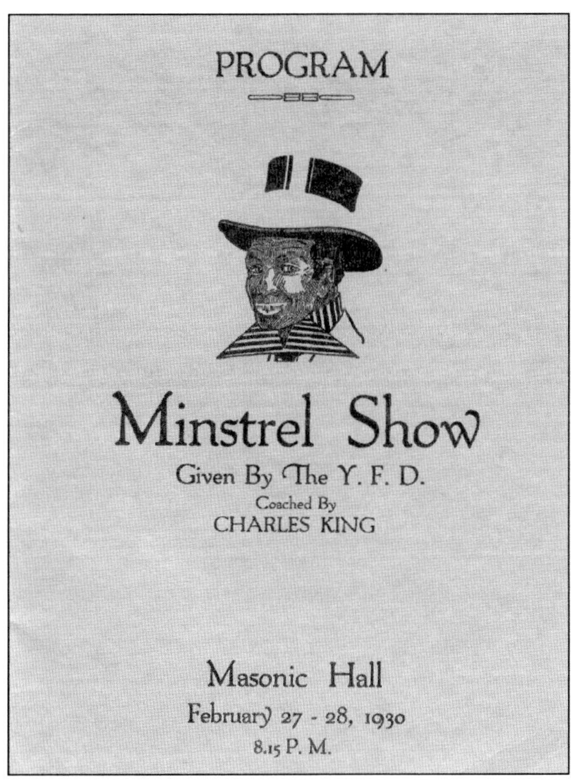

PROGRAM

Minstrel Show

Given By The Y. F. D.

Coached By

CHARLES KING

Masonic Hall

February 27 - 28, 1930

8.15 P. M.

This 1930 program is for a minstrel show sponsored by the Yarmouth Fire Department. Some of the musical numbers included "Dapper Dan," "The Fireplace is Rosy," "Stepping Hot," "Mammy," "Sidewalks of Yarmouth," and "Dance Sketch." The program's introduction from the Yarmouth Fire Department extends "sincere thanks to those who participated in the Annual Show."

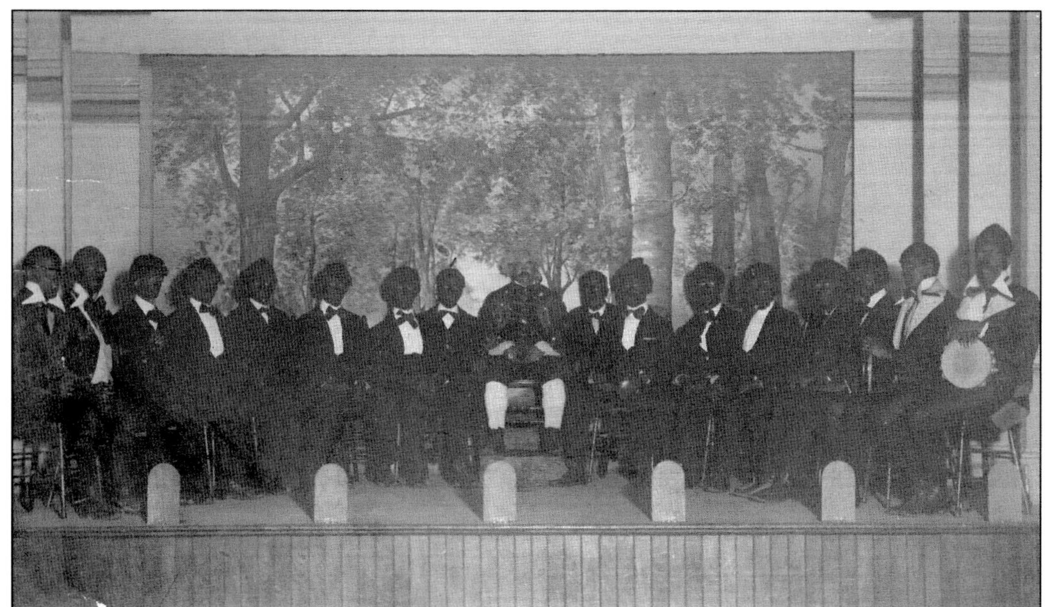

Participants in this 1930 minstrel show include Cyril Perry, John Gaudet, Alfred Carter, Lester Morrison, Lester Blake, John McKinnon, Warren Raynes, Gardiner Mansfield, George Carter, James Ward, Charlie King, E.S. Towne, and Dorothy Cleaves.

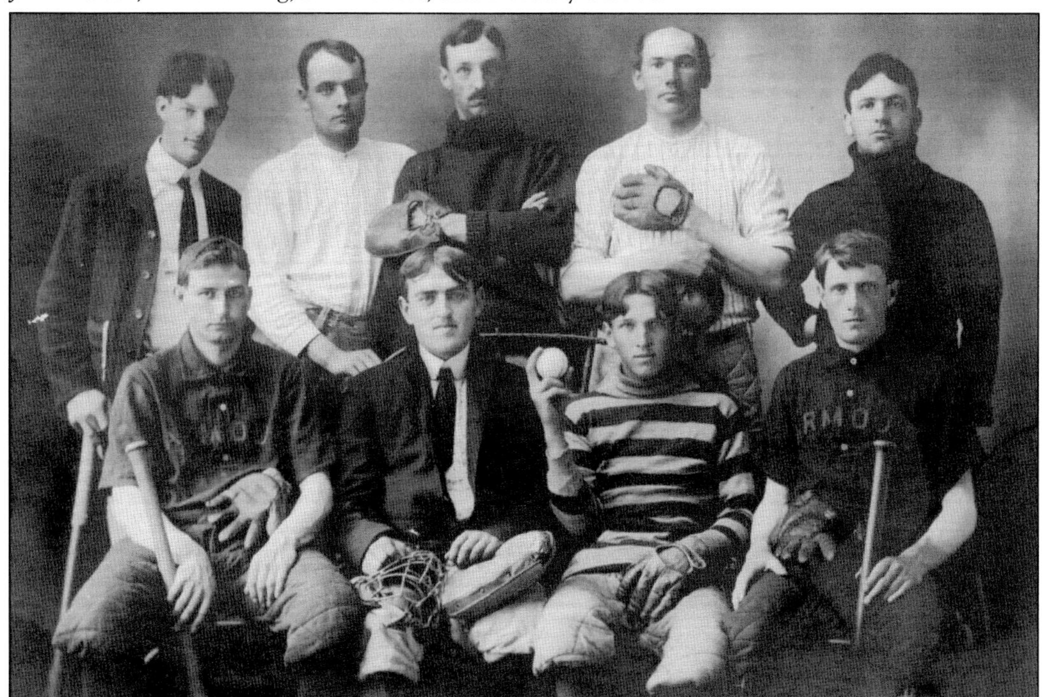

Shown in this photograph is the baseball team of the Portland Yarmouth Company, the company that ran the trolley. Pictured are, from left to right, (first row) George Raynes, center field; Ralph Anderson, catcher; Henry Merrill, pitcher; Phil Hodsdon, second base and shortstop; (second row) M. Rowe, right field; Harland Merrill, third base; George Libby, first base; Harry Turner, center field; and George Colesworthy; shortstop.

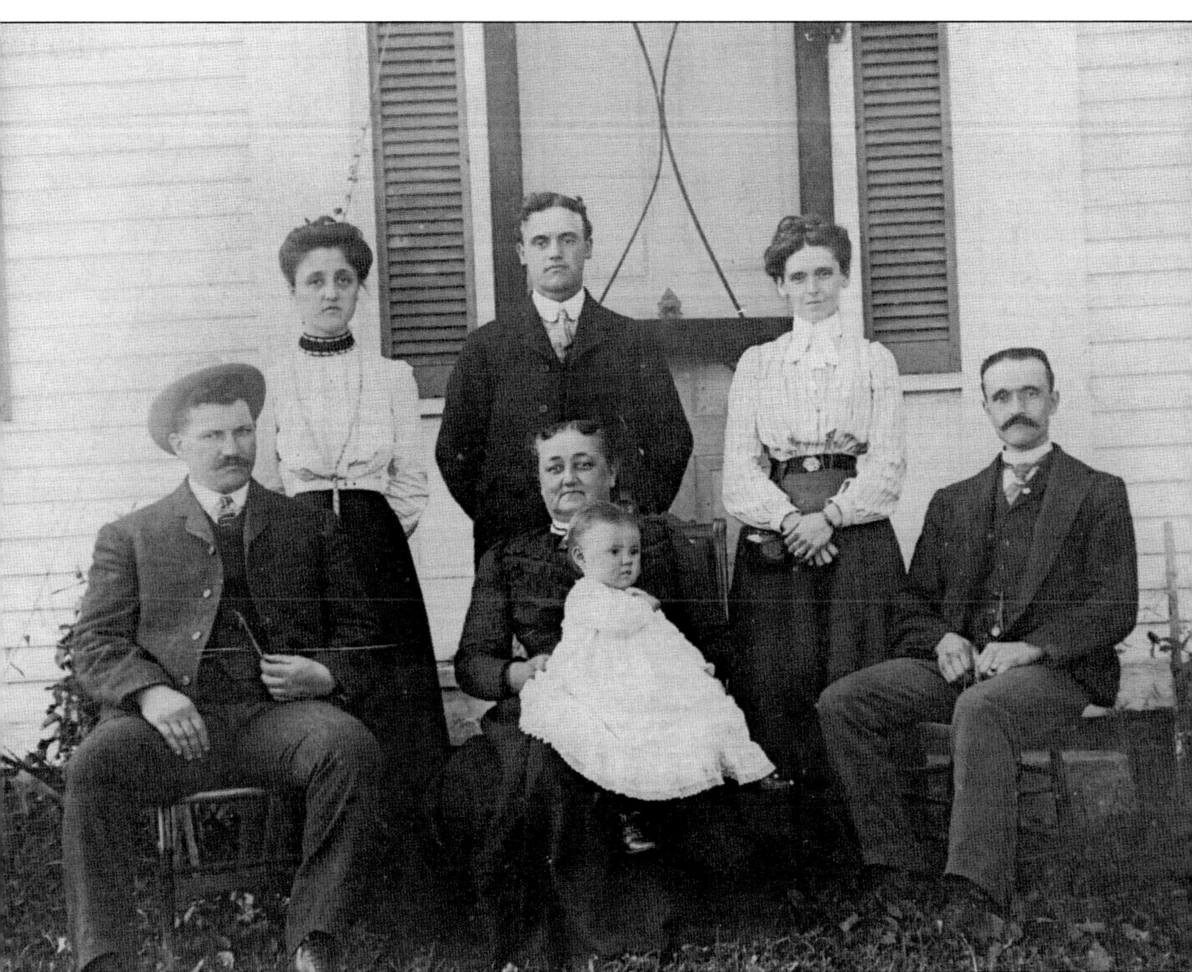

Edward C. Plummer, on the far right, wrote the book *Reminiscences of a Yarmouth Schoolboy*. Plummer cited his purpose in writing the book as "to call back upon the elm-shaded streets of this attractive village; to bring within Fancy's vision those staunch old wharves as I saw them." Plummer served as vice chairman of the US Shipping Board.

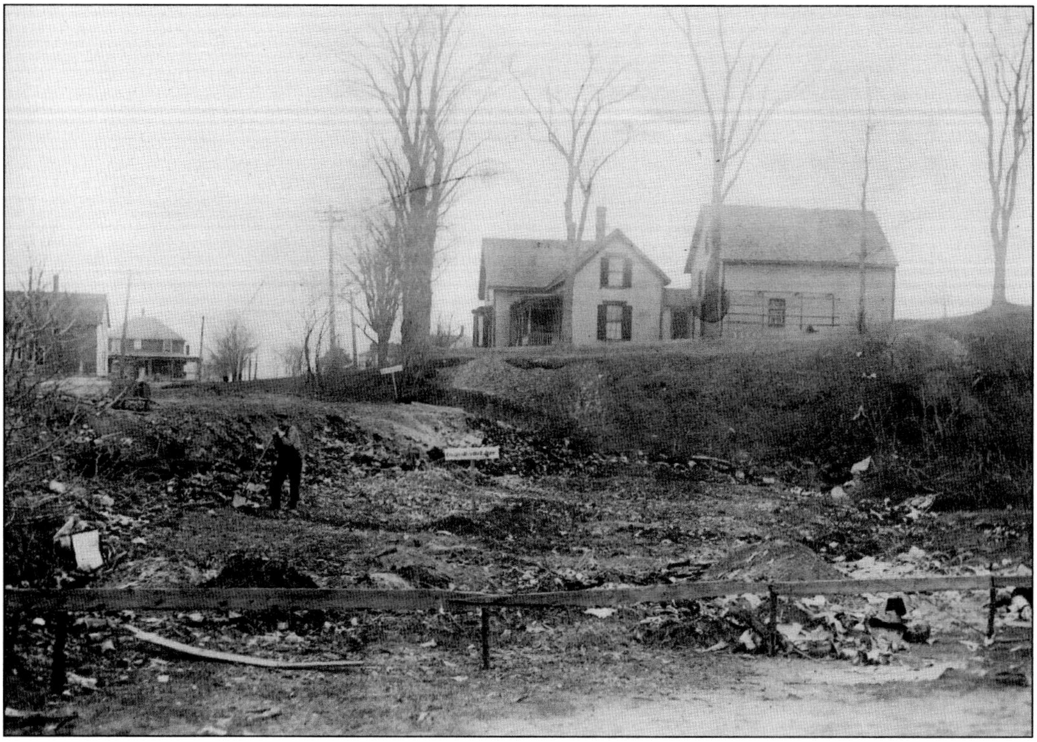

In 1912, there was a town dump just a few feet from the doors of the redbrick schools on West Main Street. The Village Improvement Society was instrumental in having the site filled in, covered, and planted with grass to make it a playground.

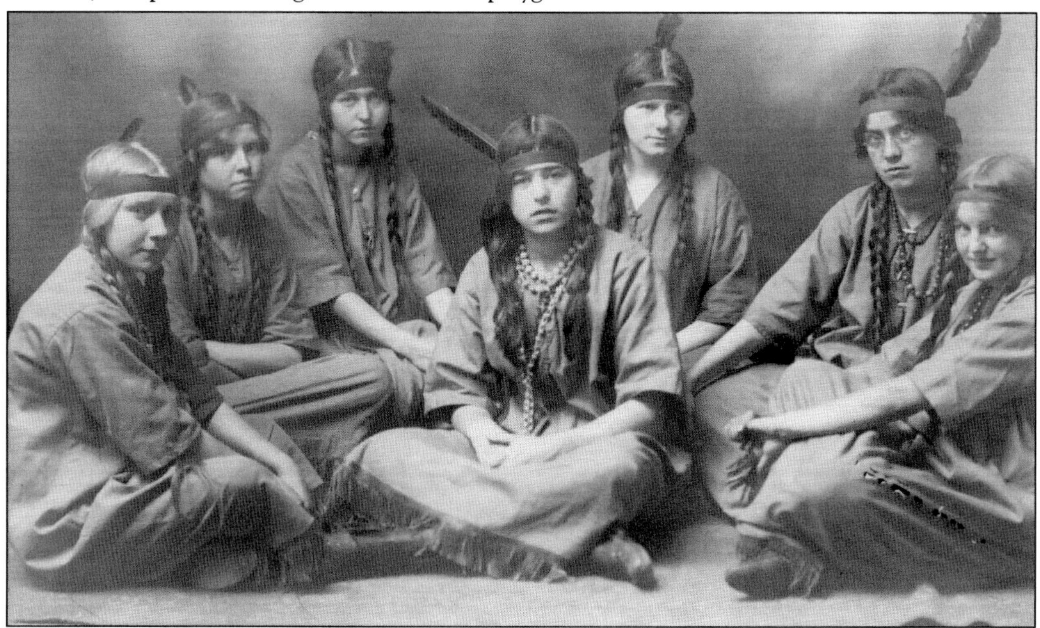

Dressed for the Village Improvement Society's Indian dance are, from left to right, Rena Blanchard, Muriel Berry, Doris Loring, Mary Leavitt, Frances Coombs, and Dorothy Williams. Hilda Loring is seated in the middle.

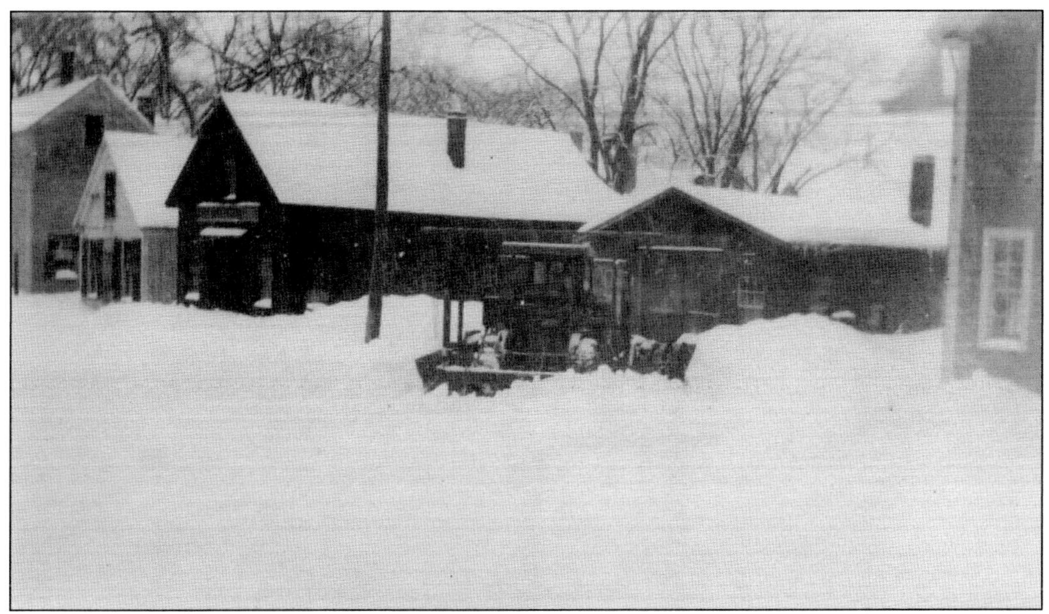

The town's first snowplow is shown on Center Street. This area of town, including South Street, was developed around 1850 and was home to some of the wealthier citizens, including Frederick Gore, Ansel Loring, and Capt. Joseph Bucknam.

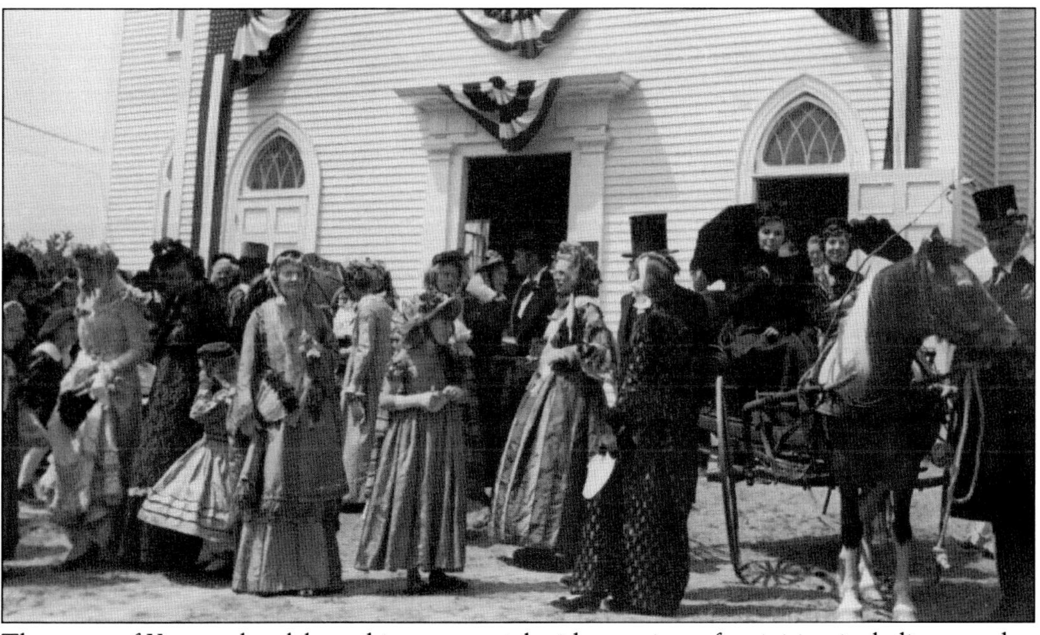

The town of Yarmouth celebrated its centennial with a variety of activities, including parades, programs, a supper, a fair, and a town birthday party. On Sunday, August 7, 1949, at 11:00 a.m., a community service was held at the Meetinghouse on the Hill at which townspeople dressed in period clothing.

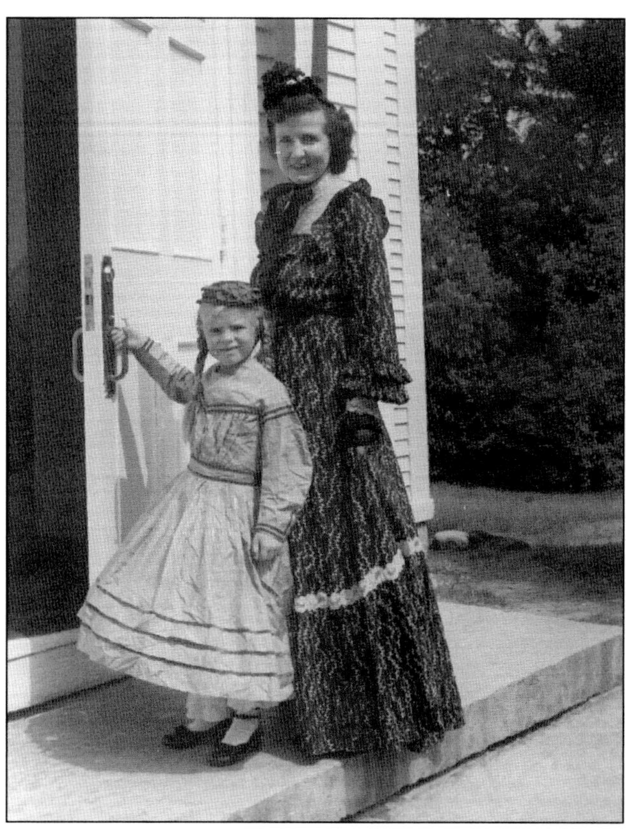

Elizabeth Merrill Barker and her daughter are shown entering the Meetinghouse on the Hill during the 1949 centennial celebration.

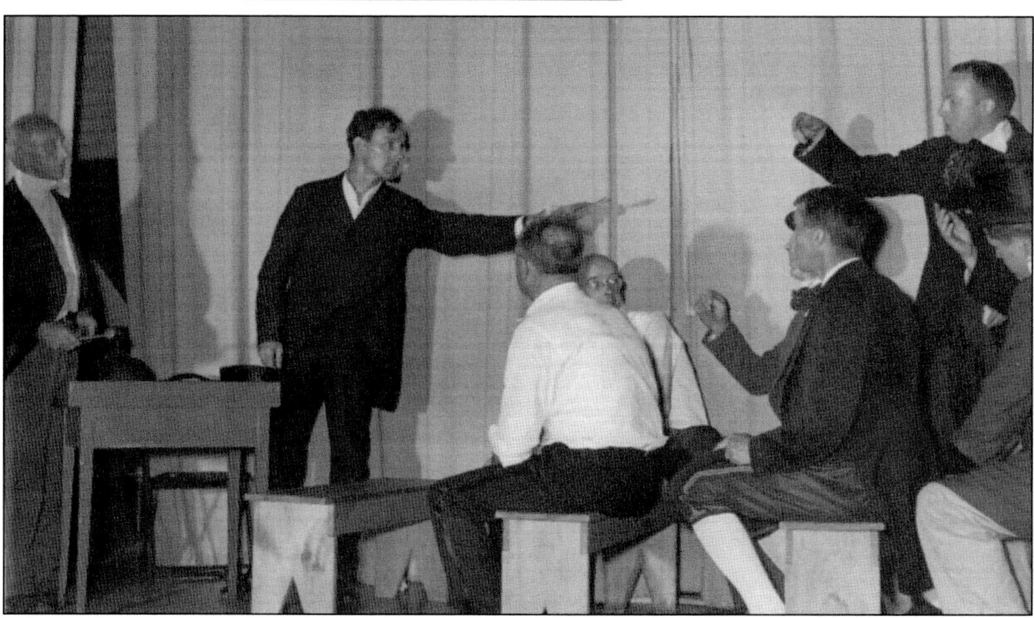

As part of the centennial celebration, town residents participated in a reenactment of the August 20, 1849, town meeting that resulted in the split of Yarmouth and North Yarmouth. In this photograph, John Strattard has taken the part of Dr. Eleazer Burbank. Dr. Burbank took an active part in town affairs as deacon of the First Parish Church and superintendent of its Sunday school.

Bud, Virginia, and Isabelle Small, the grandchildren of Capt. Alfred T. Small, are shown here in 1914. Captain Small continued to lead a productive life after his retirement from the sea, serving on the committee of public improvements.

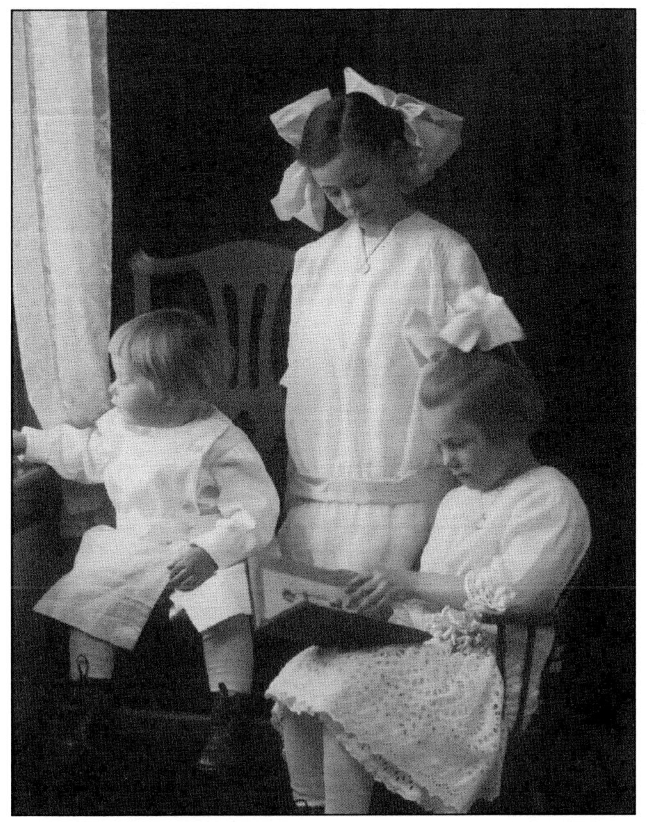

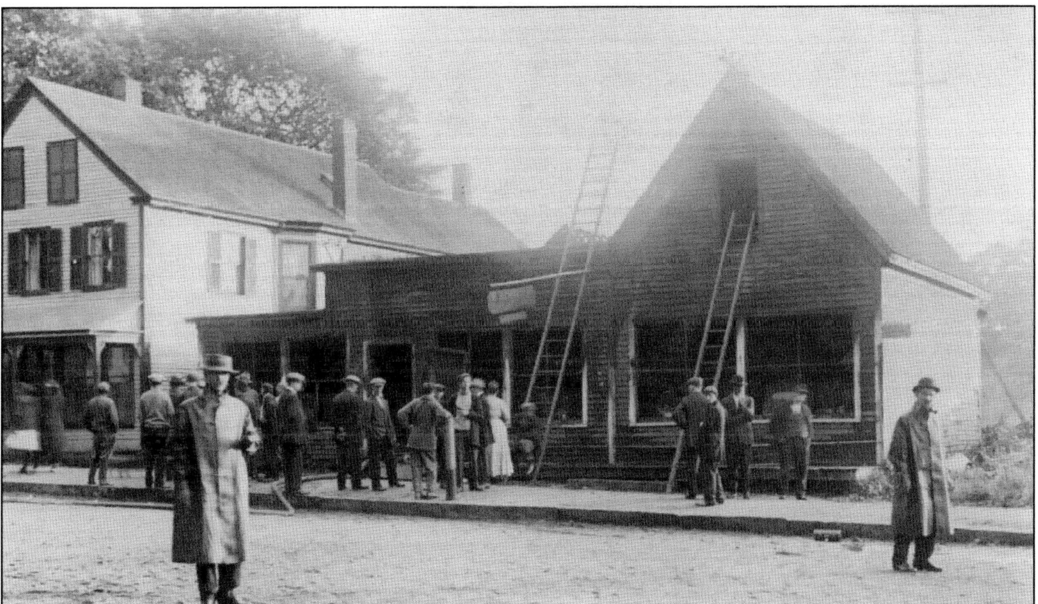

The 40 men of the Yarmouth Fire Department were awakened at 3:00 a.m. one morning in July 1913 to fight a fire at Bernstein's Department Store on Main Street, opposite South Street (next to the railroad tracks). Robert Bernstein, born in Germany, had been a traveling salesman before opening his Yarmouth store in 1905.

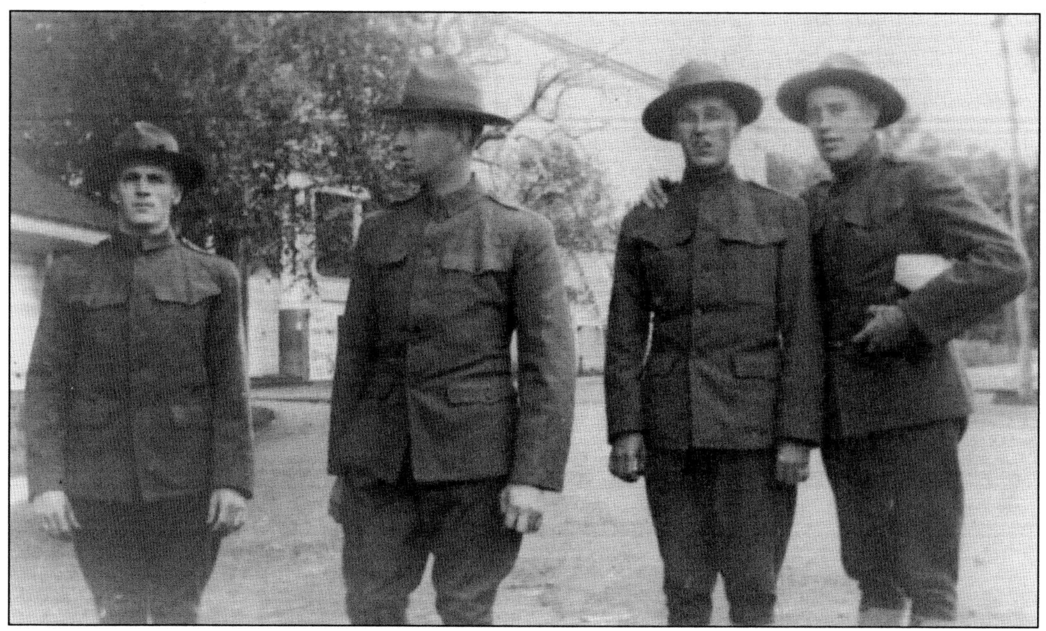

Shown in this photograph taken at Fort Williams are, from left to right, Bill Carr, Harry Porter, Clyde Bates, and Edgar Grant. A total of 106 Yarmouth residents served in World War I. Locally, residents contributed to the war effort by participating in wheatless and meatless days to conserve food. Sugar was rationed to three pounds a month per person.

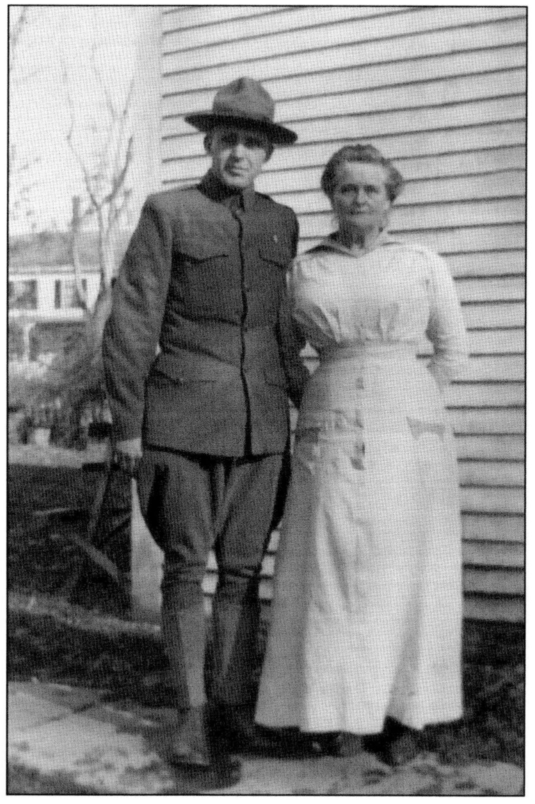

Howard Dunning is shown here with his mother while on furlough from the war. Dunning wrote to his future wife, Anna Stockwell, while at Fort Williams and throughout his service overseas.

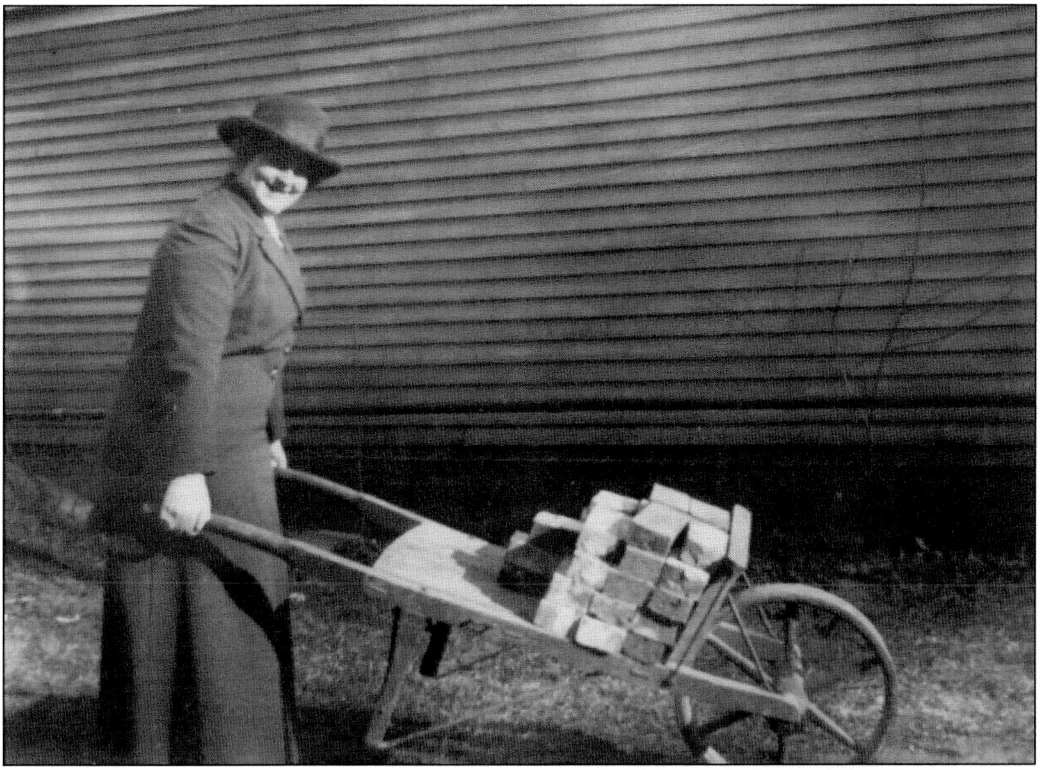

Pushing a cart with bricks for the Central Church chimney is Elsie Wellcome. Elsie Wellcome debated Harriet Bird in favor of the vote for women. At the end of the war in September 1818, Spanish influenza broke out in Massachusetts and rapidly spread to Maine. All public gatherings were closed. Elsie Wellcome was one of 14 people in Yarmouth who died of influenza.

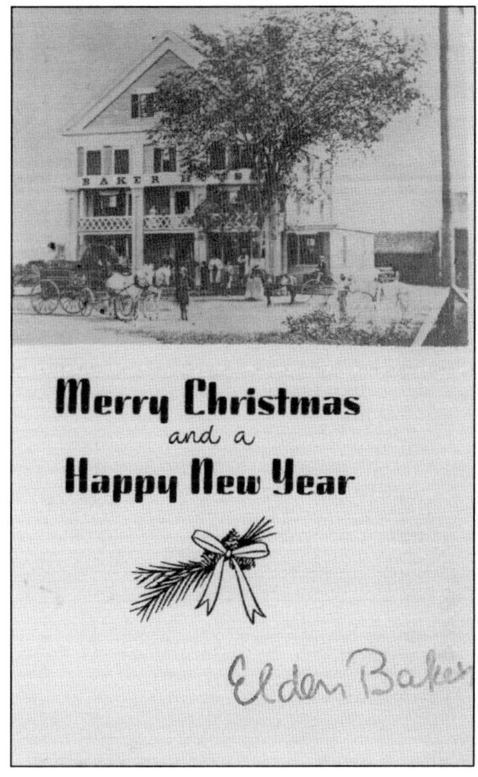

This Christmas card from the Baker House was sent from Elden Baker. On the back of the card, he wrote from New York, "To think I never knew the Bakers were ever connected to the hotel." The Baker House, located across from the Grand Trunk Railroad, was built in 1849 and served as a hotel under several different names, including Royal River House, Westcustogo House, and Yarmouth Hotel. It was destroyed by fire in 1928.

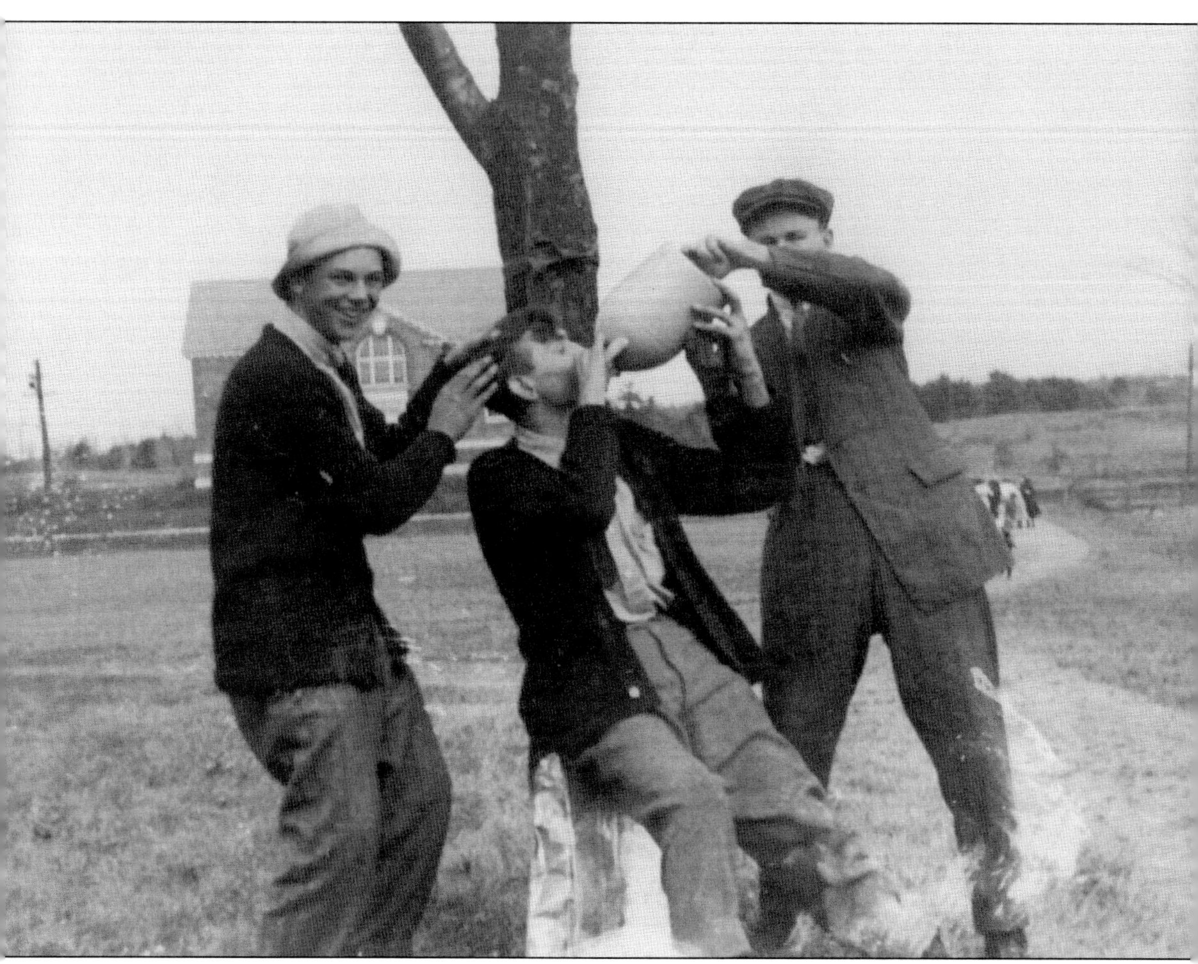

From left to right, Tom Sweetser, Clifford Jones, and Ralph Loring are shown having fun on the lawn of the schools. Across the street, Merrill Memorial Library can be seen. Alexander Longfellow, nephew of Henry Wadsworth Longfellow, designed the library, built in 1904. Joseph Merrill named the building in honor of his parents.

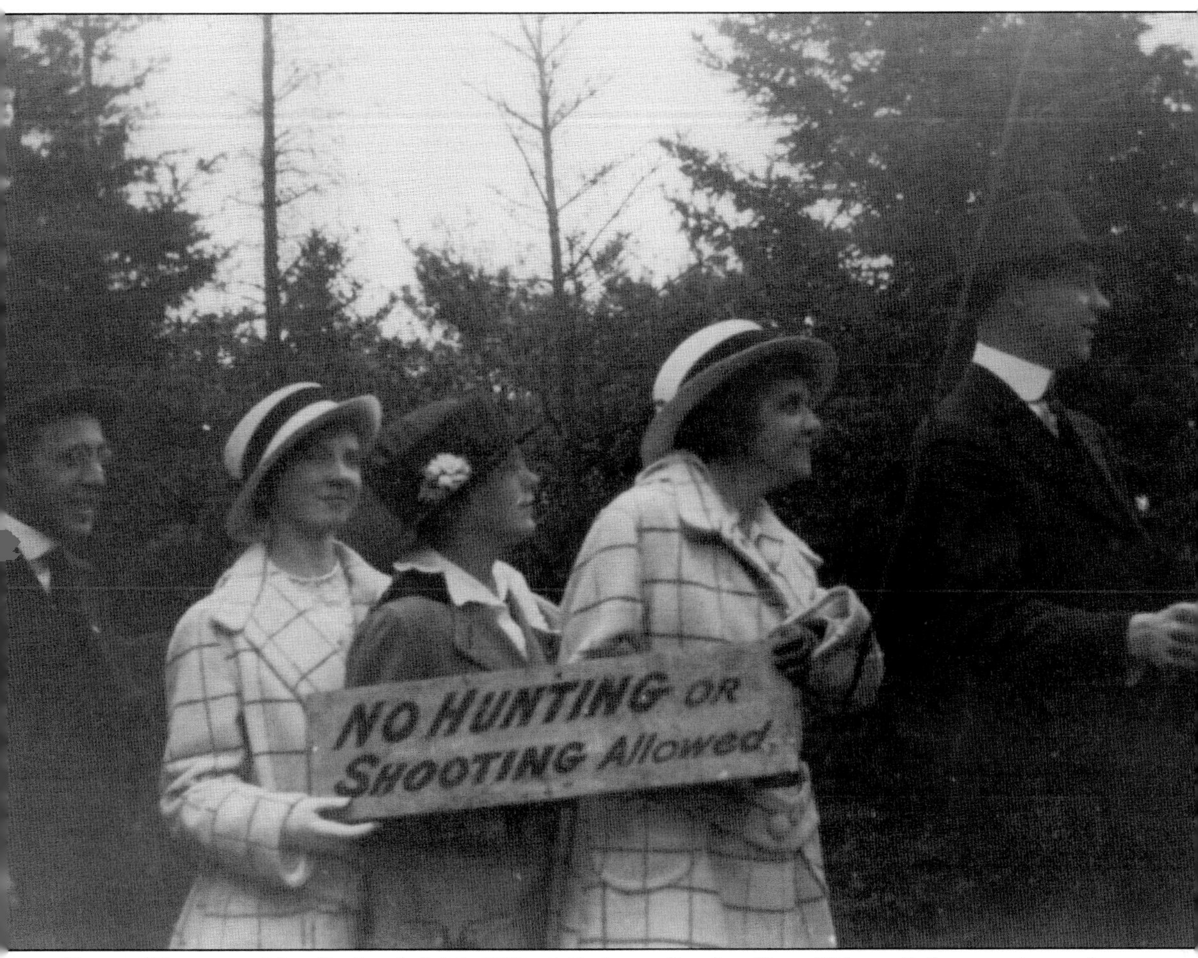

Howard Dunning, Miss Burbank, Mabel Windell, Anna Stockwell, and Henry Baker are pictured on a Sunday afternoon hike on the ledge. The sign says, "No hunting or shooting allowed."

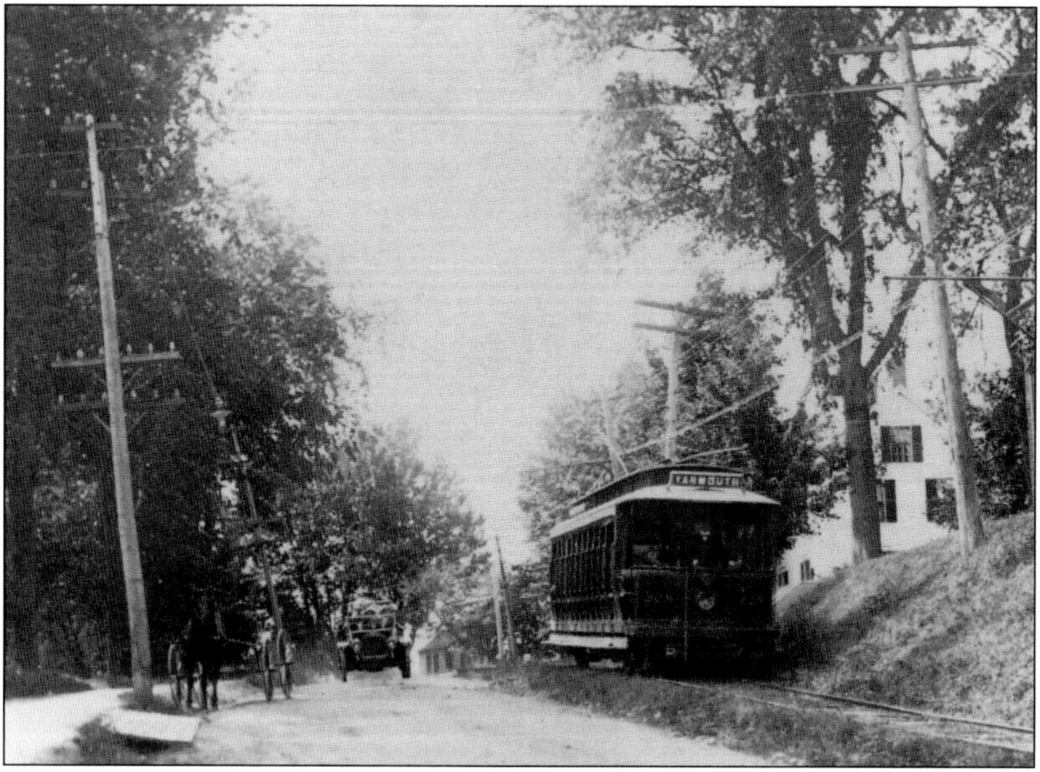

This photograph captures the transition period through various modes of transportation, including horse, automobile, and electric street railway, or trolley system.

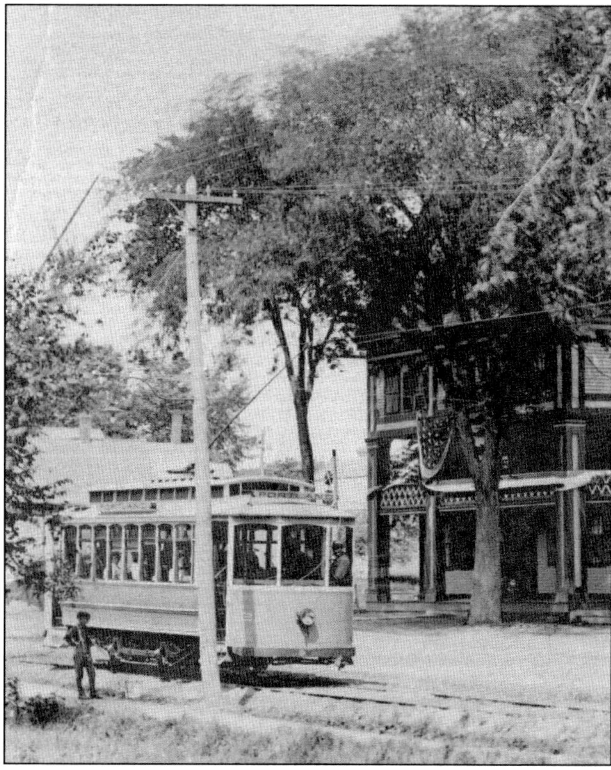

The Yarmouth Town Council approved the electric railway system in 1895, and the Portland & Electric Railroad began operation on August 18, 1898. The tracks followed Pleasant Street to the village.

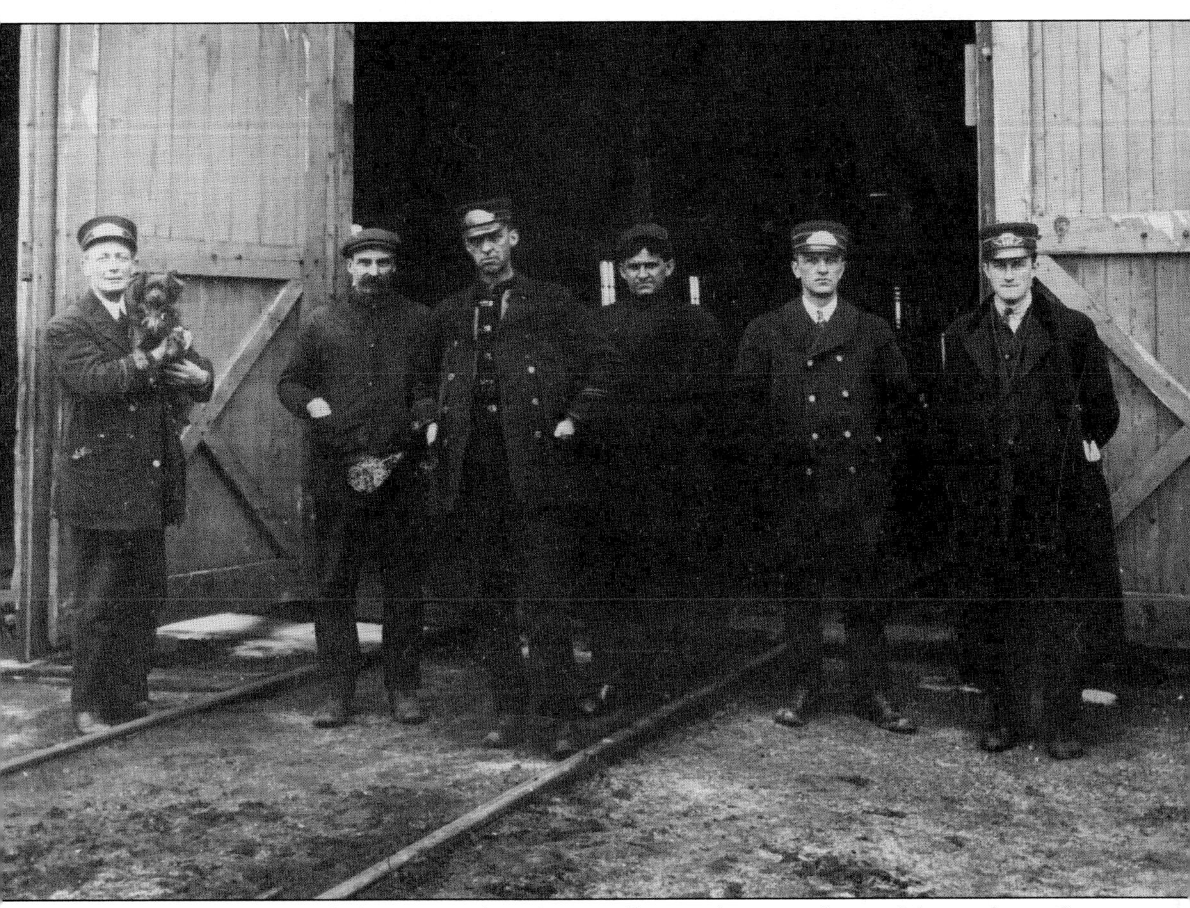

Shown in this photograph from around 1915 are trolley employees in front of the car barn. On the far left is Ervin Starling holding a puppy. Also pictured are Walter Meyers, third from right, and Claude Kingsley, far right.

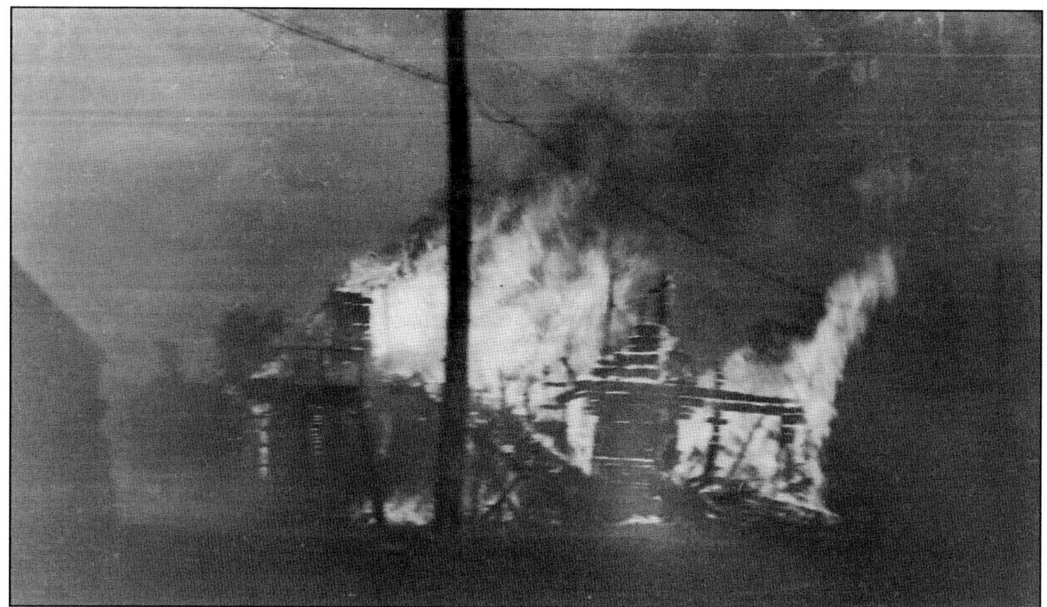

The trolley barn was located in Brickyard Hollow. In 1920, the barn caught fire. After the fire, the car barn was replaced with a new brick building. Trolley service between Portland and Yarmouth ended in June 1933.

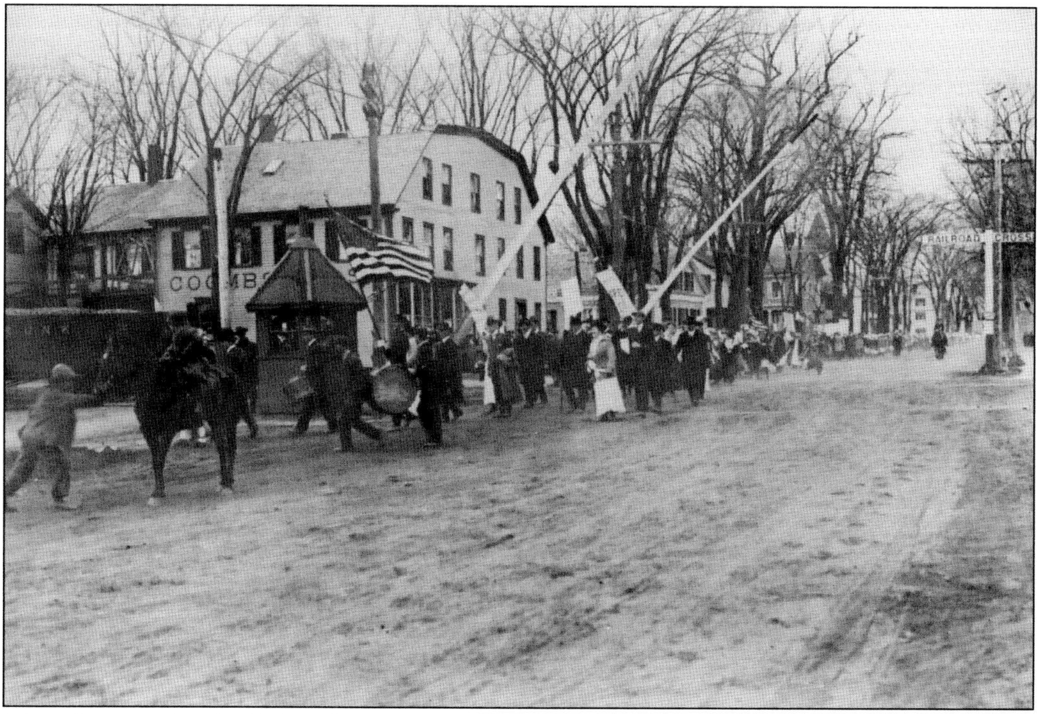

This photograph of a Village Improvement Society parade gives a view of the Coombs Bros. Building, located next to the Grand Trunk Railroad station. Coombs Bros. was located on the corner of South and Main Streets.

George E. Coombs and his brother Albert learned the confectionary business and established a candy manufactory in a two-story building on Main Street just above the Grand Trunk Railroad tracks. Coombs' Cough Drops achieved widespread popularity. Coombs Bros. had a retail department in the front of their factory and the first telephone system in the town.

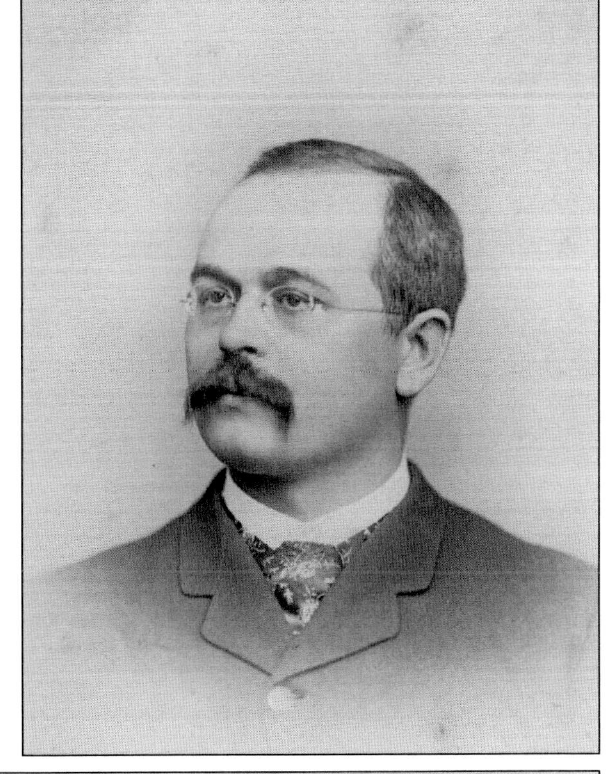

Yarmouth junction was the crossing point for the Maine Central Railroad and the St. Lawrence & Atlantic Railroad (formerly Grand Trunk Railroad). The station was located just north of Main Street and west of present-day East Elm Street.

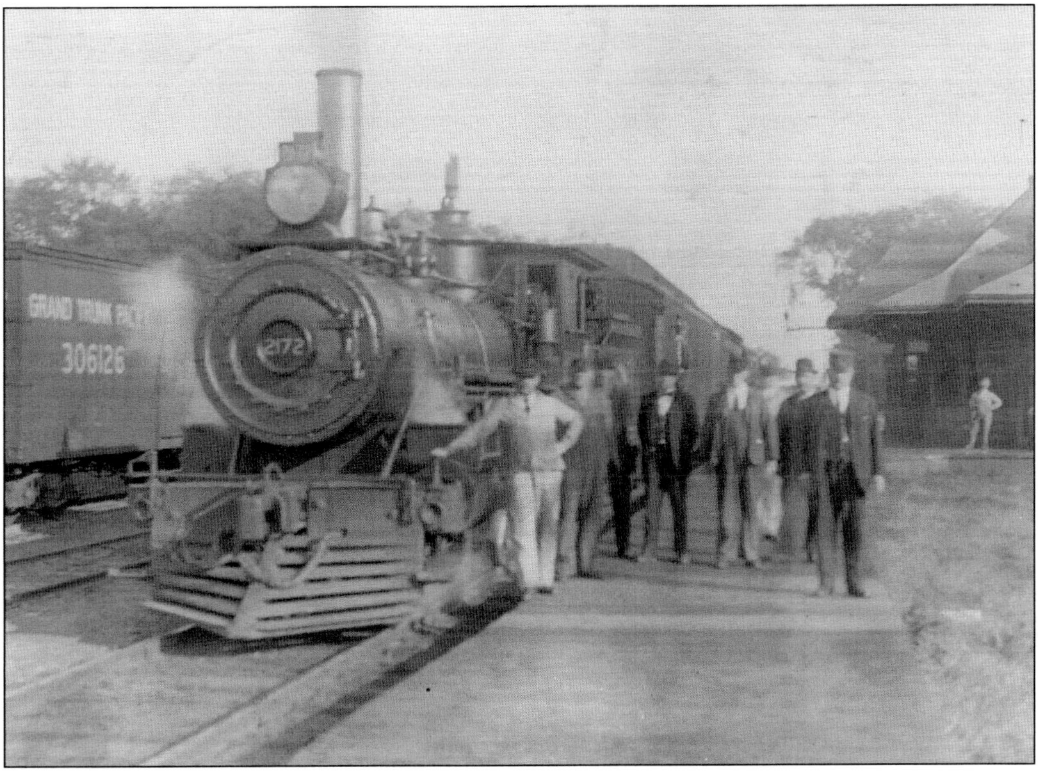

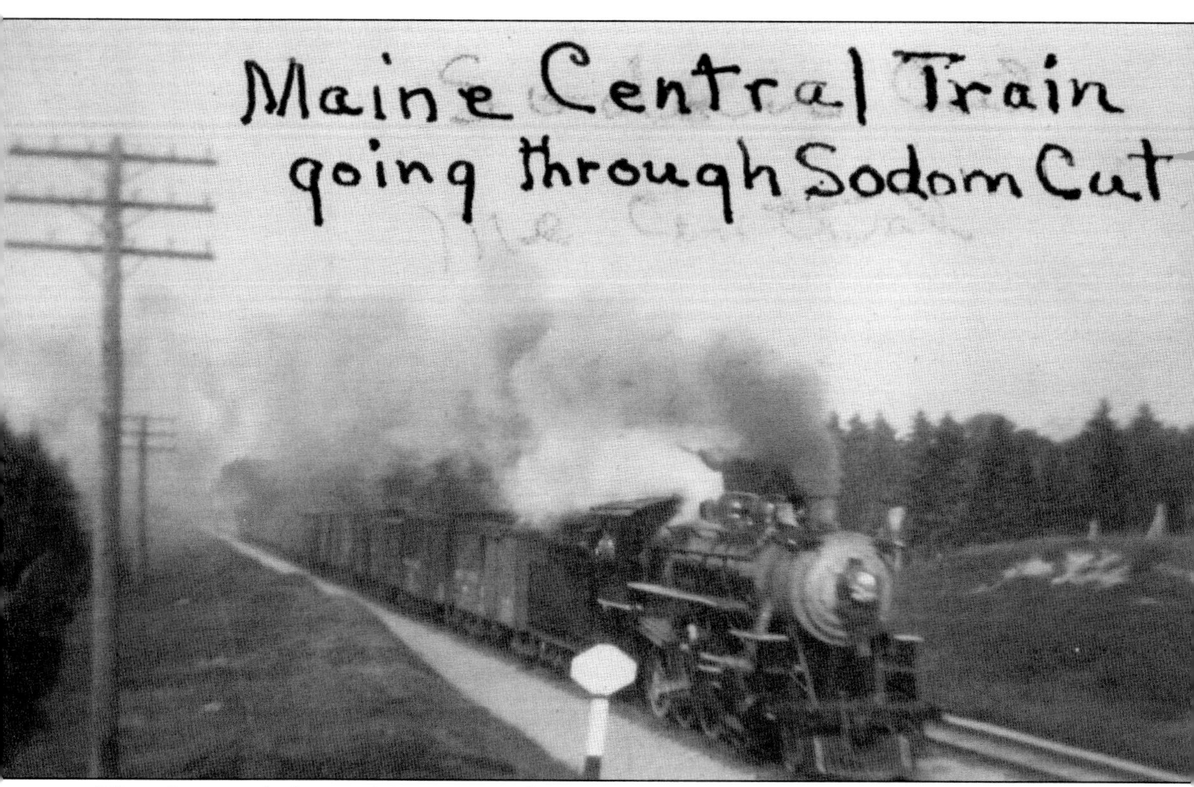

This photograph shows a Maine Central train passing through Sodom. Sodom was a nickname for the area near present-day Granite Street.

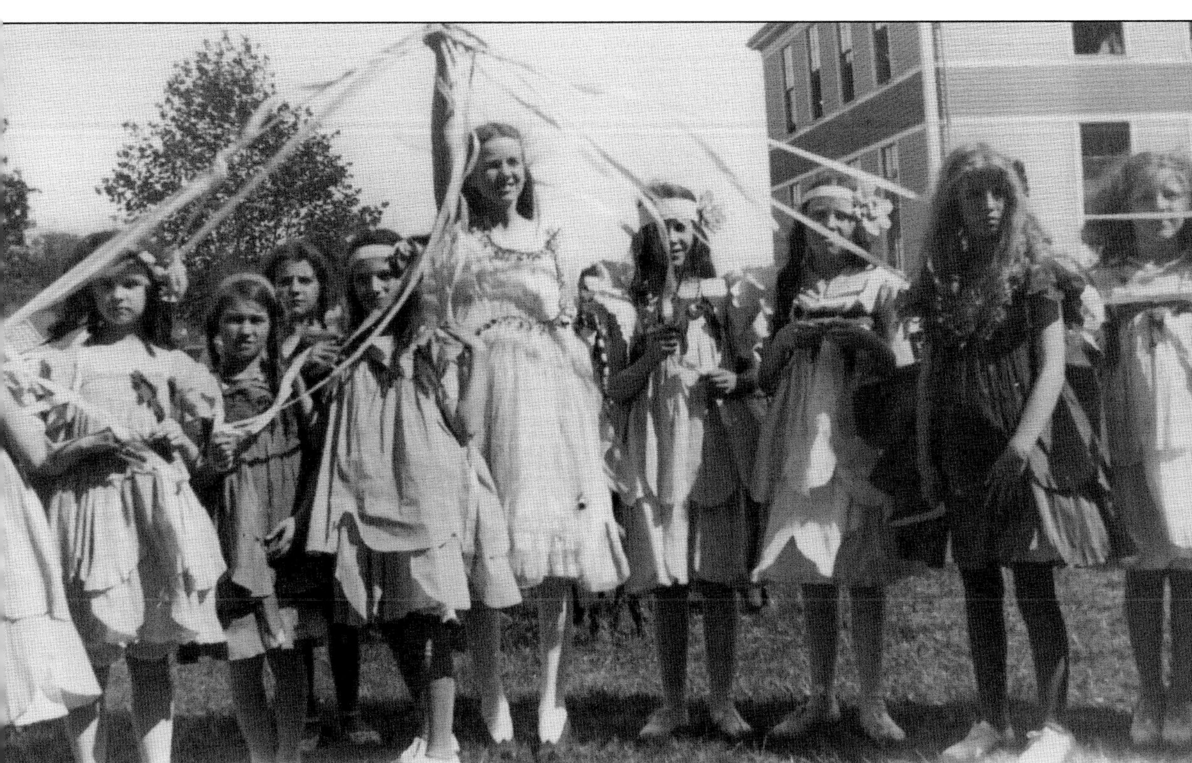

Shown is a May Day parade at the Central Grammar school. In 1931, the Yarmouth School Committee discussed with North Yarmouth Academy trustees the possibility of again educating Yarmouth students at the academy. The change was made, and this arrangement continued for another 30 years. By the late 1950s, plans to build a new Yarmouth high school got underway, and the school opened in time for the 1961 academic year.

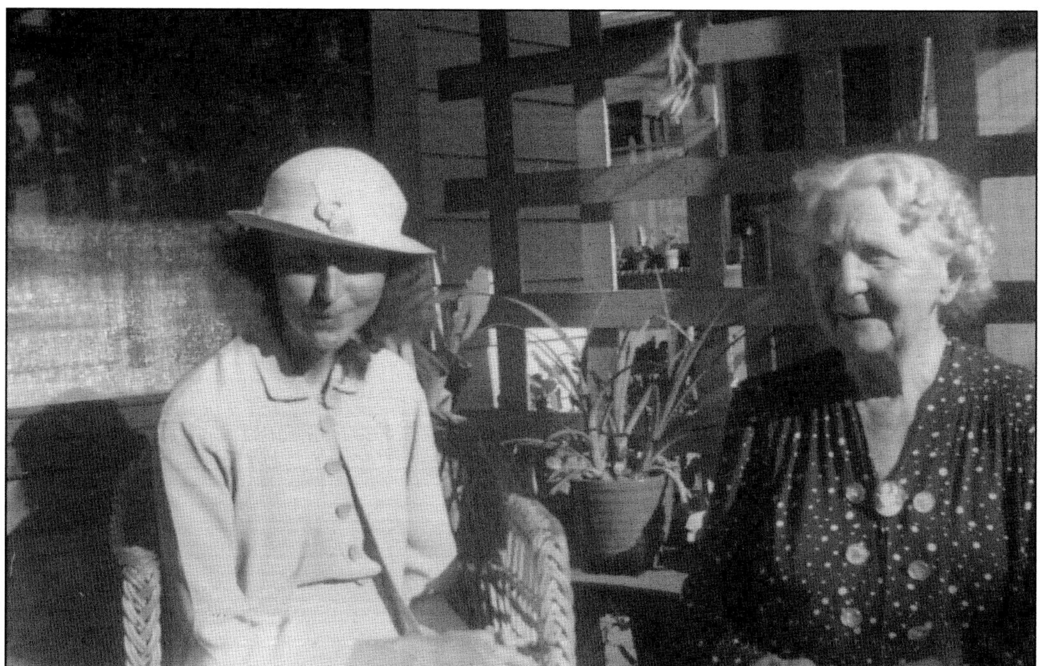

Abbie Buxton Oakes and her daughter Mary are pictured here in 1942. Abbie and Charles Oakes retired to California after their seafaring years in Yarmouth.

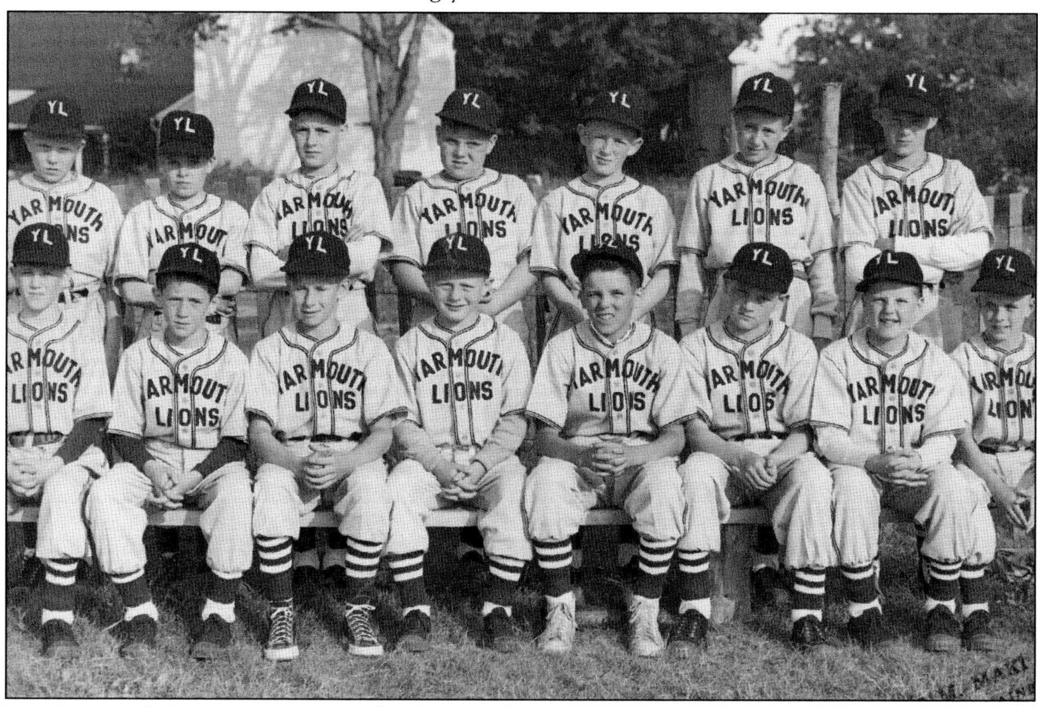

The Yarmouth Lions were one of the first Little League teams in the town. From 1951 through 1974, Little League was for boys only. In 2011, the Yarmouth 11-to-12-year-old Little League baseball team scored three runs in the top of the eighth inning to win the Maine State Championship game. Yarmouth advanced to the New England Region Tournament in Bristol, Connecticut.

Ella Woods is shown going down a boat ramp to Cousins Island. The steamer *Nellie G.* operated as a ferry service to the islands for many years. Cousins and Littlejohn Islands were the home of many summer residents. The Hotel Rockmere was in operation on Littlejohn Island.

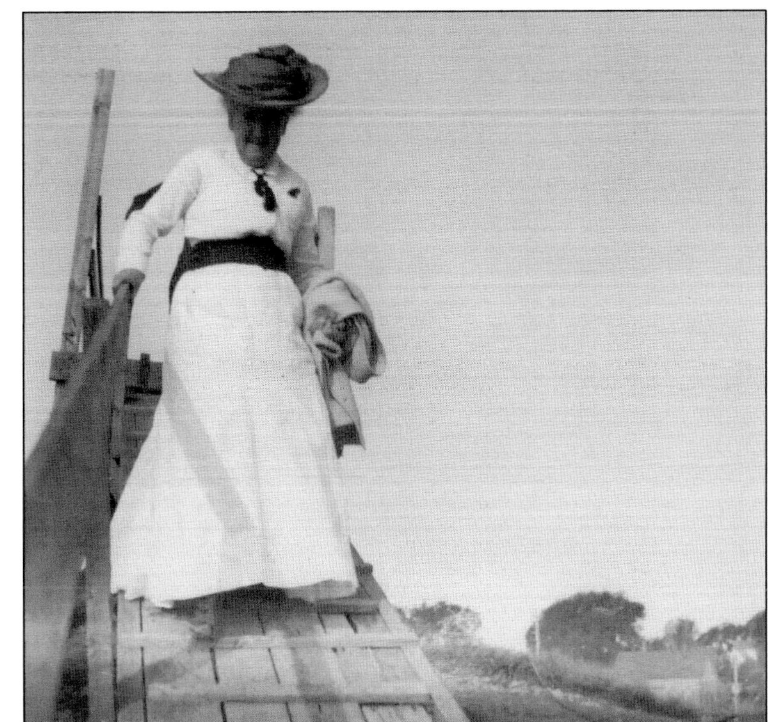

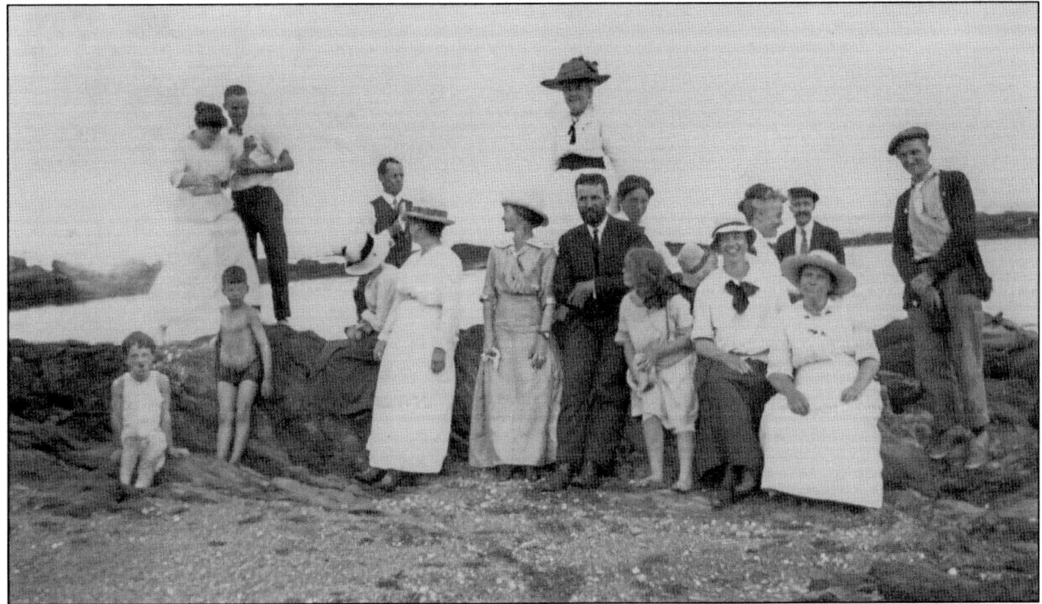

This group on the rocks evokes the summer experience many came to expect from Cousins and Littlejohn Islands. In 1908, there were 10 year-round families on the two islands. Spruce Point Road used to be the location of a girls' camp. Groves Farm, now the power plant, had an ice pond. There was a store with a post office on the corner of Wharf and Cousins Roads that burned down in 1992. Littlejohn also had its own post office that could sell ice cream, because it had a generator. "Tinker field" was the Talbot farm, then owned by Katherine Prescott Tinker. The 15 acres, now known as Tinker Property, are in the care of the school system.

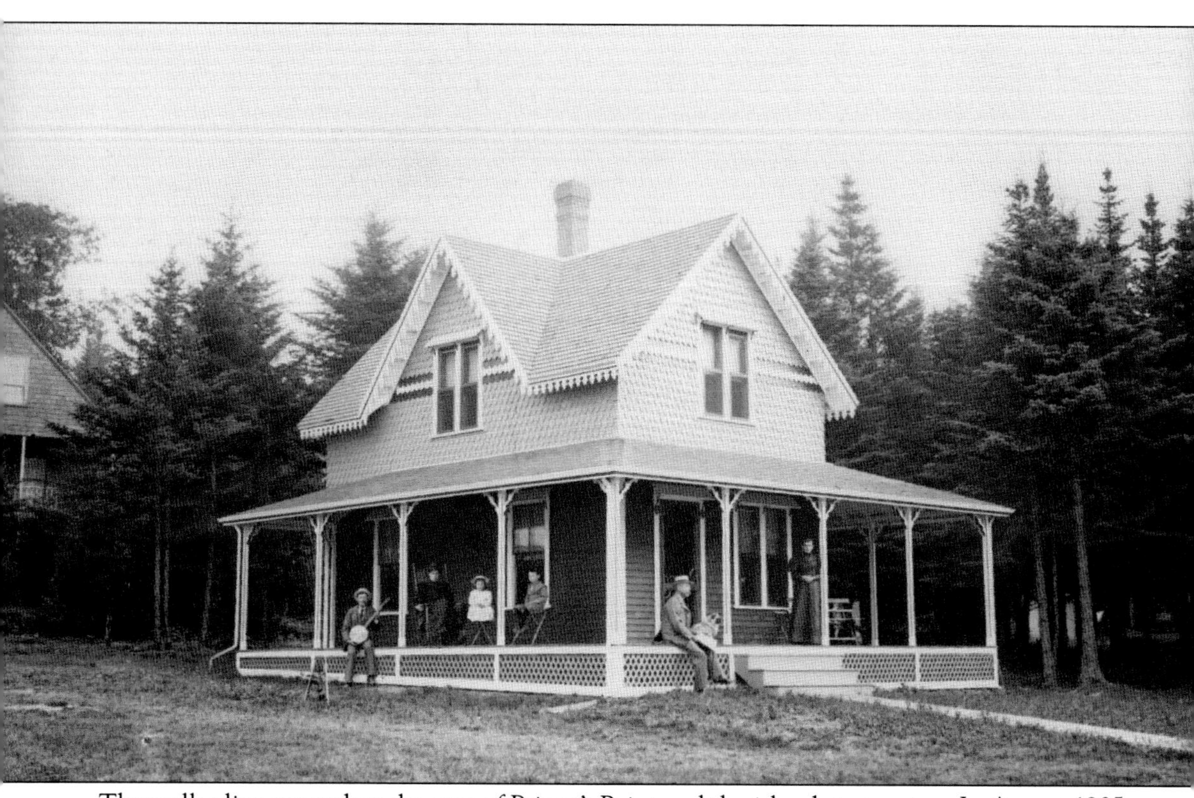

The trolley line opened up the area of Prince's Point and the islands to tourism. In August 1905, a group of property owners met with the intent of forming the Prince's Point Improvement Association. The PPIA constitution stated that its purpose was to "define and conserve the duties, rights and privileges of the property owners of the Point, to increase its value and attractiveness as a Summer Resort, and to promote the comfort, enjoyment, and safety of the cottages and all who are interested in the Point."

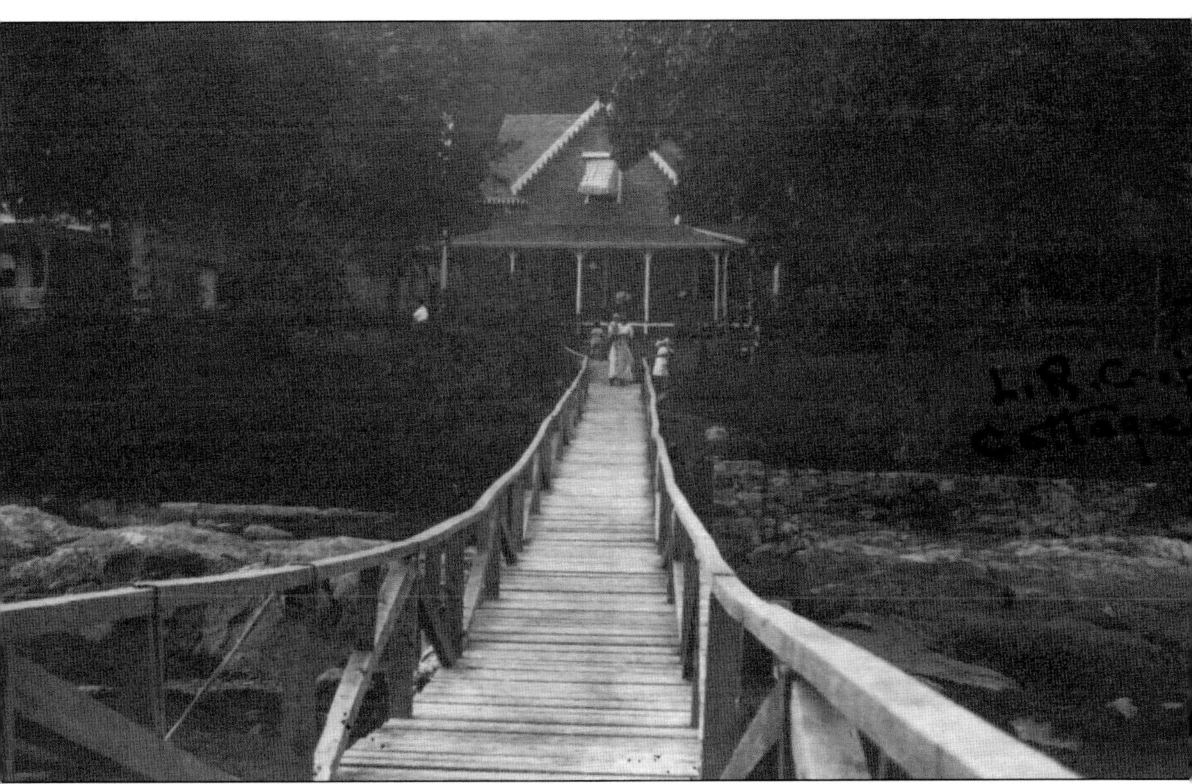

According to the records of the PPIA, the executive committee made the following arrangements: passenger delivery by Frank Russell between the point and Rock Ledge station and grocery and provision delivery from Gerow & Son grocers. Also noted in these records was that Captain Cleaves proposed to deliver vegetables and eggs. The annual dues were 50¢.

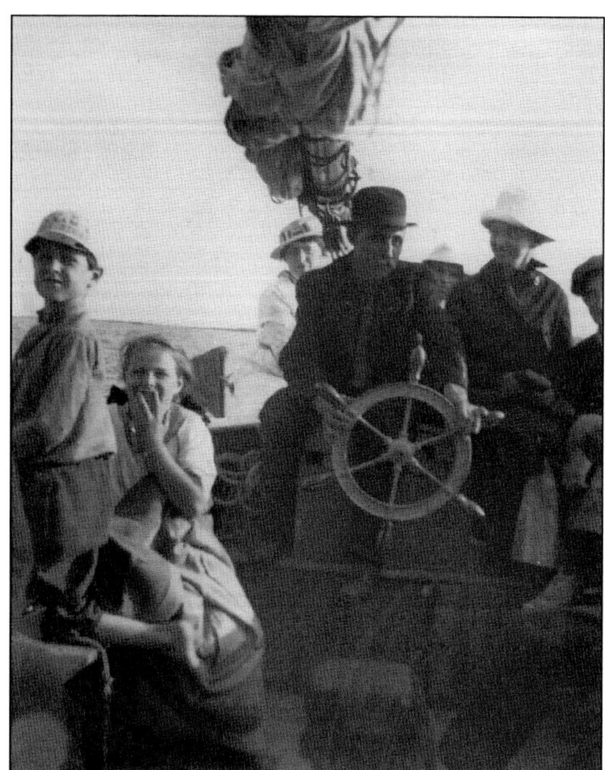

While Capt. John Kinghorn looks perfectly comfortable at the helm of this gaff-rigged sloop, for most of his life, his primary employment was at the Forest Paper Company. Captain Kinghorn moved to Portland in 1922.

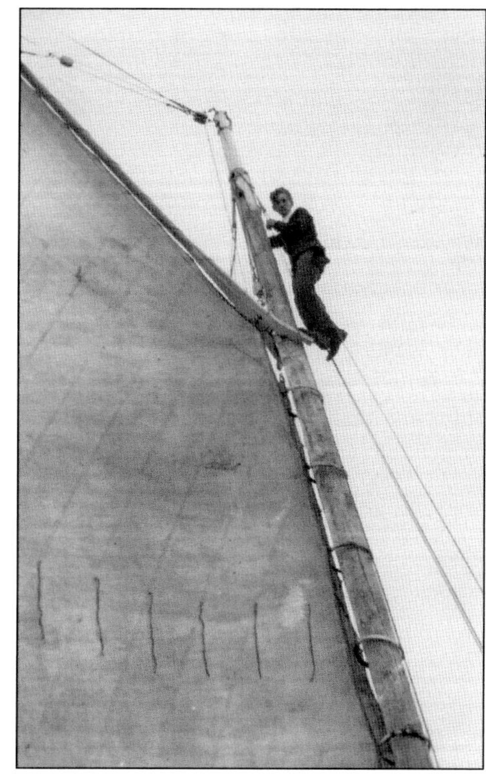

Clifford Jones is shown up on a mast. The Casco Bay Islands continue to be well known for recreational sailing as well as regattas.

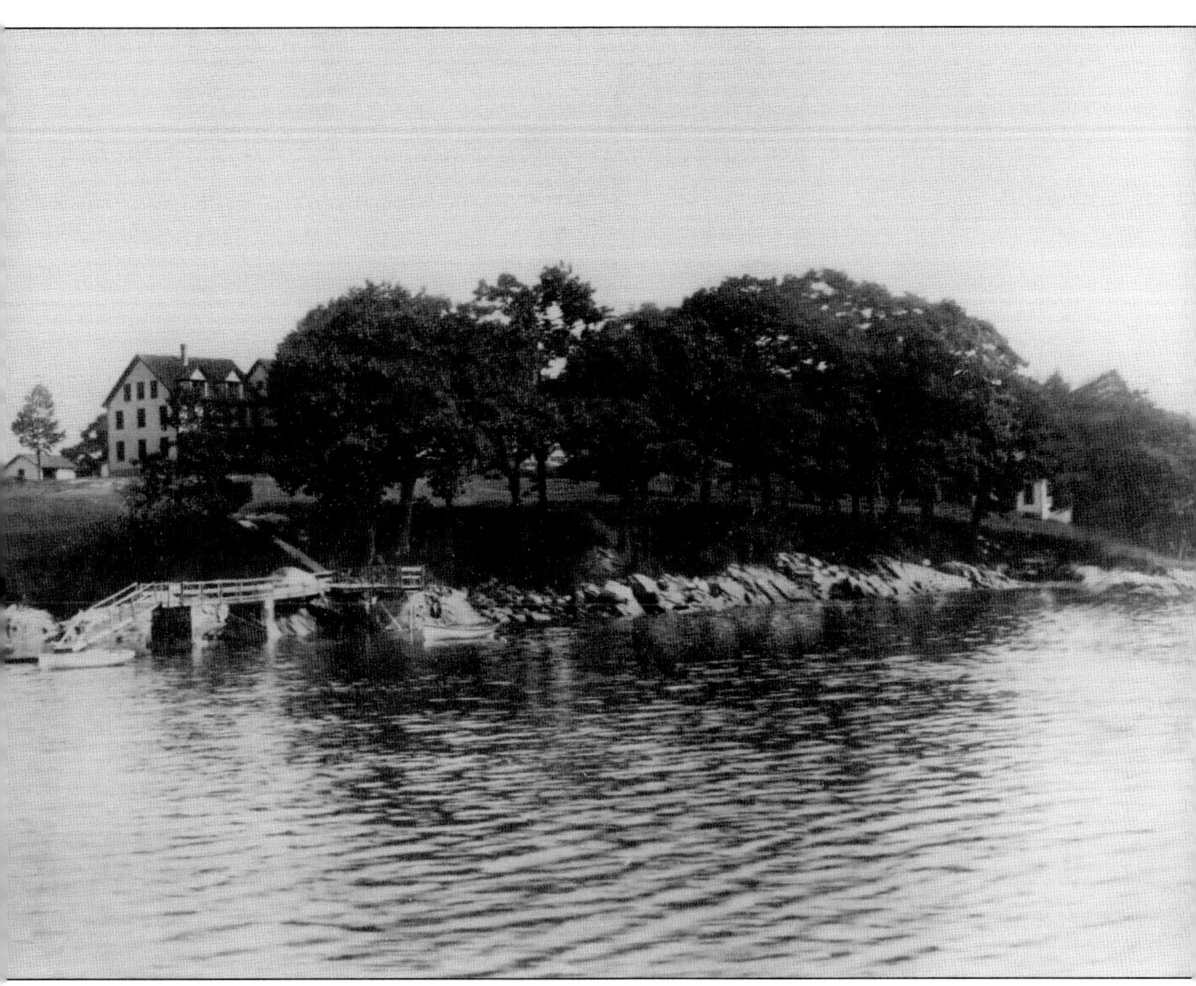

The Drinkwater Inn, a boardinghouse for summer visitors, was in business between 1906 and 1948. The building, now gone, once stood near what is now Seaborne Drive.

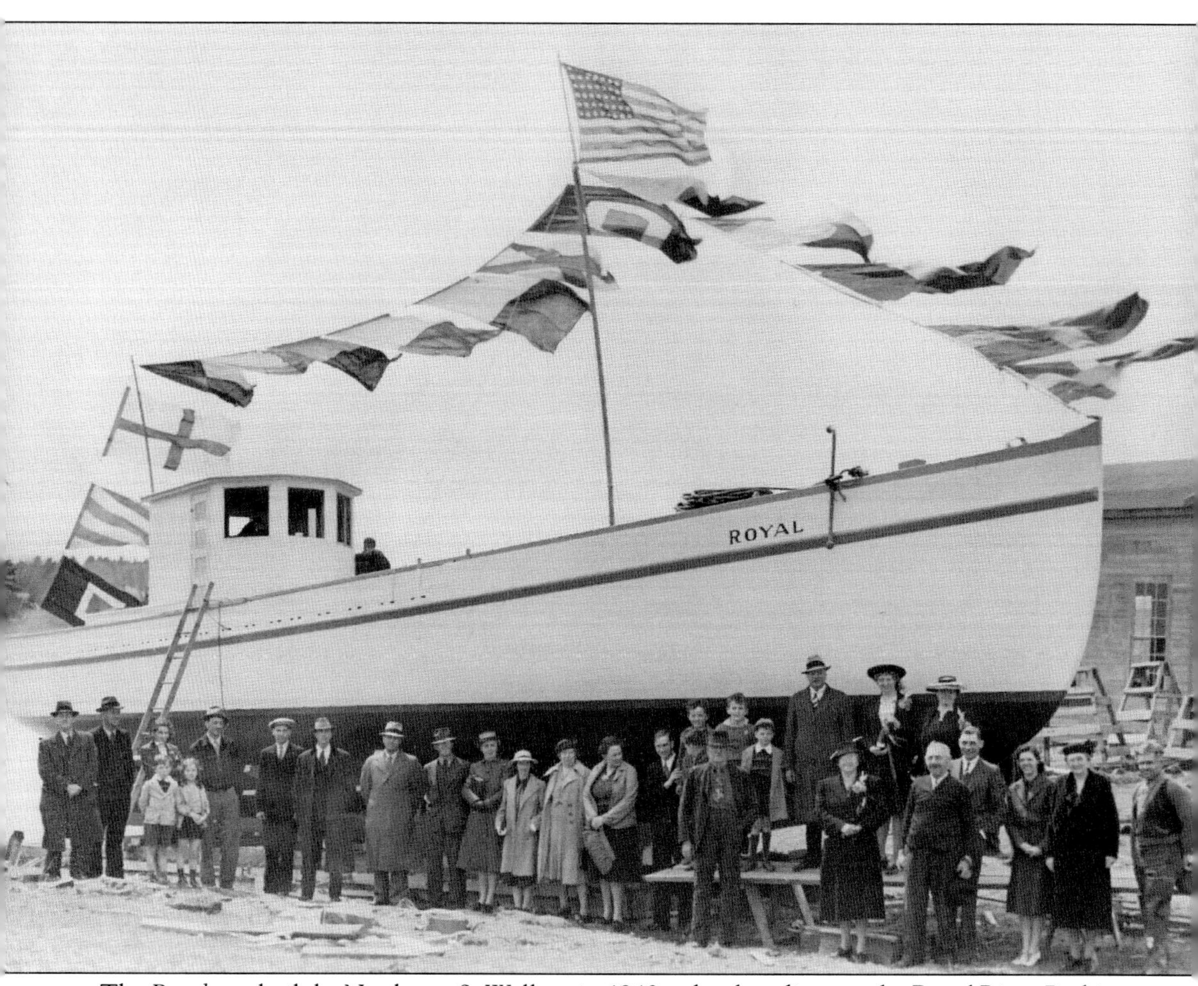

The *Royal* was built by Newberry & Wallace in 1940 to haul sardines to the Royal River Packing Corporation, located on the river's west bank. Area residents attending the spring launching at the Gray Boatyard were, from left to right, Howard Plummer, Charles Lombard, Amy Ulrickson behind Jack and Jill Hildreth, John Gorman, Willis Reed, Herman Royal, Harry Porter, Mr. and Mrs. Carl Linscott, Arlene Storer, Mrs. Howard Pulsifer, Barbara Gorman, George Pulsifer, Tim Summers, Mary Plummer, Tone Peterson, George Peterson, Reba Peterson, Mrs. Tone Peterson, and Capt. John Beal. On the platform are, from left to right, Jimmy Gorman, Leon Gorman, Tommy Gorman, Ralphie Stevens, Ralph Stevens, Mary Stevens, and Ruth Stevens.

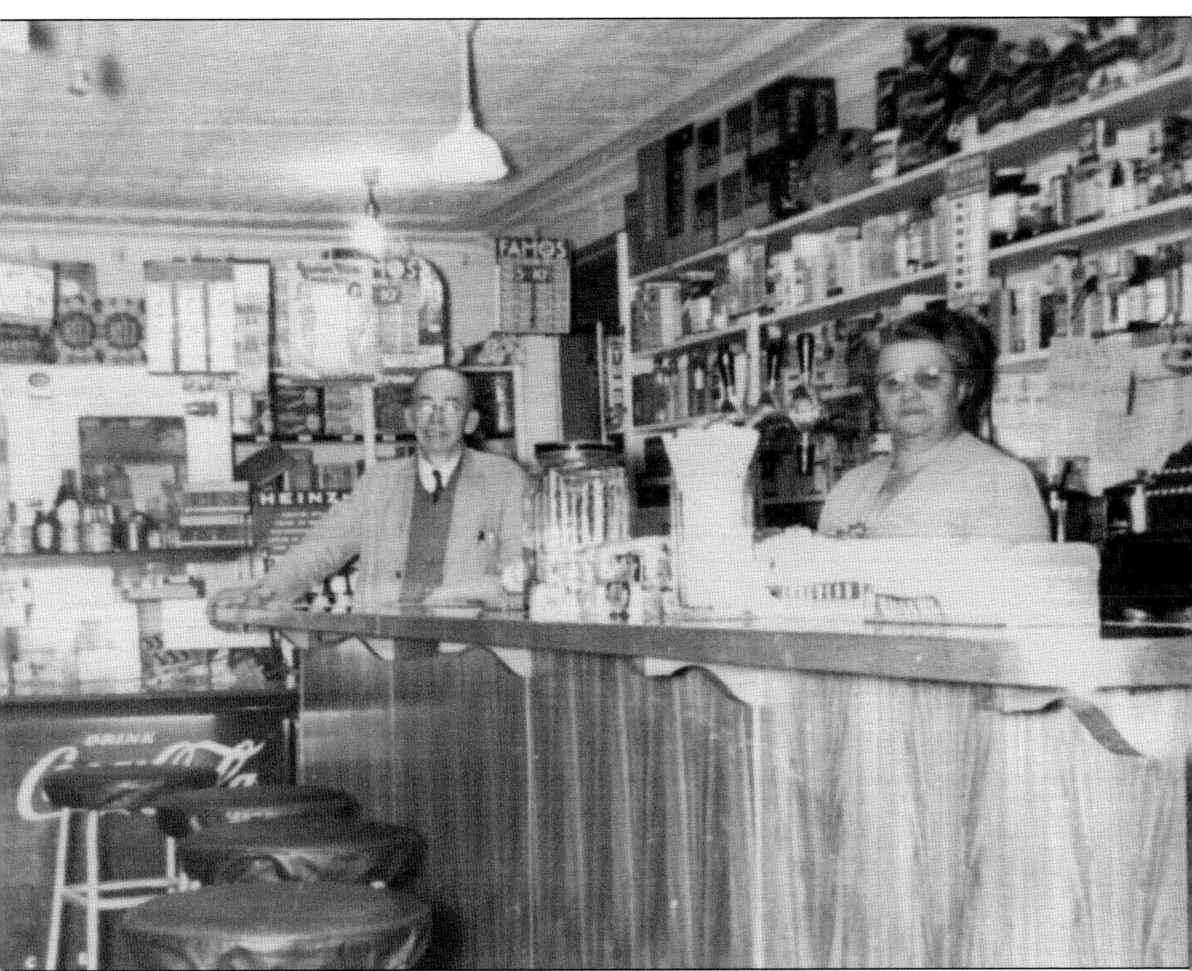

Harold B. Allen clerked for two Yarmouth merchants, William Rowe and C.M. Shaw, before establishing his own variety store. Allen's Variety was located at the corner of Main and Portland Streets. Martha and Harold Allen are shown behind the counter. The store had a lunchroom and soda fountain and operated from 1942 to 1953.

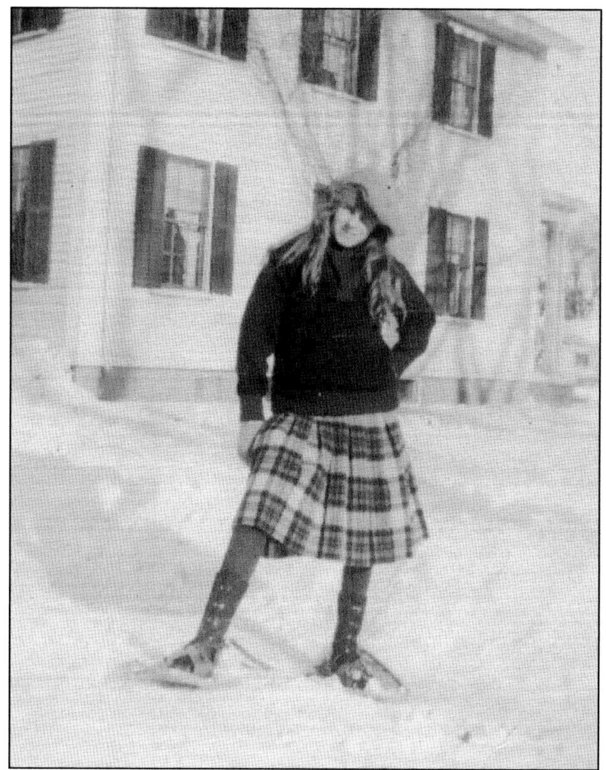

Dressed stylishly in a plaid skirt and snowshoes, Frances Mann is shown outside her Center Street house. Frances married Frank Knight, and the couple was married for more than 60 years. A small woman with wavy dark hair and blue eyes, she loved to garden and tended a nearly 30-foot row of peonies that ran beside their home. (Courtesy of the collection of Dick Knight.)

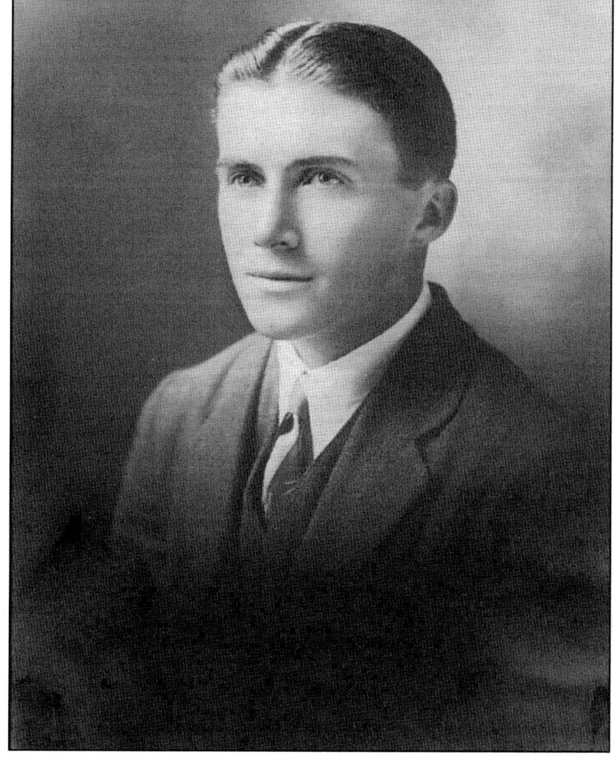

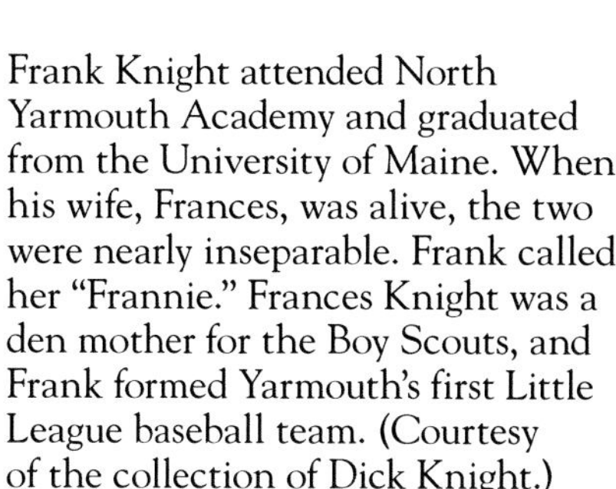

Frank Knight attended North Yarmouth Academy and graduated from the University of Maine. When his wife, Frances, was alive, the two were nearly inseparable. Frank called her "Frannie." Frances Knight was a den mother for the Boy Scouts, and Frank formed Yarmouth's first Little League baseball team. (Courtesy of the collection of Dick Knight.)

Frank and Frances Knight are shown here with their son Dick. Every year, they wrote each other Christmas, birthday, and anniversary cards and signed them with initials that were not their own. Their son Dick still has not figured out what the initials stood for. The tradition, he says, carried on until the day his mother died in 1994. (Courtesy of the collection of Dick Knight.)

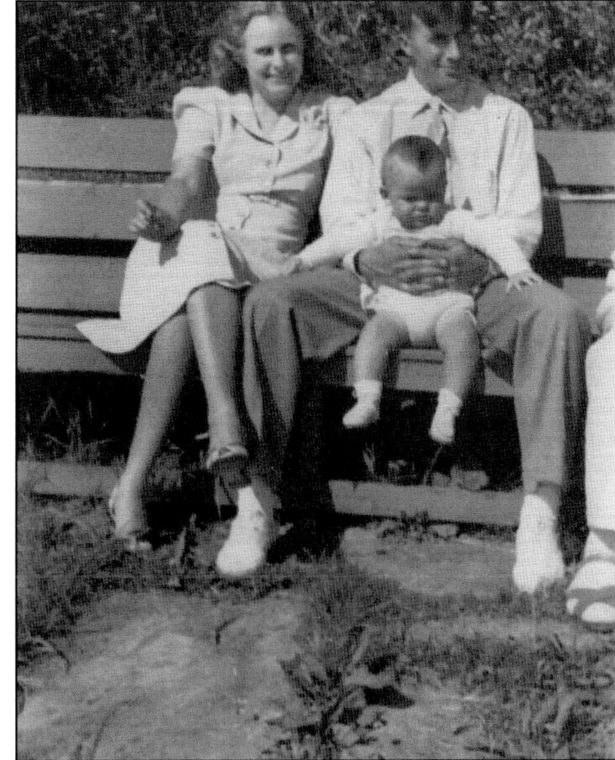

In this photograph, taken in 1954, Esther Allen Page is shown standing next to a 1949 Chevrolet on High Street. Behind her is Bastron's Greenhouses, owned by Arthur Bastron. The floral business specialized in carnations and operated between 1950 and 1970.

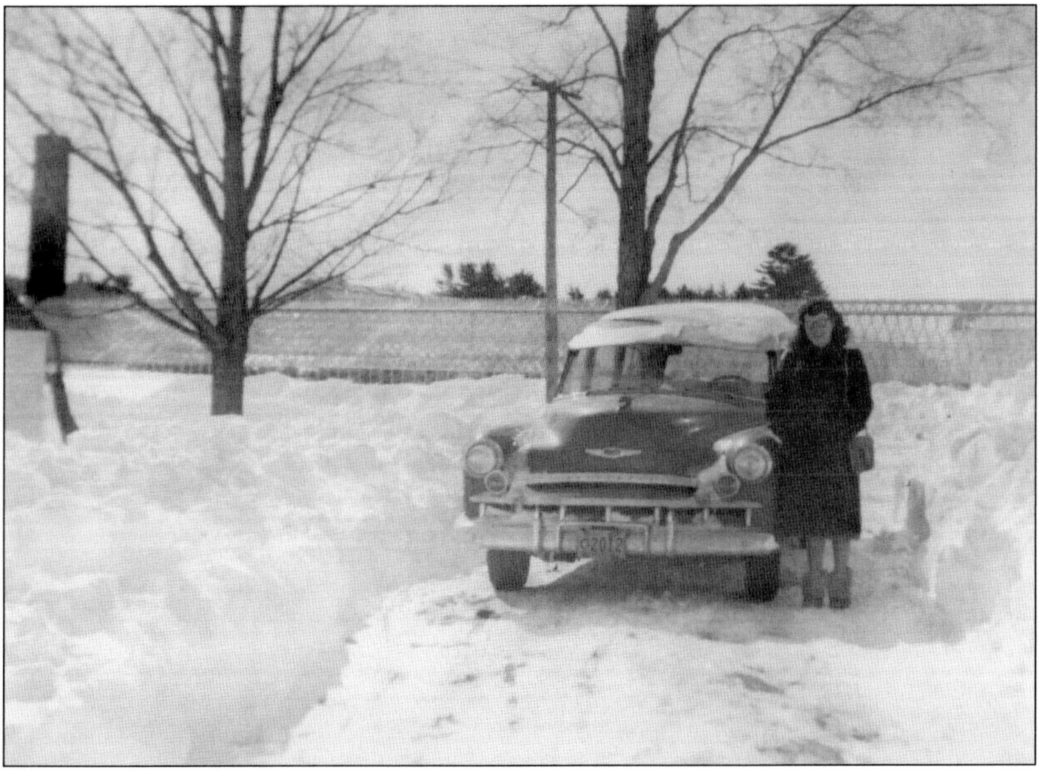

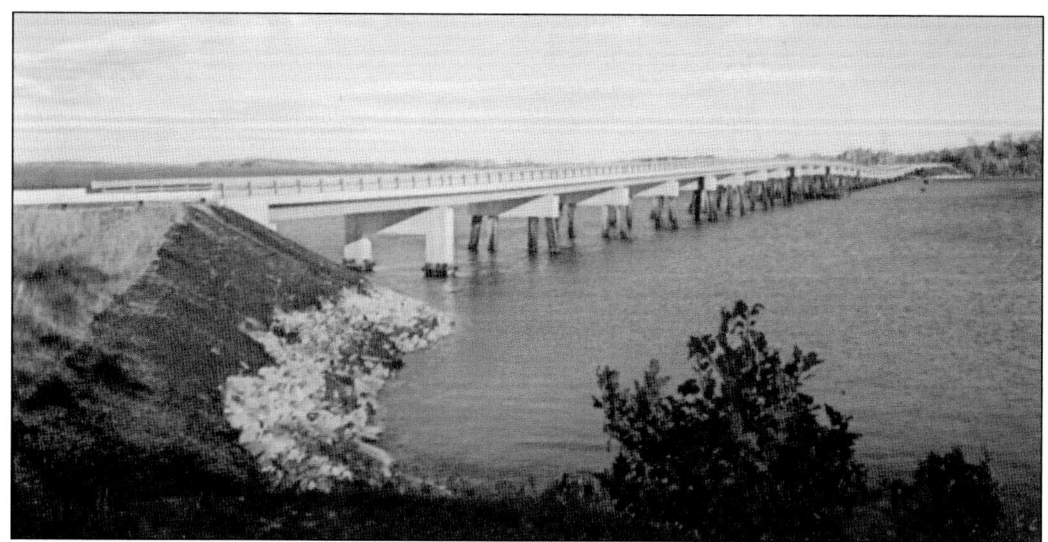

The bridge to Cousins Island was built in 1955 to aid in the construction of a power plant. Prior to the bridge, steamboats brought guests to cottages on Cousins and Littlejohn Islands. Not everyone was happy about the proposed bridge. In a letter to the Maine Public Utilities Commission, a summer resident of Littlejohn writes, "People who choose islands for a summer vacation largely do so to get away from crowds, automobiles, picnickers, and other sources of trouble."

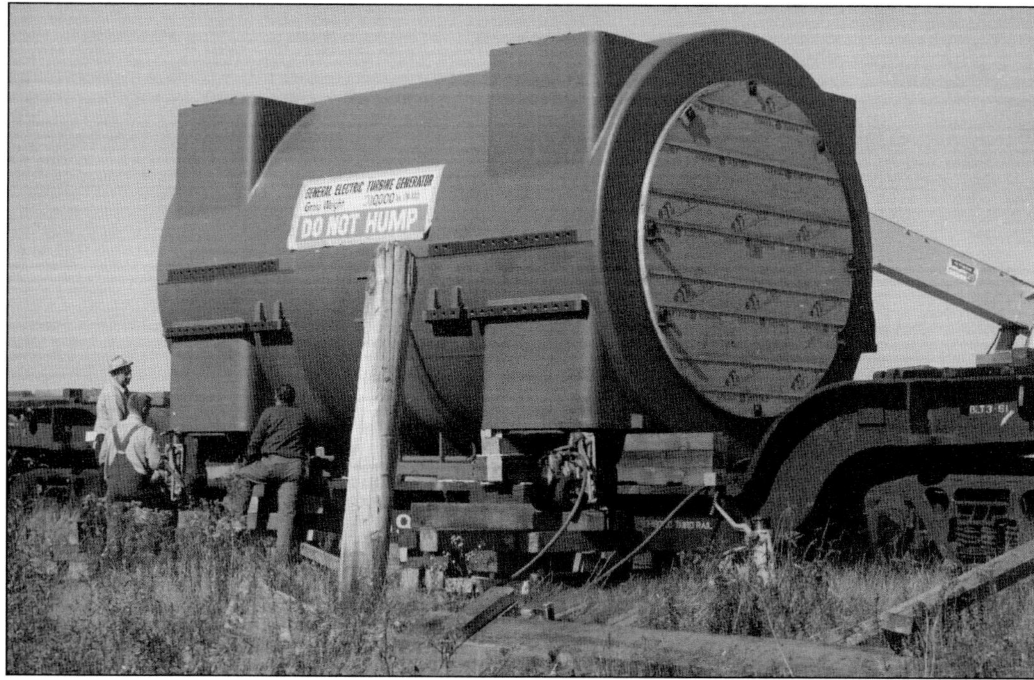

This photograph of a turbine generator was taken in 1964 on Sligo Road in Yarmouth. When Central Maine Power opened the Wyman plant, it owned a 10-acre property on Sligo Road that served as a utility pole storage yard from 1925 until it closed in 1995. The area was found to be contaminated with a toxic chemical, which required removing the topsoil of the 10 acres. It was later discovered that creosote had spilled there in the 1950s. In May 1957, a fire broke out that burned 1,000 logs and contributed to the release of chemicals into the soil.

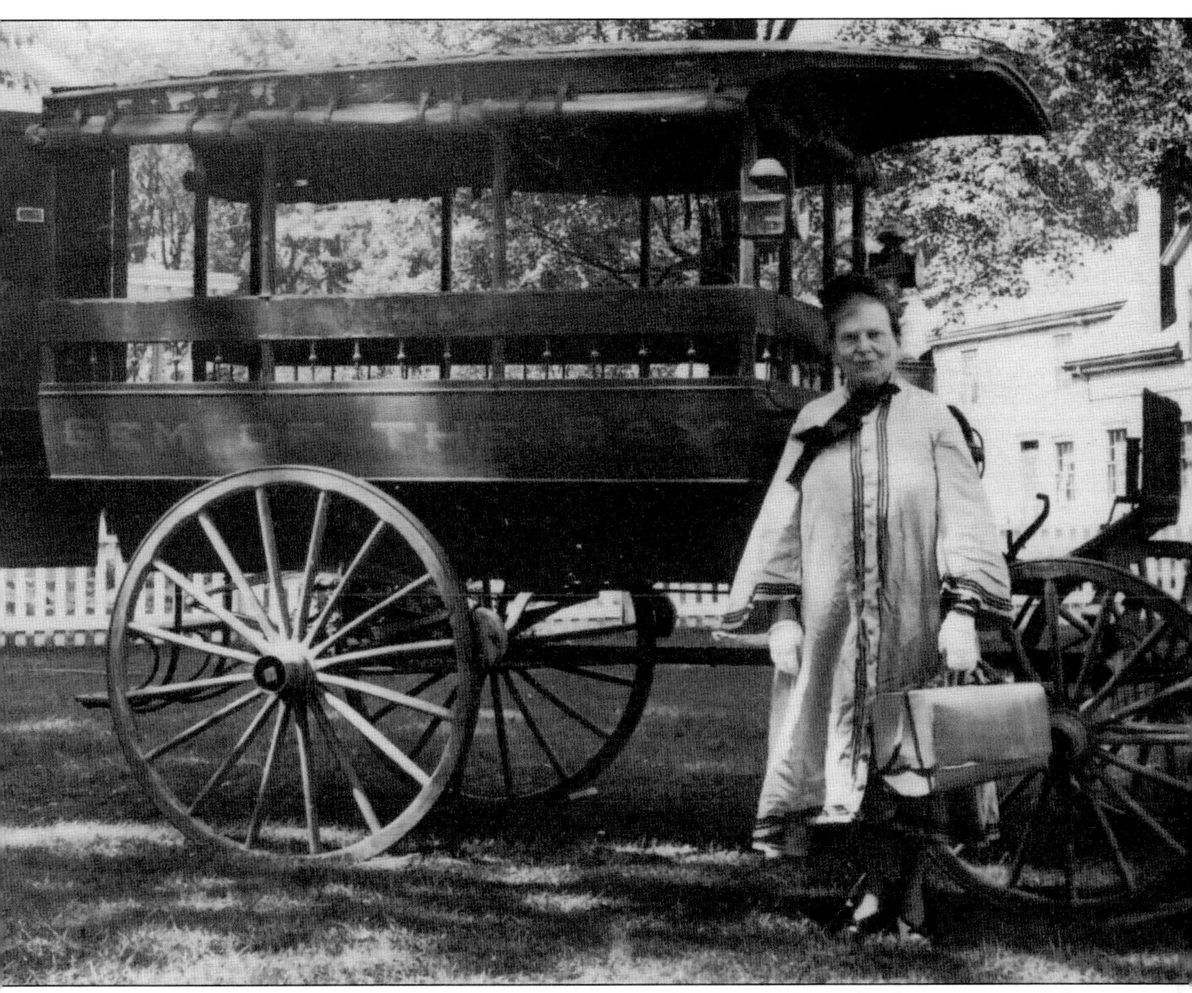

Shown in this photograph is Georgia Titcomb Mann with a wagon from the former Gem of the Bay. On the back of this Christmas greeting, the following is written: "Old chariot, Old costume, Old Friend, Affectionately, Georgia." (Courtesy of the collection of Dick Knight.)

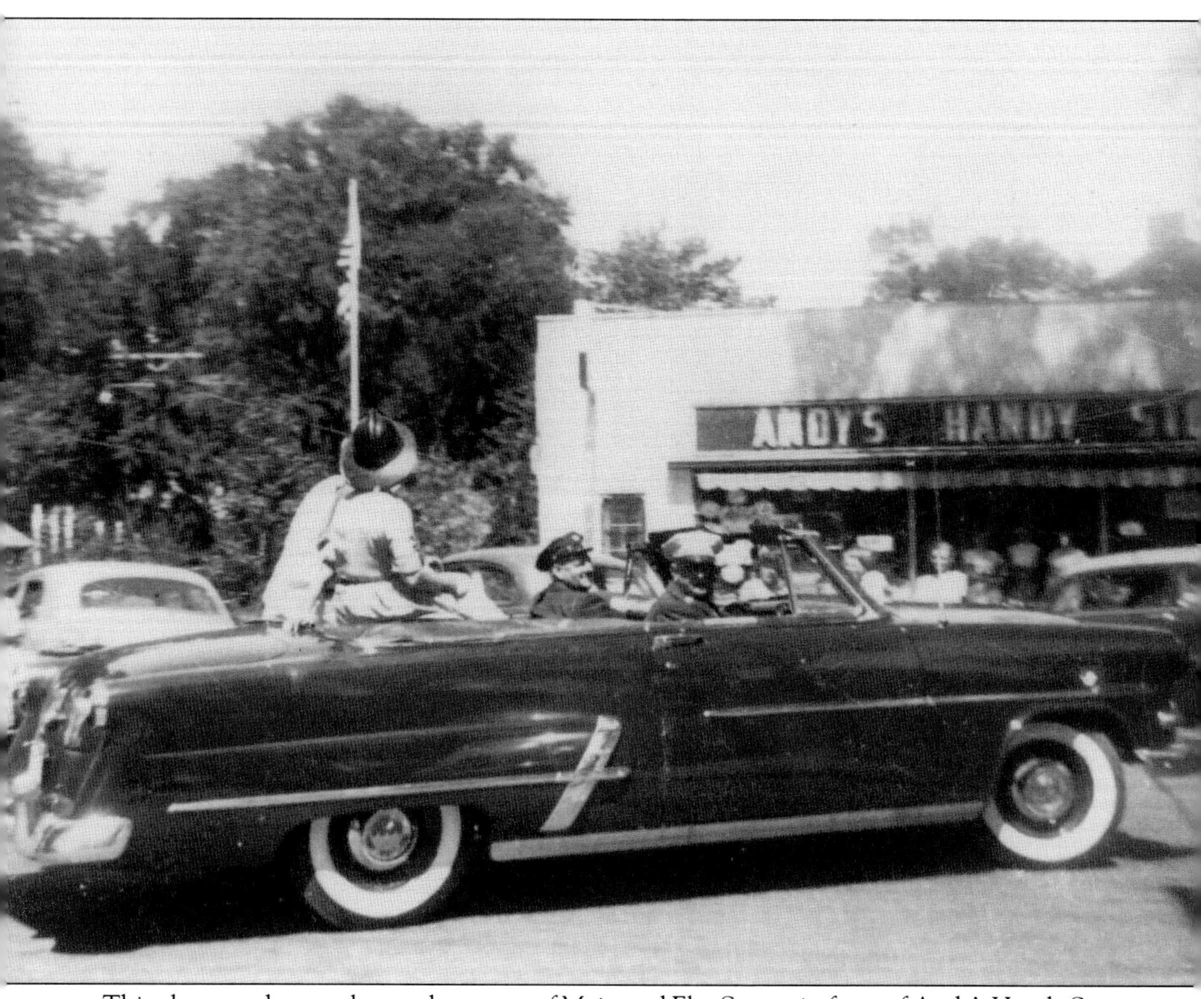

This photograph was taken at the corner of Main and Elm Streets in front of Andy's Handy Store, a local institution. This building had been a bakery owned by Freeland Knight starting in 1905. The business went through several different owners until Lester and Orland Blake purchased the building. In 1935, Leland "Andy" Anderson started what is today Andy's Handy Store.

The Yarmouth Drive-in was a popular spot in the 1950s. No longer in operation, the drive-in was located where the current Hannaford Supermarket is today on Route 1. A seasonal business, the drive-in would open the last weekend of April and run movies until the end of October.

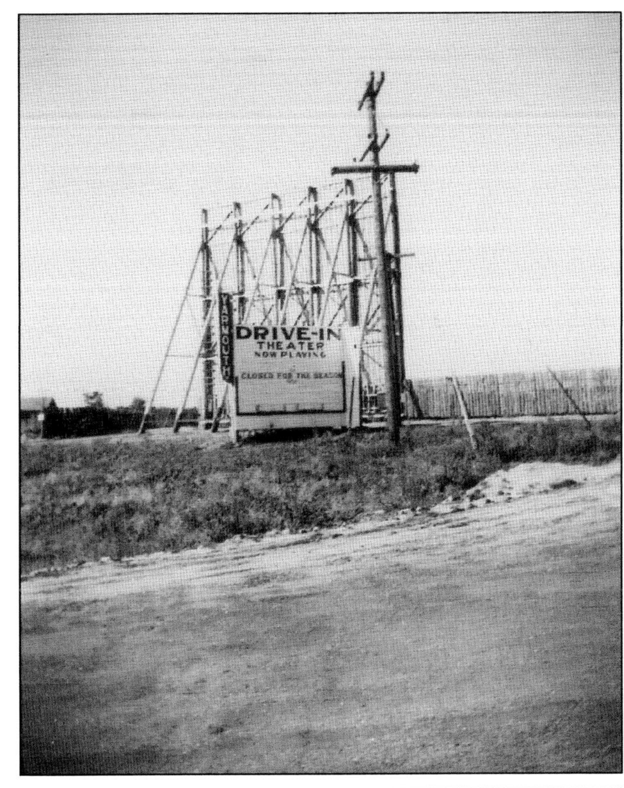

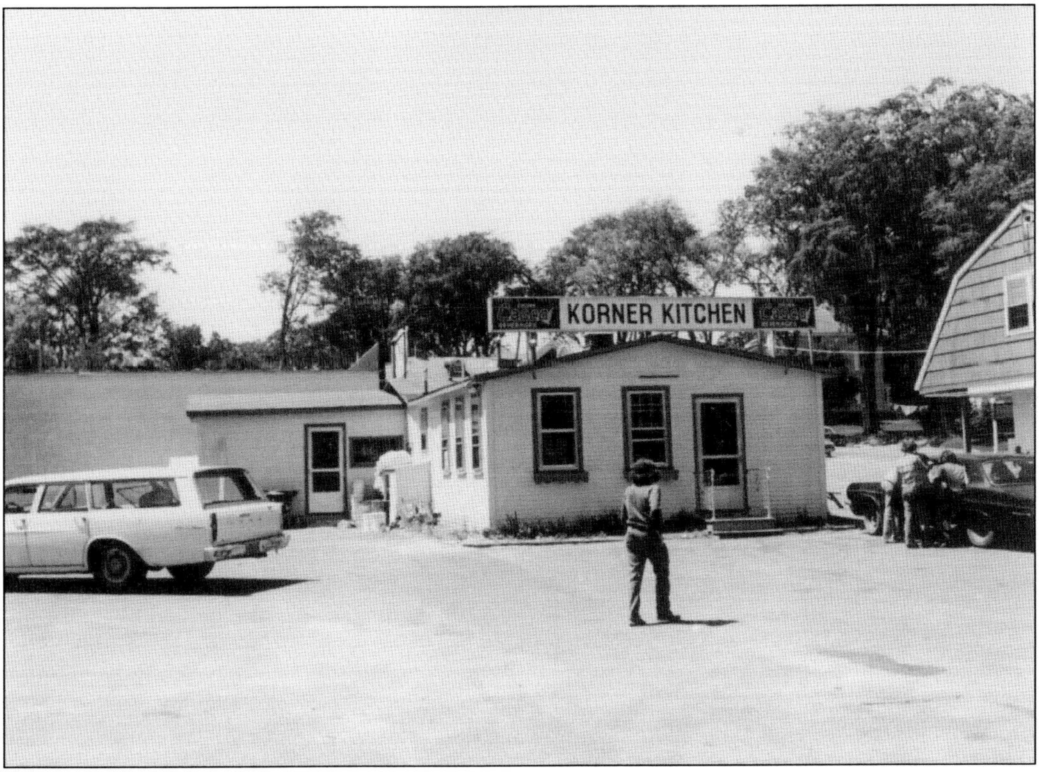

Located on the corner of Main and Cleaves Streets, the Dairy Joy and the Korner Kitchen were popular gathering spots. The Snack Shack was the name of the restaurant in the mid- to late 1960s. Locals fondly remember the banana boats at the Dairy Joy and the fried clams at the restaurants.

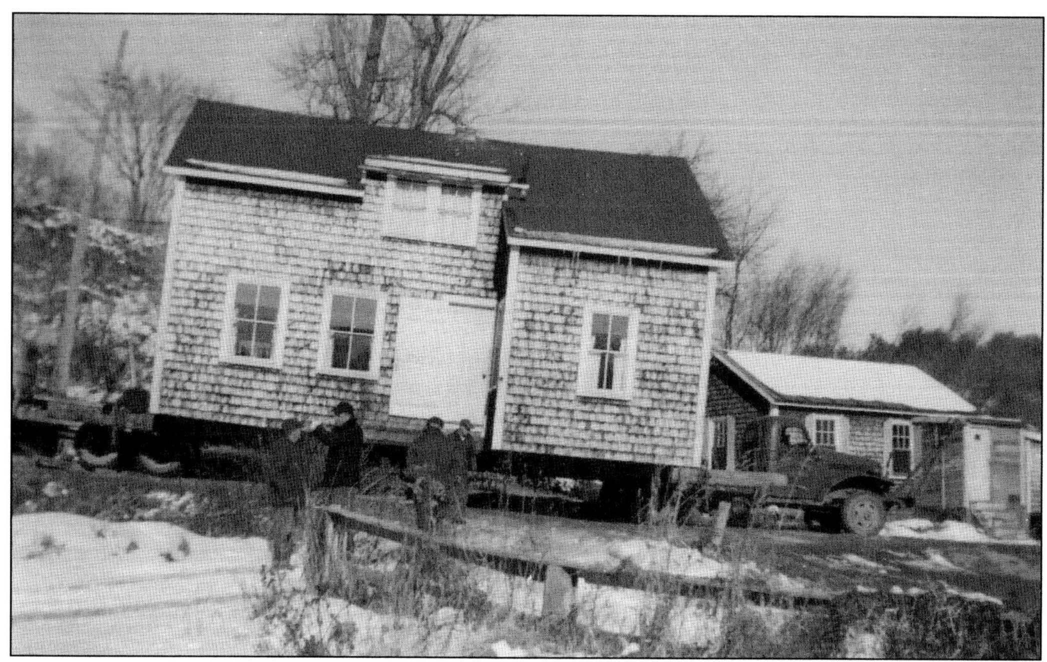

Edward Grant's house is being moved from Grantville to East Main Street. Grantville was a neighborhood located in the Bayview and East Main Street area. When US 295 was constructed, the highway overpass went through the neighborhood, which consisted of a number of members of the Grant family.

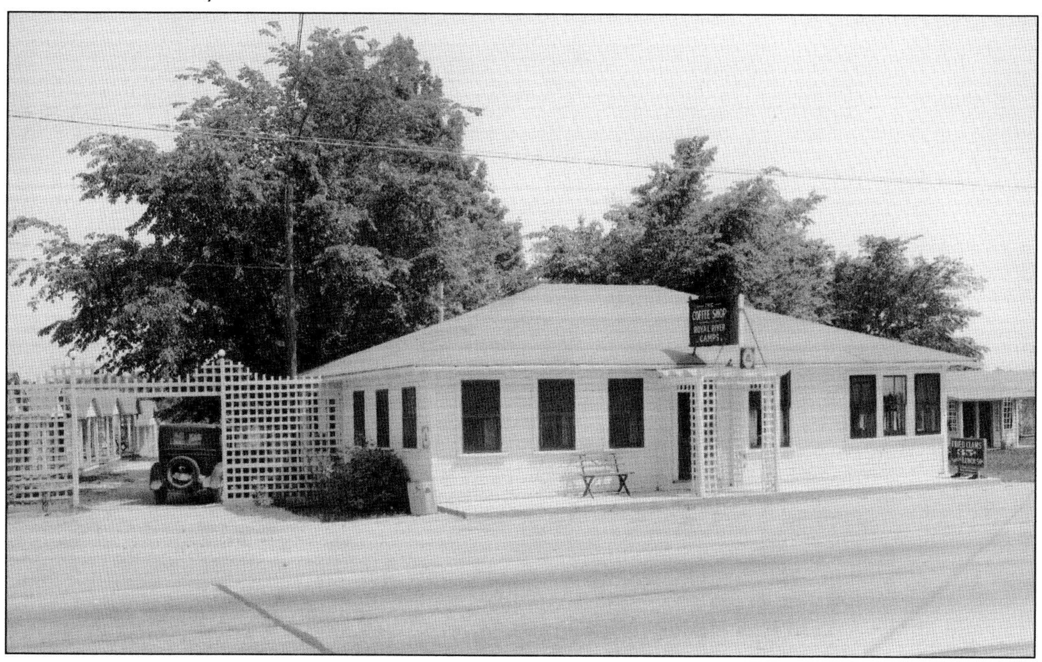

Royal River Cabins were in operation from the early 1930s to 1951. There were 20 cabins that could accommodate two to five people. They all had hot and cold water and were equipped with "flushes." In 1946, Eleanor Roosevelt stayed there when the Eastland Hotel in Portland refused to allow her dog Fala in the lobby.

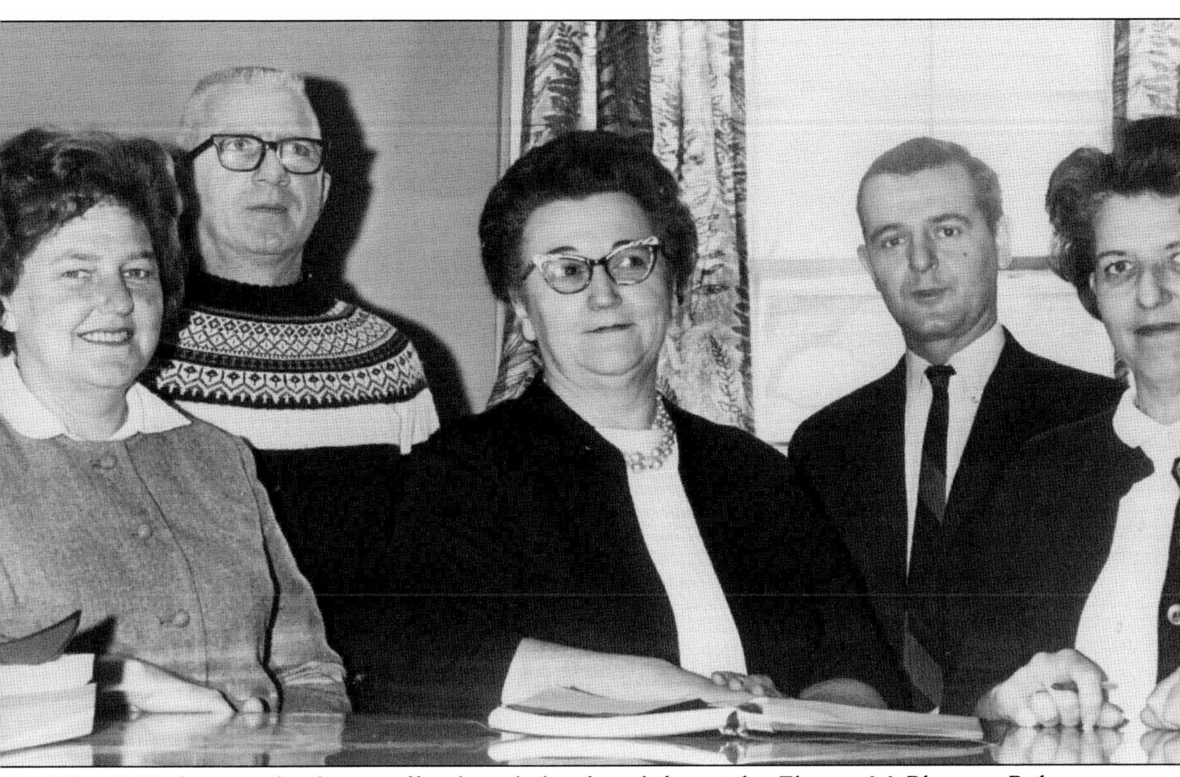

This 1968 photograph of town officials includes, from left to right, Eleanor M. Blarcom, Robert C. Hall, Frances E. Bayers, Paul A. Devine, and Phyllis Tinker.

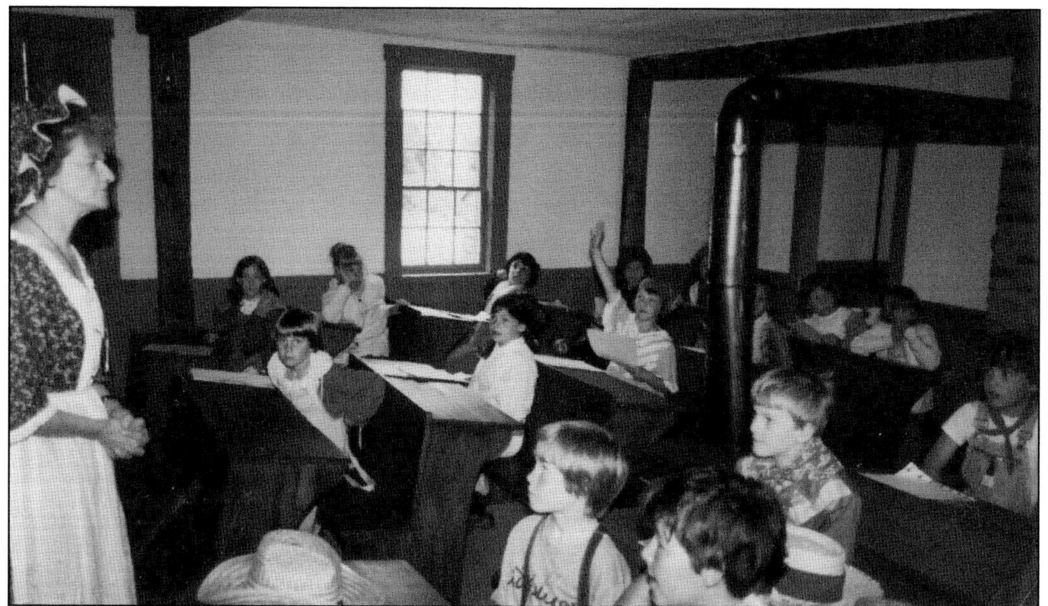

In 1970, planning began for the preservation of the Old Ledge School. It was moved to the present site on West Main Street and extensively reconstructed. In this c. 1975 photograph, a class is being held in the schoolhouse.

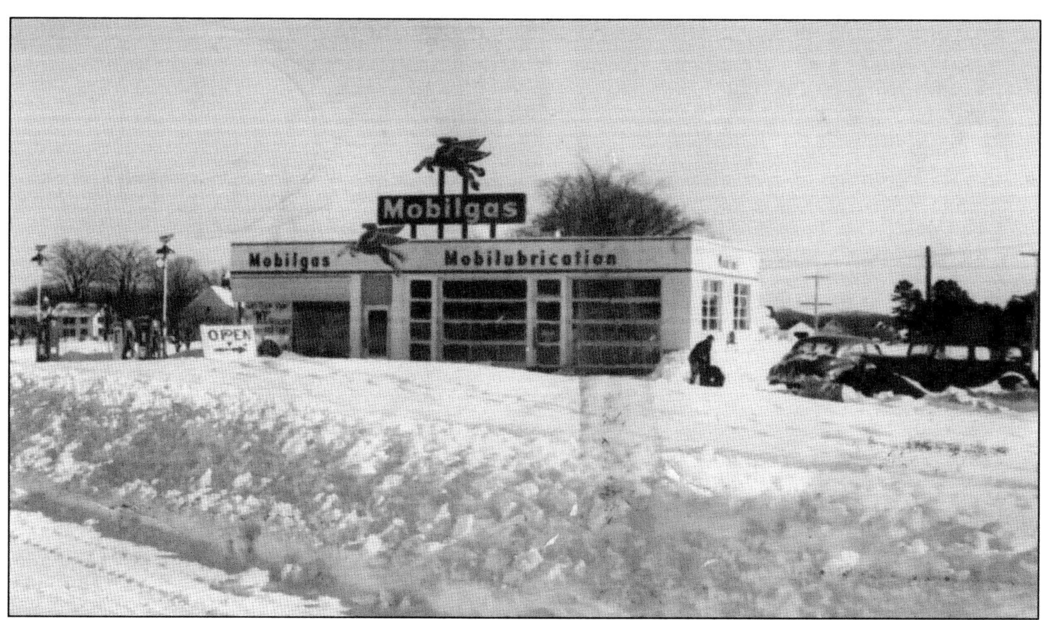

This photograph of the Mobil station shows the previous station that included two mechanic bays. This station was located on the corner of Route 1 and Portland Street on the spot where the current Mobil station stands today.

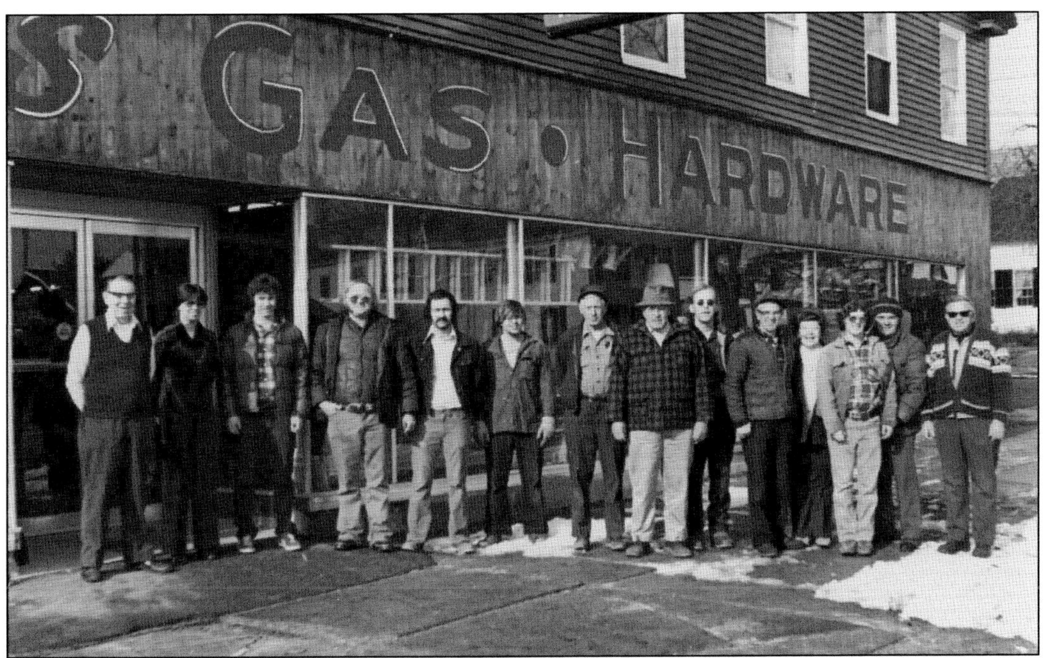

Standing at center, Elmer Ring is shown with part of the Ring's Gas and Hardware crew. Ring's was located in the former space of Coombs Bros. In addition to the hardware store, Ring also ran a "washerette," a heating and plumbing service, and a coal yard. This photograph was taken around 1977.

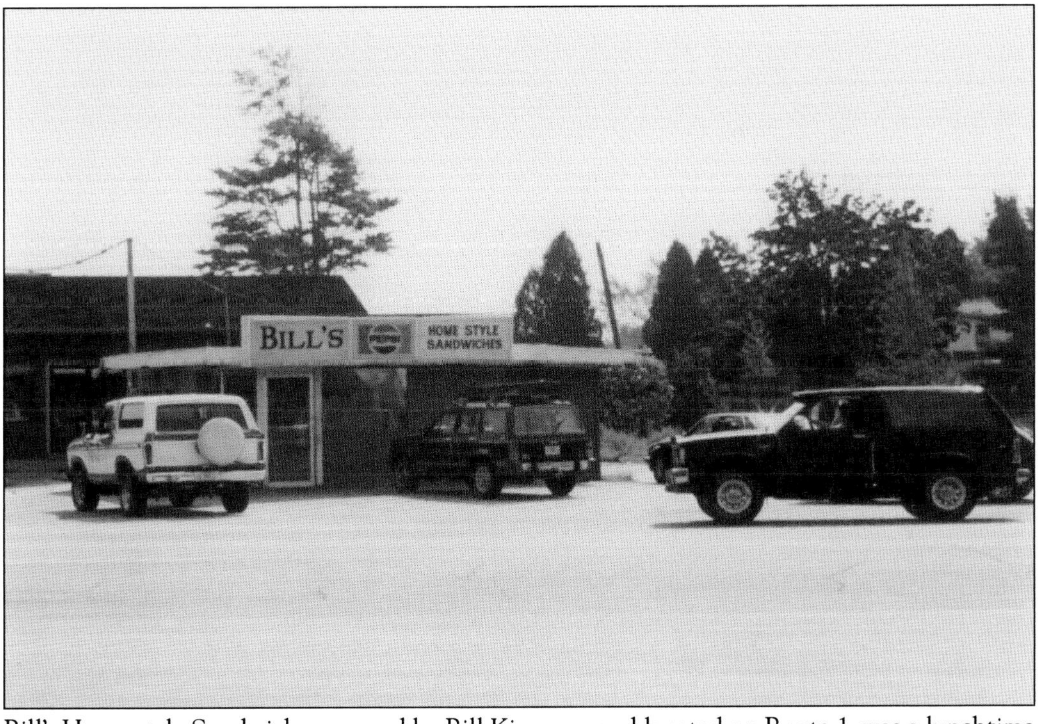

Bill's Home-style Sandwiches, owned by Bill Kinsman and located on Route 1, was a lunchtime mainstay for many locals for nearly 35 years.

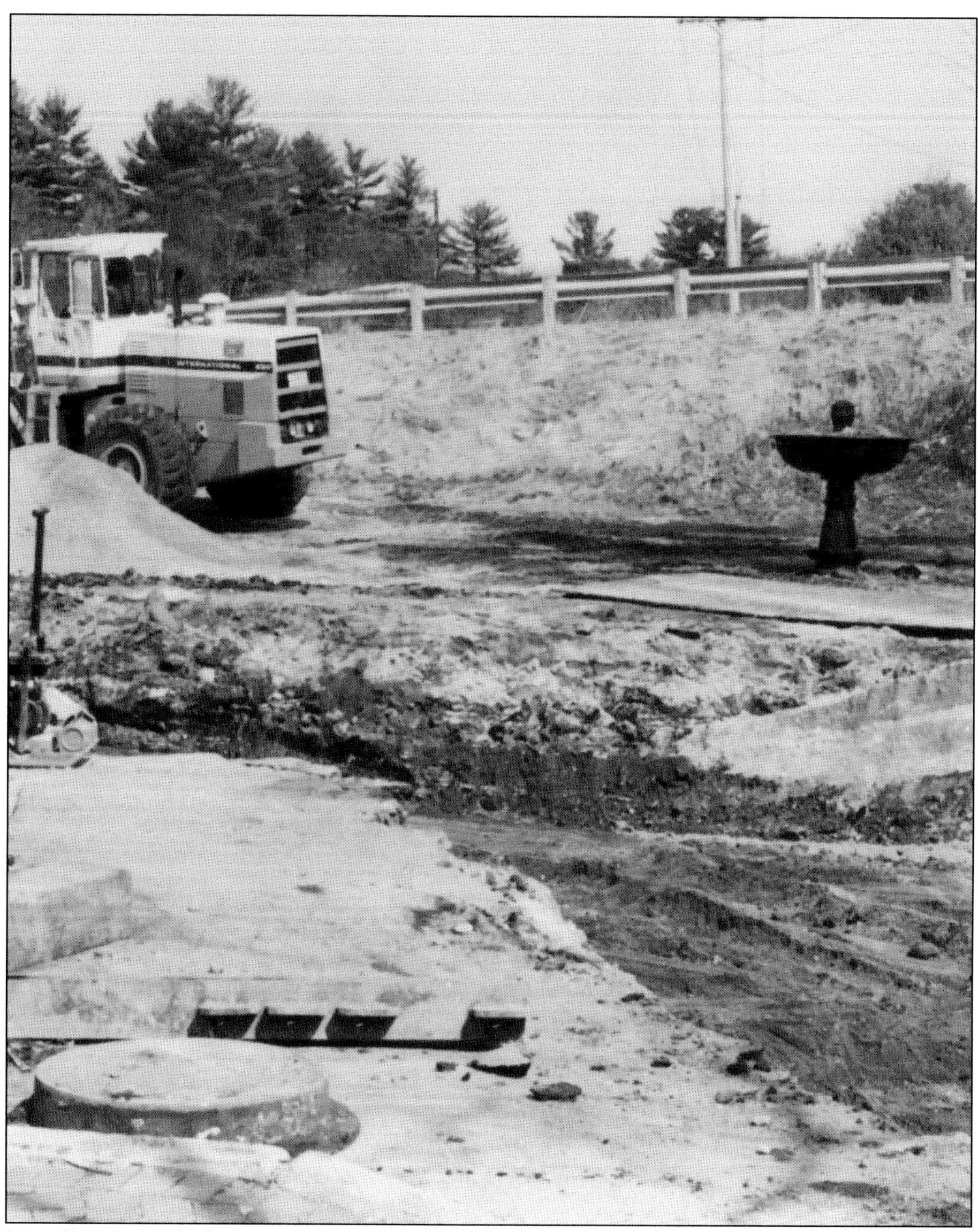

Merrill Memorial Library underwent renovations in 1988 when a wing was added to the rear of the original building. The addition doubled the size of the library. In this photograph, one of the original water troughs that were installed with the water system is shown. Another can be seen at the intersection of Center and Main Streets.

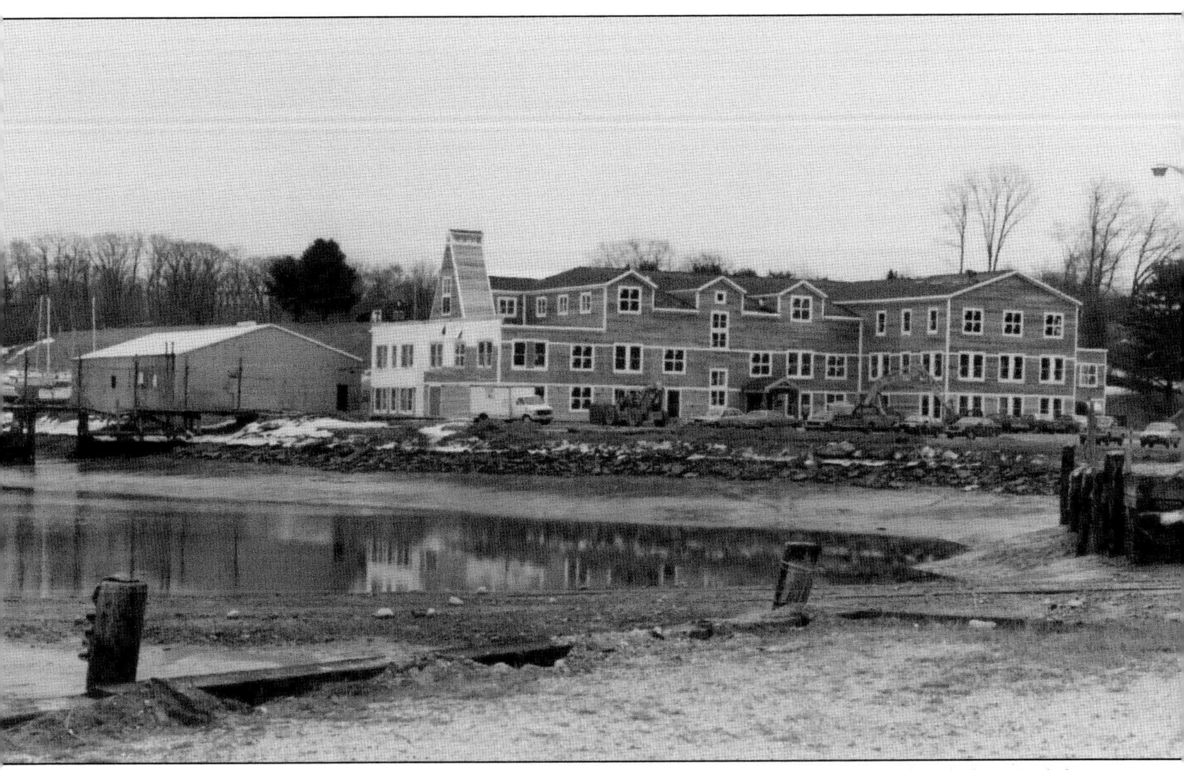

Ralph Stevens started work at the Royal River Packing Corporation in 1955 when his father, Ralph, the cannery's founder, hired him as plant manager. Stevens took the opportunity to purchase four acres of the seven-acre hillside nearby in 1964 and the remaining three acres by 1967. He was able to purchase the cannery after it closed. In 1986, Ralph Stevens formed a partnership, and the cannery was developed into today's Lower Falls Landing complex.

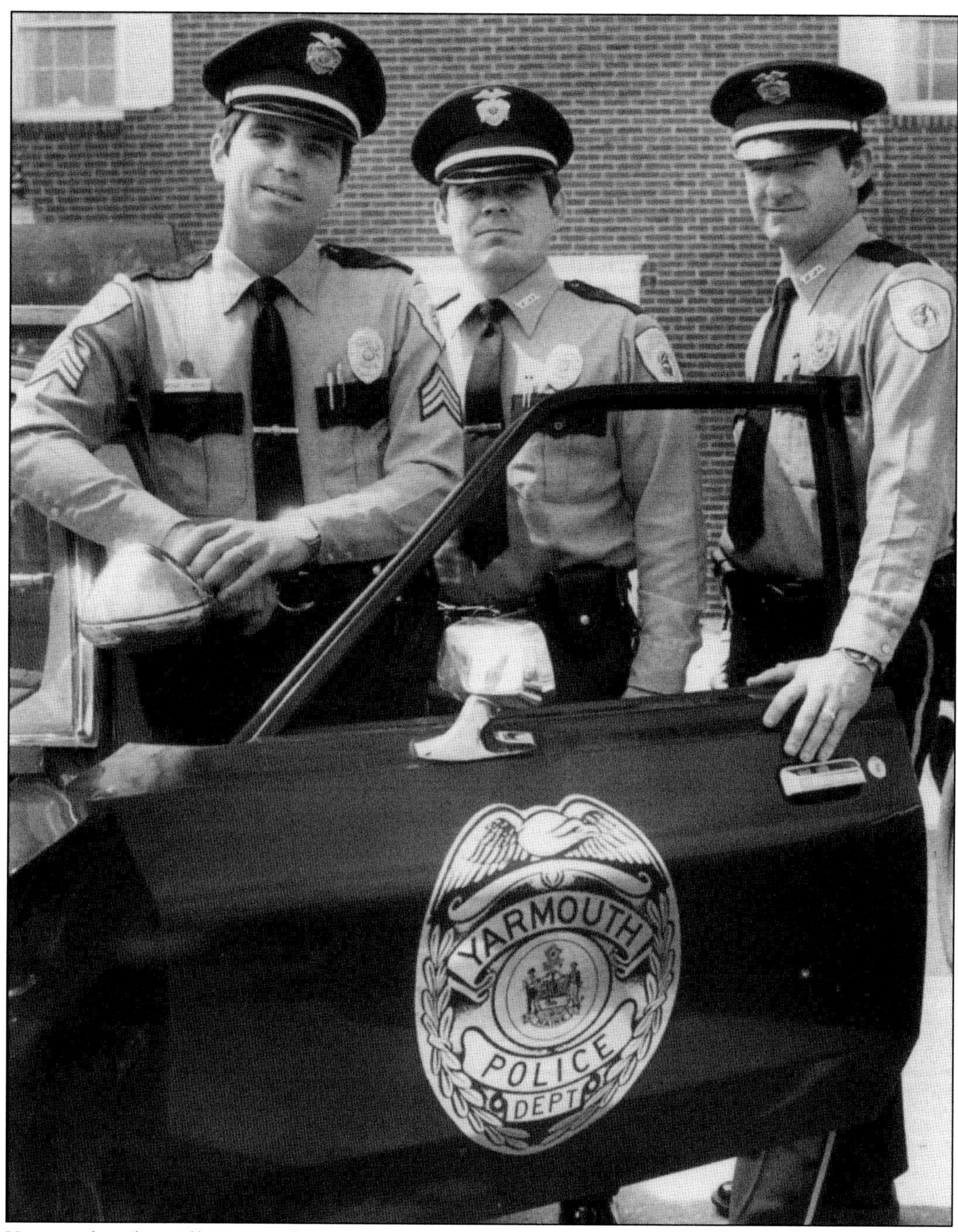

Yarmouth police officers are shown in this photograph from May 1982. From left to right are Sgt. Michael Morrill, Patrolman Bruce Moody, and Patrolman David A. Hall. Sergeant Morrill now serves as the chief of police of Yarmouth.

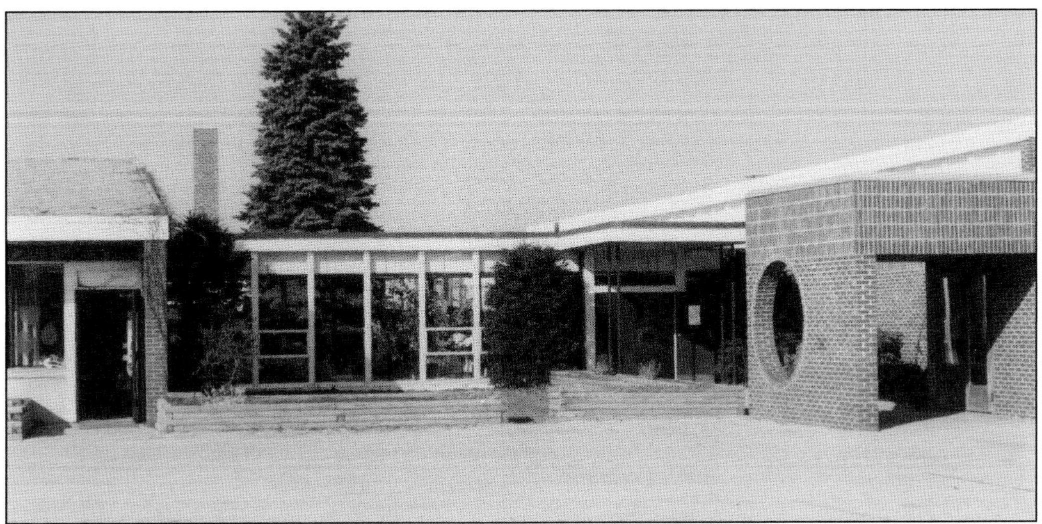

Rowe School is a kindergarten-through-first grade school. It was named for William H. Rowe, a local historian and author of books on Yarmouth and the shipbuilding industry in Maine. Rowe owned a pharmacy for many years on Main Street and served as the town clerk. The new school was completed in 2003, replacing the original school built in the 1950s.

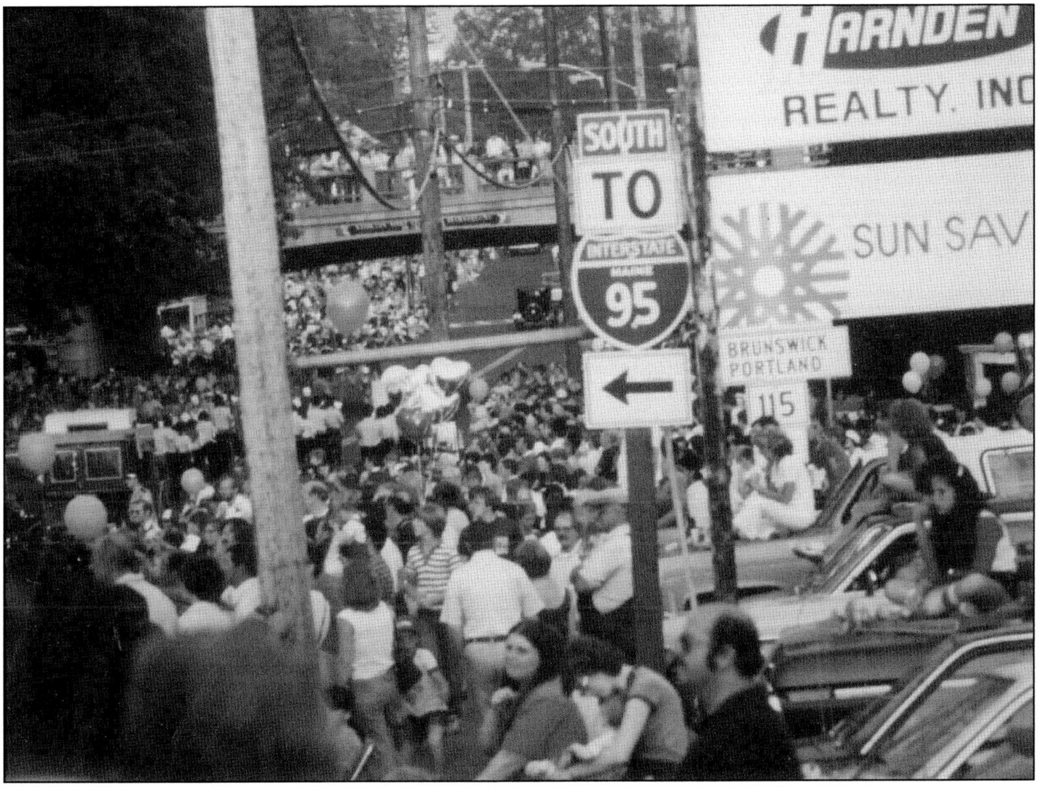

The Yarmouth Clam Festival is held every third weekend in July. The festival has drawn up to 150,000 people over the three-day weekend. In the early years, a giant clambake took place on Saturday afternoon. The trademark white booths first appeared in 1981 and are operated by local nonprofit organizations and volunteers.

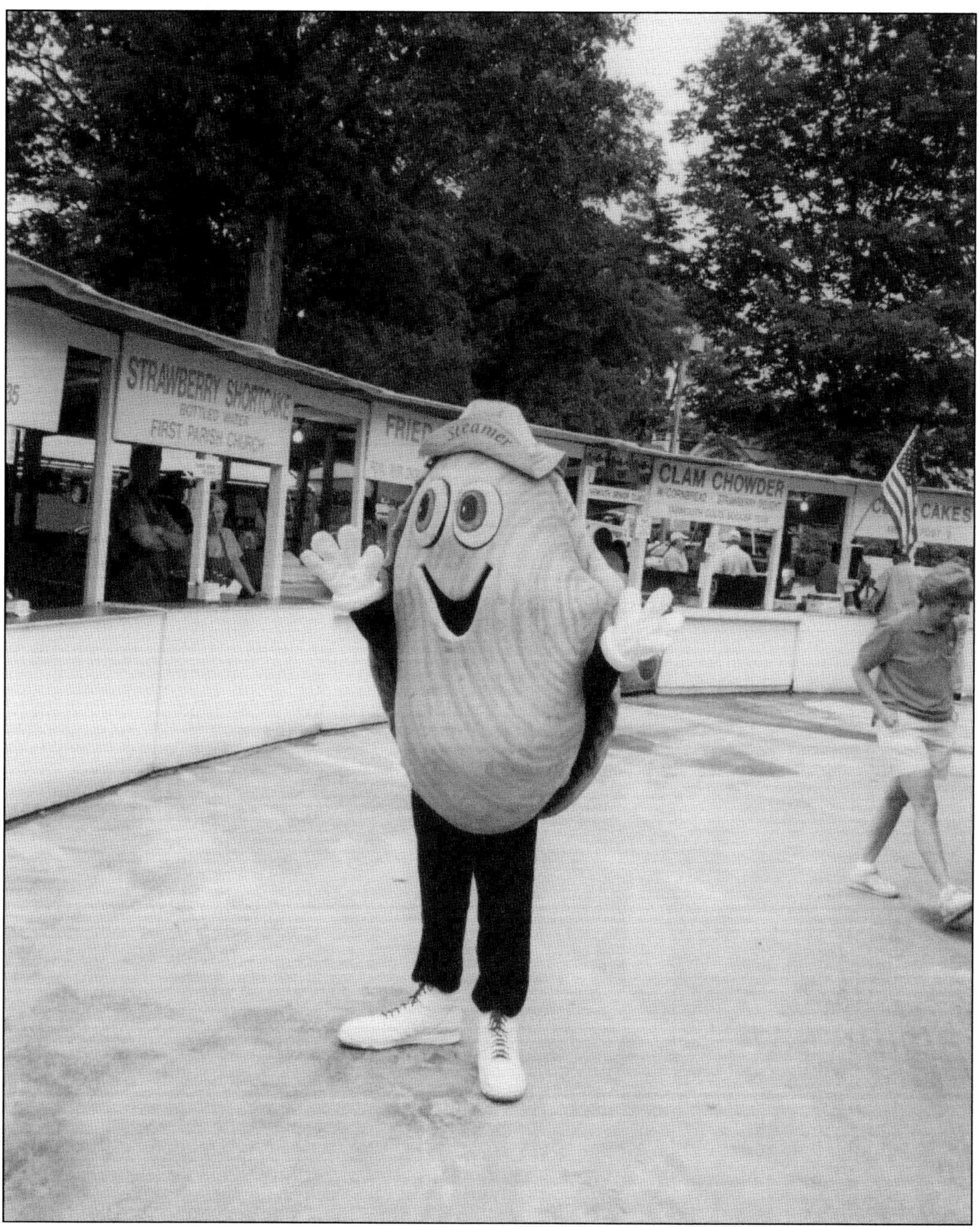

Steamer the Clam is the well-known mascot of the Yarmouth Clam Festival. A local tradition of townspeople putting out chairs days ahead of the Friday evening parade has escalated in past years with chairs being placed in their spots a full week prior to the parade. On Saturday, a firemen's muster is held, which dates back to the early militia musters.

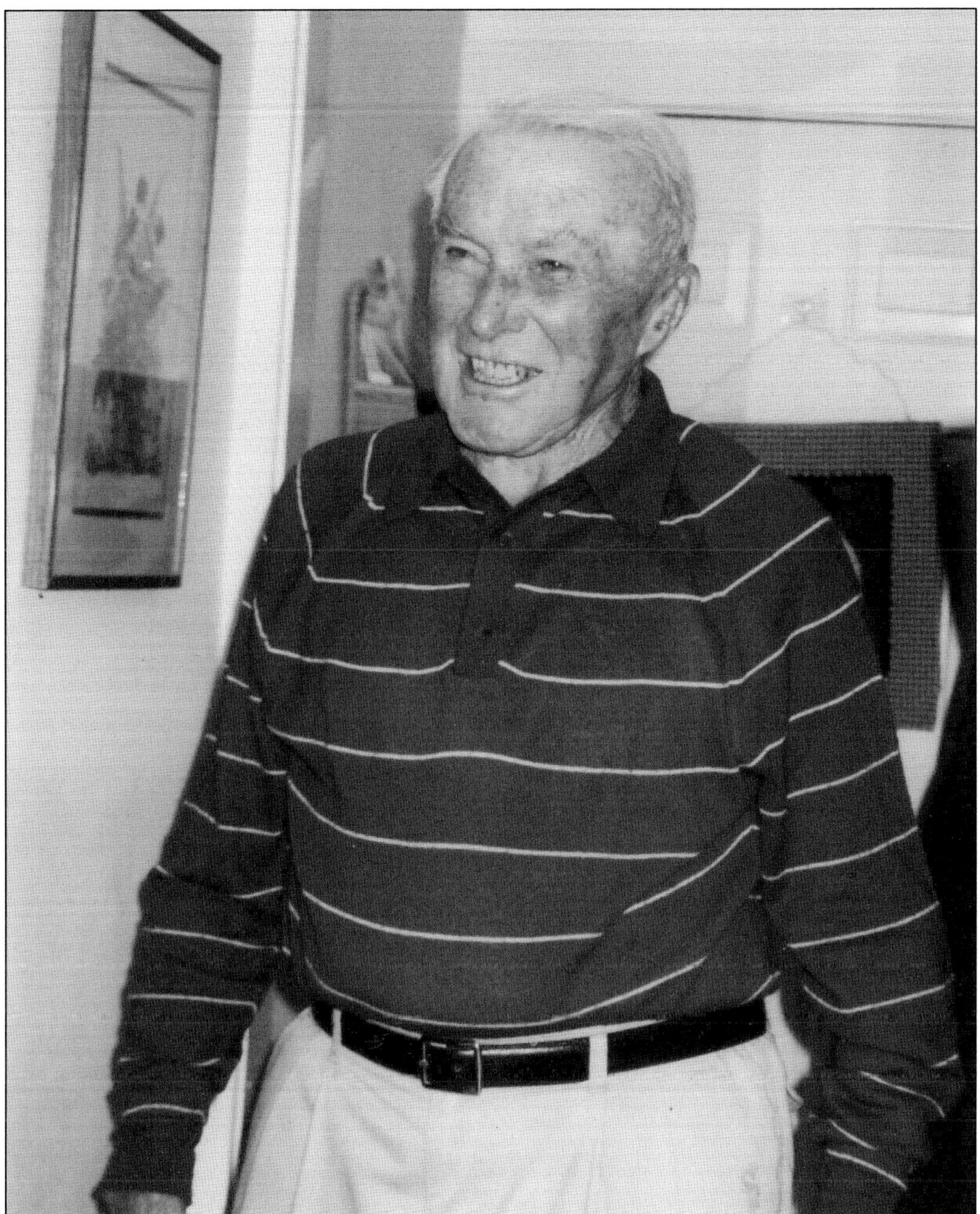

Frank Knight was born in Pownal, attended North Yarmouth Academy, and graduated from the University of Maine with a degree in forestry. Frank and Frances Mann Knight were married for more than 60 years. Frank Knight was a dedicated and active citizen of Yarmouth. In 2009, he gained national fame for his effort to save Herbie, a 217-year-old tree that succumbed to Dutch elm disease; unfortunately, it was cut down in January 2010.

Consistent with our mission to preserve history on a local level, this book was printed in South Carolina on American-made paper and manufactured entirely in the United States. Products carrying the accredited Forest Stewardship Council (FSC) label are printed on 100 percent FSC-certified paper.

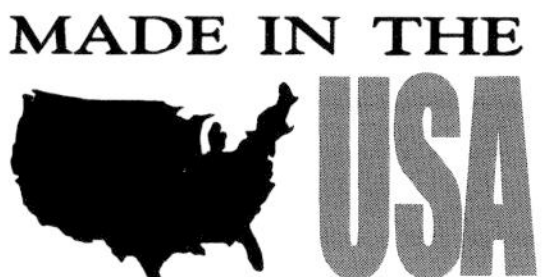